MAKING CHRIST KNOWN

Making Christ Known

*Historic Mission Documents
from the Lausanne Movement
1974–1989*

• •

*'We affirm that God has committed
to the whole church and every member of it
the task of making Christ known
throughout the world.'*

(Affirmation 12 of the Manila Manifesto, 1989)

• •

Edited by
John Stott

WILLIAM B. EERDMANS PUBLISHING COMPANY
GRAND RAPIDS, MICHIGAN / CAMBRIDGE, U.K.

© 1996 Lausanne Committee for World Evangelization

Published jointly 1997 in the United States of America by
Wm. B. Eerdmans Publishing Company
255 Jefferson Ave. S.E., Grand Rapids, Michigan 49503
and in the U.K. by Paternoster Press
P.O. Box 300, Carlisle, Cumbria CA3 0QS

Printed in the United States of America

02 01 00 99 98 97   7 6 5 4 3 2 1

Library of Congress Cataloging-in-Publication Data

Making Christ known: historic mission documents from the
Lausanne Movement, 1974-1989 / edited by John Stott.
p.   cm.
Includes bibliographical references and indexes.
ISBN 0-8028-4315-8 (pbk.: alk. paper)
1. Lausanne movement — History — Sources. 2. Missions — Theory —
History of doctrines — 20th century — Sources. 3. Evangelistic work —
Philosophy — History of doctrines — 20th century — Sources.
4. Evangelicalism — History — 20th century — Sources.
I. Stott, John R. W.
BV2063.M18   1997
266'.009'047 — dc21   97-14961
CIP

Printed or xeroxed copies of the original Lausanne Occasional Papers, whether included in this book or not, are obtainable from either of the following addresses:
(i)   The Lausanne International Communication Center, St Olavsgate **23**, 0166 Oslo, Norway.
(ii) MARC, 121 W. Huntington Drive, Monrovia, CA 91016, USA.

In encouraging the publication and study of the material contained in this book, the Lausanne Committee for World Evangelization does not necessarily endorse every viewpoint expressed in it.

CONTENTS

FOREWORD

When the International Congress on World Evangelization convened in Lausanne, Switzerland in July, 1974, none of us could have predicted its full impact. However, not only did it prove to be an immediate catalyst for evangelism throughout the world, but God has continued to bless and expand its vision in a variety of ways.

The Lausanne Covenant, for example, has helped challenge and unite evangelical Christians in the great task of world evangelization.

The Lausanne Movement has also stimulated fresh biblical thinking to help evangelical Christians understand more clearly God's calling for his people.

Much of this has taken place through smaller conferences and working groups focusing on such issues as the relationship between evangelism and social responsibility, prayer and evangelism, conversion, and the gospel and culture. At times their conclusions were intended only as a first step, or were even controversial. Others, however, have proved to be definitive statements with broad influence. Each deserves careful study and reflection, for the issues they raise are vital.

I am very glad that the historic mission documents beginning with Lausanne (1974) and ending with Manila (1989) have now been brought together in one volume. I pray that the study of these statements will lift our vision and lead each of us to a new commitment to the task of world evangelization.

BILLY GRAHAM

ABBREVIATIONS

BGEA	The Billy Graham Evangelistic Association
CAG	LCWE's Communications Advisory Group
CCCOWE	The Chinese Co-ordination Centre of World Evangelism
COWE	The Consultation on World Evangelization, Pattaya, 1980
CRESR	The Consultation on the Relationship between Evangelism and Social Responsibility, Grand Rapids, 1982
CWME	The WCC's Commission on World Mission and Evangelism
ERCDOM	The Evangelical-Roman Catholic Dialogue on Mission
GCOWE	The Global Congress on World Evangelization, Seoul, 1995
HUP	The Homogeneous Unit Principle
ICOWE	The International Congress on World Evangelization, Lausanne, 1974
IMC	The International Missionary Council
IWG	LCWE's Intercession Working Group
LB	The Living Bible
LC	The Lausanne Covenant, 1974
LCWE	The Lausanne Committee for World Evangelization
LOP	Lausanne Occasional Paper
LTEG	The Lausanne Theology and Education Group (later TWG)
MARC	The Mission Advanced Research and Communication Center
MM	The Manila Manifesto, 1989
SLS	Simple Lifestyle
SWG	LCWE's Strategy Working Group
TWG	LCWE's Theology Working Group (formerly LTEG)
WCC	The World Council of Churches
WE	*World Evangelization*, LCWE's magazine
WEF	The World Evangelical Fellowship
WMC	World Missionary Conference

SELECT BIBLIOGRAPHY

The following publications are all 'Lausanne-related' either because they were officially commissioned or endorsed by the Lausanne Committee, or because they are independent evaluations of aspects of the Lausanne movement.

Beyerhaus, Peter: *Evangelicals, Evangelism and Theology*, a missiological assessment of the Lausanne movement (The Evangelical Review of Theology Vol. 23 No. 2, April, 1987)

Bosch, David J.: *Witness to the World*, the Christian mission in theological perspective (Basingstoke: Marshall, Morgan and Scott, 1980)

Bosch, David J.: *Transforming Mission: Paradigm Shifts in Theology of Mission* (Maryknoll: Orbis, 1991)

Bright, Vonette and Ben A. Jennings, eds.: *Unleashing the Power of Prayer* (Chicago: Moody 1989)

Dayton, Edward R. and David A. Fraser: *Planning Strategies for World Evangelization* (Grand Rapids: Eerdmans, 1980)

Dayton, Edward R.: *That Everyone May Hear*, strategies for reaching unreached people groups (CA: Monrovia MARC, 1980; 3rd edition, 1983). Also a companion work book and an audio-visual.

Douglas, J. D. ed.: *Let the Earth Hear His Voice*, the compendium of the International Congress on World Evangelization, Lausanne, Switzerland (Minneapolis: World Wide Publications, 1975)

Douglas, J. D. ed.: *Proclaim Christ Until He Comes*, the compendium of the second International Congress on World Evangelization, Manila, Philippines (Minneapolis: World Wide Publications, 1990)

Ford, Leighton: *A Vision Pursued*, the Lausanne movement 1974–1986, Fuller Lectures, 1986 (unpublished)

Hedlund, Roger E.: *Roots of the Great Debate in Mission*: mission in historical and theological perspective (1981; Bangalore, India: Theological Book Trust, 1993)

Henry, Carl F. H. and W. Stanley Mooneyham, eds.: *One Race, One Gospel, One Task* (Minneapolis: World Wide Publications, 1967)

Houston, Tom: *Scenario 2000*, a personal forecast of the prospects for world evangelization (MARC — LCWE, 1992)

Johnston, Arthur P.: *The Battle for World Evangelism* (Wheaton: Tyndale, 1978)

Kane, J. H.: *Christian Missions in Biblical Perspective* (Grand Rapids: Baker, 1976)

McCurry, Don M. ed.: *The Gospel and Islam*: a 1978 Compendium (Monrovia CA: MARC, 1979). An abridged edition was also published in 1984.

Nicholls, Bruce J. ed.: *In Word and Deed*, Evangelism and Social Responsibility (Exeter: Paternoster, 1985)

Nichols, Alan. *Exposition and Commentary of An Evangelical Commitment to Simple Lifestyle* (LOP 20, 1980)

Nichols, Alan ed.: *The Whole Gospel for the Whole World*, the story of the Lausanne II Congress on World Evangelization, Manila, 1989 (Wheaton: LCWE and Regal Books, 1989)

Padilla, C. René ed.: *The New Face of Evangelicalism* (London: Hodder & Downers Grove: IVP, USA 1976)

Sampson, Philip, Vinay Samuel and Chris Sugden, eds.: *Faith and Modernity* (Oxford: Regnum Books International, 1994)

Samuel, Vinay K. and Albrecht Hauser, eds.: *Proclaiming Christ in Christ's Way*, studies in integral evangelism (Oxford: Regnum, 1989)

Shenk, David W.: *God's Call to Mission* (Scottdale: Herald Press, 1994)

Sider, Ronald J.: *Evangelism, Salvation and Social Justice* (Nottingham: Grove Books, 1977)

Sider, Ronald J. ed.: *Lifestyle in the Eighties*, an evangelical commitment to simple lifestyle (Exeter: Paternoster, 1982)

Stott, John R. W.: *Christian Mission in the Modern World* (Downers Grove: IVP, USA 1975)

Stott, John R. W. and Robert T. Coote, eds.: *Down to Earth: Studies in Christianity and Culture* (London: Hodder, 1981)

Wagner, C. Peter: *On the Crest of the Wave*, becoming a world Christian (Ventura: Regal Books, 1983)

Wells, David F.: *God the Evangelist*, how the Holy Spirit works to bring men and women to faith (Grand Rapids: Eerdmans and Exeter: Paternoster, 1987, 1997)

Wells, David F.: *Turning to God*, biblical conversion in the modern world (Grand Rapids: Baker Book House and Exeter: Paternoster, 1989, 1997)

Winter, Ralph D. and Steve C. Hawthorne, eds.: *Perspectives on the World Christian Movement: A Reader* (Pasadena: William Carey Library, 1981)

Yates, Timothy: *Christian Mission in the Twentieth Century* (Cambridge: Cambridge University Press, 1994)

Series

World Christianity (incorporating country profiles):
Vol. I Middle East, ed. Donald M McCurry (Monrovia: MARC, 1979)
Vol. II Eastern Asia, ed. David C. E. Liao (Monrovia: MARC, 1979)
Vol. III South Asia, ed. Roger E. Hedlund (Monrovia: MARC, 1980)
Vol. IV Central America and the Caribbean, ed. Clifton L. Holland (Monrovia: MARC, 1981)

The Annual Directory of Unreached Peoples, ed. (1979–1982) C. Peter Wagner
and Edward R. Dayton
   1979 The Challenge of the Church's Unfinished Business (Elgin IL: David
      C. Cook, 1978)
   1980 Focus on Muslim Peoples (Elgin IL: David C. Cook, 1980)
   1981 Focus on Asian Peoples (Elgin IL: David C. Cook, 1981)
   1982 Focus on Urban Peoples (Elgin IL: David C. Cook, 1982)
   1983 *The Refugees Among Us*, ed. Edward R. Dayton and Samuel Wilson
      (Monrovia: MARC und.)
   1984 *The Future of World Evangelization*, ed. Edward R. Dayton and
      Samuel Wilson (Monrovia: MARC, 1984)
   1987 *Clarifying the Task*, ed. Harley Schreck and David Barrett
      (Monrovia MARC, 1987)

Periodicals

World Evangelization, the LCWE's quarterly news magazine.
World Evangelization Information Service, a monthly news release.

AN HISTORICAL INTRODUCTION

During the last quarter of the twentieth century, and so of the second millennium AD, a new word has entered the Christian vocabulary. It is the word 'Lausanne'. Of course in one sense we knew it already. Lausanne is a beautiful town in western Switzerland, situated on the shore of Lake Geneva, capital of the canton of Vaud, and home to a famous university dating from the sixteenth century. But now for many Christians the old word has a new meaning, since in July 1974 the city of Lausanne became the venue for the first International Congress on World Evangelization. 'Lausanne' soon came to be used as an adjective. People spoke of the Lausanne Congress, the Lausanne Covenant, the Lausanne Committee, the Lausanne movement, and the Lausanne spirit.

Time magazine called the Congress 'possibly the widest ranging meeting of Christians ever held', since it assembled 2,700 participants from 150 nations and from the whole spectrum of Protestant denominations. It was 'a formidable forum' on the task of world evangelization.[1]

Nevertheless, the Lausanne Congress was not an isolated event. From one point of view its antecedents go right back to the beginning when the resurrected Lord, claiming universal authority, commissioned his disciples to take the gospel to the nations (Mt. 28:18–20). And those disciples were told not to 'stand here looking into the sky', but rather to be Christ's witnesses 'to the ends of the earth' (Acts 1:8, 11). They were to be evangelists, not star-gazers.

From another and more recent point of view Lausanne was the culmination of a whole series of smaller missionary conferences. During the second half of the nineteenth century a number of national and regional missionary conferences took place, especially in Asia (India, China and Japan), but also in South Africa, North America and Mexico. In addition, World Missionary Conferences (WMC), which were self-consciously international in their membership, were held in Liverpool (1860), London (1888) and New York (1900). These three were highly significant events, providing guidelines for the church's global task, but they were also stepping-stones to the much more influential WMC held in Edinburgh in 1910, whose Continuation Committee became the International Missionary Council (IMC), which in its turn was one of the streams which flowed into the World Council of Churches.

---

[1] *Time* magazine, 5 August 1974.

From Edinburgh 1910 to Berlin 1966

The Edinburgh WMC was pioneered and chaired by John R. Mott, although he was still in his early forties. It had been preceded by a thorough world-wide study process and it ended on a note of euphoria, even triumphalism. Speakers drew attention to what they regarded as the weaknesses of the ethnic religions, and declared them bankrupt, even moribund. Soon now, it was confidently asserted, they would capitulate to the victorious Christ. As John Mott began his final address, 'The end of the conference is the beginning of the conquest'. That was the mood in which the participants left Edinburgh.

But the mood did not last long, and the predictions proved to be false. Why was this? What were the influences which undermined the expectations engendered at Edinburgh? There were two, socio-political on the one hand and theological on the other.

When the delegates left Edinburgh, who could have guessed that only four years later the world would be plunged into war, or that less than twenty years would separate it from World War Two? These devastating conflicts sapped the moral as well as the financial strength of the west, and signalled to the rest of the world the collapse of western culture and of its foundation, Christianity.

Theologically, the fatal flaw at Edinburgh was not so much doctrinal disagreement as apparent doctrinal indifference; since doctrine was not on the agenda. Vital themes like the content of the gospel, the theology of evangelism and the nature of the church were not discussed. The reason is that Randall Davidson, Archbishop of Canterbury, as a condition of Anglican participation in Edinburgh, secured a promise from John R. Mott that doctrinal debate would be excluded. In consequence, the theological challenges of the day were not faced. And, during the decades which followed, the poison of theological liberalism seeped into the bloodstream of western universities and seminaries, and largely immobilized the churches' mission.

These two movements undermined the self-confidence which had characterized the Christian leaders who met in Edinburgh in 1910, and their successors. When the first assembly of the World Council of Churches convened in Amsterdam in 1948, mission was not at the top of their agenda. Some ecumenical pioneers tried hard to remedy this by securing at the third assembly in New Delhi in 1961 the integration of the International Missionary Council with the World Council of Churches. Then, it was said, when the IMC became the missionary arm of the WCC, mission would be at the heart of the Council's concerns and so of its member churches. In the event, however, mission became marginalized by being largely reinterpreted in socio-political terms. Thus the vision of Edinburgh 1910 suffered an almost total eclipse.

The 1960s was the decade of radical revolt. The hopes raised by the election of the young John F. Kennedy as President of the United States in 1961 were dashed by his assassination two years later. The Berlin wall was built. The free speech movement broke out at Berkeley. Students and workers took to the street barricades in Paris. Cultural revolution was proclaimed by violent young Red Guards in China, while North American society became bitterly divided over civil rights and the Vietnam war, and tens of thousands of disillusioned young people dropped out into communes, loosely connected with which was 'the Jesus movement'. The continent of Africa was in turmoil, as the European colonies demanded 'uhuru'. There was confusion also in the churches. Bishop John Robinson's provocative book *Honest to God* was published in 1963. The Second Vatican Council was in session in Rome from 1963–1965. Liberation theologies began to spread from Latin America throughout the world. And the charismatic movement grew in strength and stature.

One person who kept his ear to the ground, and who struggled to understand these contemporary trends, was Dr. Billy Graham. He resolved to respond Christianly to these social upheavals. He knew that, although the gospel is unchanged and unchanging, it cannot be preached in a vacuum. He was convinced that the historic, crucified, resurrected and reigning Christ is himself good news for the world, and that he speaks to alienated youth, the drug subculture, racial conflict, the breakdown of moral values, the cult of violence, the search for freedom and the longing for love.

So this widely experienced Christian leader determined not only to continue his own crusades, but also to encourage the evangelical constituency to unite in reaching the world for Christ. The evangelist became a promoter of evangelism, the preacher a statesman. He was mainly responsible for convening the World Congress on Evangelism in Berlin in 1966. It was co-sponsored by the Billy Graham Evangelistic Association (which largely funded it) and *Christianity Today*. Its motto was 'one Race, one Gospel, one Task', and its moving spirit Dr. Carl Henry, the editor of *Christianity Today*.[2] It was followed by a series of regional conferences on evangelism in Singapore (1968), Minneapolis and Bogota (1969) and Australia (1971).

Lausanne 1974

During these years Billy Graham began to dream about another and larger Congress for the 1970s, which would develop strategies for world evangelization. He consulted about 200 evangelical leaders world-wide, asking if they considered such a Congress to be needed, and if so whether they would be willing to serve on the convening committee. The response was overwhelmingly positive.

The Congress slogan, emblazoned over the platform at Lausanne, was: 'Let the earth hear his voice.' In his opening speech, entitled 'Why Lausanne?', Dr. Billy Graham first drew attention to the representative

---

[2] The proceedings of the congress were published in two volumes under the title *One Race, One Gospel, One Task*, edited by Carl F. H. Henry and W. Stanley Mooneyham (World Wide Publications, 1967).

nature of the gathering, and then outlined some contemporary signposts of both 'promise' (God at work in a remarkable way) and 'danger' (economic crisis, moral relativism, false religion etc.). He went on to elaborate the Congress's 'four basic presuppositions':

1. 'The Congress stands in the tradition of many movements of evangelism throughout the history of the church', while being itself 'a conference of evangelicals'.
2. The Congress convenes 'as one body, obeying one Lord, facing one world, with one task', namely evangelization.
3. The Congress convenes 'to re-emphasize those biblical concepts which are essential to evangelism', especially five, namely —
   (a) commitment to the authority of Scripture,
   (b) the lostness of human beings apart from Christ,
   (c) salvation in Jesus Christ alone,
   (d) Christian witness 'by both word and deed' (neither denying Christian social responsibility, nor making it 'our all-consuming mission'), and
   (e) the necessity of evangelism for the salvation of souls.
4. 'The Congress convenes to consider honestly and carefully both the unevangelized world and the church's resources to evangelize the world.'

Billy Graham concluded his stirring speech with four hopes and two needs. His four personal hopes were that the Congress would (1) 'frame a biblical declaration on evangelism', (2) challenge the church 'to complete the task of world evangelization', (3) 'state what the relationship is between evangelism and social responsibility', and (4) help to develop 'a new "koinonia" or fellowship among evangelicals of all persuasions . . . throughout the world'.

And the 'two basic needs' he saw were (a) that during the Congress there would be 'a tremendous emphasis on prayer', and (b) that we would all leave the Congress 'filled with the power of the Holy Spirit'.[3]

The Lausanne Covenant

If Billy Graham's introductory address set the scene for the Congress, the Lausanne Covenant was a conscientious attempt to encapsulate its main concerns. Its full text appears on pages 3–55 below, together with an exposition and commentary which seek to draw out its meaning and implications. Here it may be sufficient to mention seven of its main emphases. First, it contains an outspoken affirmation of biblical authority, calling Scripture 'the only written Word of God, without error in all that it affirms' (§ 2). Secondly,

---

[3] The full text of Billy Graham's opening message *Why Lausanne?* may be found on pages 22–36 of *Let the Earth Hear His Voice*, the Congress compendium, ed. J. D. Douglas.

in response to Billy Graham's specific hope, there is a biblical declaration on evangelism, which brings together the proclamation of Christ, the offer of salvation, the call for repentance and faith, and the cost of discipleship (§ 4). Thirdly, solid grounds are laid for Christian social responsibility, namely the character of God, the value of human beings made in his image, the requirement of neighbour-love, and the righteousness of the Kingdom (§ 5).

After the opening foundational clauses, the Covenant moves on to the church's evangelistic responsibility, and the fourth emphasis to mention should perhaps be the costliness of the task. For it will involve a deep penetration of society, sacrificial service, being 'marked by the cross', strict honesty and integrity, 'visible unity in truth', a renunciation of 'sinful individualism and needless duplication' (§§ 6 and 7), and the development of 'a simple lifestyle' (§ 9).

A fifth emphasis was the urgency of the evangelistic task. Dr. Donald McGavran and Dr. Ralph Winter of the Fuller School of World Mission shared with participants the startling figure that 2,700 million people remained unevangelized, but that nevertheless they could be reached if we were to break down the world's population into 'people groups', distinguish between E1, E2 and E3 evangelism, and remember the 'great new resource for world evangelization' constituted by the younger churches (§§ 8 and 9).

Sixthly, many were introduced for the first time at Lausanne to the problems raised by culture. Since culture is a human construct, it reflects the ambiguity of human beings, who both bear God's image and are fallen. Some missionaries export a 'culture Christianity' which glorifies their own culture and is correspondingly disrespectful of the culture to which they go. The need for sensitivity to culture, by national churches and leaders as well as missionaries, was strongly stressed (§§ 10 and 11).

The last four paragraphs of the Covenant may be taken together as indicating its seventh emphasis, namely that evangelism involves us in unseen spiritual warfare. The malign influence of the powers of darkness may be detected in false ideologies outside the church, in false gospels and false values inside it (§ 12), and in persecution (§ 13). So we need God's armour and weapons, and in particular the power of the Holy Spirit, since he is the chief witness to Christ and 'without his witness ours is futile' (§ 14). Despite Satanic opposition, our witness must continue throughout the interim period between Christ's ascension and return (§ 15).

Here then are seven major emphases to look for in the Lausanne Covenant: the authority of Scripture, the nature of evangelism, the grounds of Christian social responsibility, the costliness and the urgency of world mission, the problems of culture and the reality of spiritual warfare.

Follow-up
Both before and during the Congress, participants were asked to express their opinion whether it should have any kind of follow-up, and if so, what form it should take. Over 90% voted for a continuing communication link, and

72% for a Lausanne Continuation Committee. When the latter first met in January 1975 in Mexico City, with Bishop Jack Dain in the chair, a major debate took place whether the Committee's mandate was limited to evangelism, or whether it should include other responsibilities contained in the Covenant. In the end the Committee's object was defined as follows:

> 'to further the total biblical mission of the church, recognizing that "in the church's mission of sacrificial service evangelism is primary" (§ 6), and that our particular concern must be the evangelization of the 2,700 million unreached people of the world.'

This definition has continued to guide the Committee's work. Any topic contained in the Covenant came within the Committee's mandate (whether culture or simple lifestyle or social responsibility or freedom and persecution) provided that it was handled in relation to world evangelization.

When the Committee met the following year in Atlanta, its defined aim was broken down into four functions (intercession, theology, strategy and communication), and four working groups were established to concentrate on them.

The Strategy Working Group (SWG), chaired first by Dr. Peter Wagner and then by Dr. Ed Dayton, developed a fruitful partnership with MARC (World Vision's Mission Advanced Research and Communication Center), and pursued pioneer research into the world's 'unreached peoples'. SWG and MARC published a series of 'country profiles', and a number of annual paperbacks entitled *Unreached Peoples* beginning in 1979. 'We have come to see the world in a new way', Dr. Dayton wrote, 'not only as over 220 nation-states, but as thousands of people groups, within which God intends his church to take root and grow.' Moreover, 'every people group is unique. Because this is true, no one method, no one means, no one strategy can be used to communicate the saving grace of Jesus Christ to every people.'[4]

LTEG (the Lausanne Theology and Education Group), which was later renamed TWG (Theology Working Group), was set up at the same time 'to promote theological reflection on issues related to world evangelization and, in particular, to explore the implications of the Lausanne Covenant'. It organized a series of consultations between 1977 and 1982, some in co-operation with the World Evangelical Fellowship. Each produced a report which was first published as an LOP (Lausanne Occasional Paper), and is now incorporated in this book, and each was undertaken in 'the spirit of Lausanne'. Billy Graham was the first to use this expression, in his opening address at the Congress. Although it has never been given an authoritative definition, it seems to denote a mood or attitude compounded of five ingredients. It combines the resolve to work together for world evangelization, the humble penitence to confess our past shortcomings, the courage to meet one another face to face in order to debate the issues which divide us, the mutual

---

[4] *That Everyone May Hear*, pp. 1, 5.

respect to listen open-mindedly to one another's viewpoints, and the determination to submit to Scripture as we conscientiously understand it, while not breaking fellowship with those who interpret it differently.

Six Consultations 1977–1982

The first Lausanne Consultation sponsored by LTEG took place in Pasadena, California, in June 1977, and related to the 'homogeneous unit principle' (HUP). Dr. Donald McGavran's definition of the HUP is that people 'like to become Christians without crossing racial, linguistic or class barriers'. As an observable fact in evangelism this is indisputable. The controversial question is whether the principle may be extended to churches, or whether homogeneous congregations contradict the unity of the church which Christ secured by his death. Thus theology and strategy were in tension.

The Consultation began by affirming human cultural diversity as a good gift of the Creator, which he intends to be preserved and celebrated. In many situations, the report acknowledged, a homogeneous church 'can be a legitimate and authentic church'. Yet 'it can never be complete in itself', since 'it cannot reflect the universality and diversity of the Body of Christ'. So every homogeneous church should move towards heterogeneity, inspired by the eschatological vision of the redeemed community (Rev. 7:9ff.), which is racially, tribally and linguistically heterogeneous, and of which our fellowship at the Lord's Supper is intended to be a foretaste.

Just over six months later, in January 1978, a second Lausanne Consultation was held, this time at Willowbank in Bermuda. It was jointly sponsored by LTEG and SWG, and was entitled *Gospel and Culture*. As already mentioned, 'culture' was a prominent topic at the Congress. The Willowbank Consultation dug into it more deeply. After a careful definition of culture, the report considers its influence in six areas — in the writers and the readers of the Bible (since they and we are both culturally conditioned), in the preaching and the receiving of the gospel (contextualization and conversion), in the formation of the church and in ethical behaviour. Cross-cultural messengers of the gospel have to ask themselves: 'How can I, having been born and raised in one culture, take the gospel from Scripture which was written in other cultures, and communicate it to people in a third culture, without either distorting the message or rendering it unintelligible?' To help us to answer this question, the report contains both a moving analysis of missionary humility and a reflection on the Incarnation as a model of Christian witness.

The Glen Eyrie conference on Muslim evangelization came next, although it was not sponsored by LTEG but jointly by the North American Lausanne Committee and World Vision International. It was held in Colorado Springs in October 1978. Its report is not an official statement, although most of it

was read to the conference, and participants' suggestions were later incorporated into it. Some key evangelical leaders from the Middle East, Asia and
Africa were present. Preceded by the circulation of forty foundation papers,
the conference was a time of considerable 'intellectual ferment'. It was also
permeated throughout by a mood of penitence and humility. The wide
diversity of cultures in the Islamic world was recognized. Although some
biblical strategies for mission were considered, and a decisive break with the
past was called for, no new strategies for Muslim evangelization were developed. The emphasis was rather on the need for integrity, transparency,
courage, patience, on the willingness to suffer and on the centrality of love.
The Samuel Zwemer Institute, later re-named the Zwemer Institute of Muslim Studies, came into being as a direct result of the Glen Eyrie consultation,
with Dr. Don McCurry as its founding director.

The most anxiously debated clause in the Lausanne Covenant is the one
which accepts 'our duty to develop a simple lifestyle' (§ 9). So in March 1980
at High Leigh Conference Centre north of London an International Consultation on Simple Lifestyle was held, jointly sponsored by LTEG (as their third
consultation) and by the WEF's Theological Commission. The report took
the form of 'An Evangelical Commitment to Simple Lifestyle'. It has been
criticized from both the left and the right, but it can be defended as a biblically
balanced statement. It avoids the opposite extremes of asceticism (since we
should celebrate the goodness of God's creation) and materialism (since a
selfish preoccupation with material things is incompatible with a faithful
stewardship of creation's resources). While wisely declining to lay down rules
and regulations, whether for ourselves or for others, it calls us (as the Bible
does) to beware of covetousness, to renounce waste, to oppose extravagance
and to cultivate contentment, simplicity and generosity. What it says about
governments, multi-national corporations and political action is regarded by
some as controversial, but it was carefully worded with the help of economists
and avoids rhetoric. The report concludes with a strong summons to world
evangelization, in the knowledge that the Lord Jesus is coming back to judge,
to save and to reign.

In June 1980 the large Consultation on World Evangelization (COWE)
took place at Pattaya in Thailand. The theme of Lausanne had been 'Let the
earth hear his voice'; the theme of Pattaya was 'How shall they hear?' COWE
was essentially a study conference, in that for five of its ten days the participants broke into mini-consultations, which were the climax of a lengthy,
world-wide study programme, and each of which was concerned with our
Christian witness to a particular section of the population. These produced
seventeen reports, a list of which may be found in Chapter 6.

At the end of COWE 'the Thailand Statement' was adopted. Endorsing
the Lausanne Covenant in its entirety as 'the basis of our common activity',
it says: 'Although evangelism and social action are not identical, we gladly
reaffirm our commitment to both.' It goes on to quote the Covenant's
statement that 'in the church's mission of sacrificial service evangelism is

primary' (§ 6). Why? Because 'of all the tragic needs of human beings none is greater than their alienation from their Creator and the terrible reality of eternal death for those who refuse to repent and believe . . .'. The Statement goes on to emphasize the urgency of bringing the gospel to those who have not heard it, and the value of thinking of them not only as individuals but also as 'people groups'. For this was one of the major concepts presented to COWE.

The Thailand Statement mentions the topics of the plenary sessions (e.g. the Bible, the local church, cultural sensitivity, and the indispensable necessity of the work of the Holy Spirit and of prayer). It also notes as prominent in all the mini-consultation reports a stress on love, humility, integrity and power. The Statement ends with the participants' resolve to 'strengthen evangelical co-operation in global evangelization', in spite of the problems, with the Lausanne Committee acting as a catalyst, and with a twelve-point pledge, which participants made together publicly in the final meeting.

The Thailand Statement alludes indirectly, at least in one paragraph, to an unofficial 'Statement of Concerns' which had been circulated during the Consultation. This Statement expressed the view that the Lausanne Committee was insufficiently concerned for social justice, and called on it to organize a world conference on this topic. What most Pattaya participants did not know at the time was that LTEG's plans were already advanced for the Consultation on the Relationship between Evangelism and Social Responsibility (CRESR), which took place two years later.

Although the Lausanne Covenant includes clear statements both on 'The Nature of Evangelism' (§ 4) and on 'Christian Social Responsibility' (§ 5), the two paragraphs stand there side by side without any attempt to relate them, except for the clause in § 6 that 'in the church's mission of sacrificial service evangelism is primary'. Yet in his opening address at Lausanne Billy Graham had specifically expressed his hope that the Congress would 'state what the relationship is between evangelism and social responsibility'. So in June 1982 CRESR convened in Grand Rapids, Michigan, jointly sponsored by LTEG and WEF. The fifty or so participants had been carefully chosen to represent different nations, churches, traditions, cultures and viewpoints. Such a diverse group did not augur well for the possibility of consensus. And indeed, when we began, conflicting opinions were voiced, even with stridency. But as we listened to one another with respect, and began to grasp what it was that we wanted to safeguard, the time for creative engagement arrived. True, in a few places the report says that 'some of us think this, while others think that'. Yet the great majority of the report expresses agreement.

The Grand Rapids Report is too long (nearly 20,000 words) to be summarized in a single paragraph. But after the three opening sections, entitled 'A Call to Worship and Thanksgiving', 'A Call to World Evangelization' and 'A Call to Social Responsibility', the crucial fourth chapter spells out a threefold relationship between evangelism and social responsibility. Social activity is a *consequence* of evangelism (since evangelism brings people to new birth, and their new life manifests itself in the service of others), a *bridge* to evangelism (since it breaks down suspicion and gains a hearing for the gospel) and a *partner* of evangelism (words and works belonging together, 'like the two blades of a pair of scissors or the two wings of a bird'). The report also clarifies that the 'primacy' of evangelism is due partly to the fact that it relates to people's eternal destiny (as the Thailand Statement had said), and partly to its logical priority, since 'Christian social responsibility presupposes socially responsible Christians', and such Christians are the fruit of evangelism.[5]

After CRESR (1982), which was the fourth consultation organized by LTEG, four more international Lausanne meetings were held, namely the International Prayer Assembly for World Evangelization (Seoul, 1984), the Consultation on the Work of the Holy Spirit and Evangelization (Oslo, 1985), a conference of young leaders (Singapore, 1987), and the Consultation on Conversion and World Evangelization (Hong Kong, 1988). Further information about these meetings is given in Chapter 8.

Manila 1989

During these years preparations were going on for the Second International Congress on World Evangelization, which came to be known as 'Lausanne II' and which took place in Manila in July 1989. It was again an enormous undertaking, with over 3,000 participants from 170 nations, including Eastern Europe and the Soviet Union, but sadly not from mainland China. The ten-day programme was crowded with activity: worship, prayer and celebration; Bible Studies; plenary addresses; national and regional meetings; and workshops on every conceivable subject related to world evangelization.[6]

Throughout the Congress a listening team and a drafting committee were hard at work, and gradually the Manila Manifesto was framed. Its second draft was circulated for criticism and comment to all the participants, and their responses were carefully considered and in most cases incorporated. The final document was submitted as an expression 'in general terms' of the participants' 'concerns and commitments', and with that understanding was accepted by an overwhelming majority.

The Manila Manifesto (MM) is essentially an elaboration of the Lausanne Covenant (LC) fifteen years later, and for this reason the Lausanne Committee have ruled that the two documents will always be published together. Nevertheless, a careful study of MM, which is twice as long as LC, shows that it goes beyond it in a number of important ways. This is true of each of its twelve paragraphs.

---

[5]   These issues were further explored the following year at a conference convened by WEF in Wheaton, Illinois, entitled *I will Build my Church*. See its summary document, *The Church in Response to Human Need*, ed. Tom Sine (MARC, 1983).

[6]   The story of Lausanne II is vividly told in *The Whole Gospel for the Whole World*, ed. Alan Nichols (Regal, 1989).

(1)   MM portrays in solemn terms our human predicament as 'self-centred, self-serving rebels', declares self-salvation impossible, and rejects both false gospels and half gospels.

(2)   MM affirms that apologetics and evangelism belong together, and explains the two senses in which the gospel is 'good news for the poor'.

(3)   MM indicates how we should think about non-Christian religions, and insists on the necessity of Jewish evangelism.

(4)   MM affirms that 'good news and good works are inseparable'; that 'the proclamation of God's kingdom necessarily demands the prophetic denunciation of all that is incompatible with it'; and that our commitment to social action is not a return to the 'social gospel' of theological liberalism, but rather 'a recognition that the biblical gospel has inescapable social implications'.

(5)   MM declares that 'God himself is the chief evangelist' (through the Holy Spirit); that 'every true conversion involves a power encounter'; and that we must reject 'both the scepticism which denies miracles and the presumption which demands them'.

(6)   MM insists on 'the ministry (as well as the priesthood) of all believers'; on the role of pastors 'not to monopolize ministries, but rather to multiply them'; and on 'the partnership in world evangelization which God intends men and women to enjoy', and young people too.

(7)   MM emphasizes the need for 'integrity' in Christian witnesses, since 'nothing commends the gospel more eloquently than a transformed life, and nothing brings it into disrepute so much as personal inconsistency'. MM deplores the 'worldliness' which allows 'the prevailing culture to subvert the church, instead of the church challenging and changing the culture'.

(8)   MM states that the local church is 'both a worshipping and a witnessing community'; that it 'bears a primary responsibility for the spread of the gospel'; and that it must not only proclaim the gospel, but embody it in its life of love.

(9)   MM points out that 'evangelism and unity are closely related in the New Testament', declares that 'the great new fact of our era is the internationalization of missions', and opens up the delicate question of evangelical relationships with those who do not profess to be evangelical.

(10)   MM recognizes that 'evangelism takes place in a context, not in a vacuum'; that one such context is the 'emerging world culture' called 'modernity', especially in the big cities of today; and that modernization brings both dangers and opportunities.

(11)   MM classifies the world population into four categories — the 'committed' (the potential missionary work force), the 'uncommitted' (nominal Christians), the 'unevangelized' (with minimal Christian knowledge) and the 'unreached' (the two million who belong to 12,000 unreached people groups, and who have never heard of Christ). 'There is nothing magical about the date', but AD 2000 is 'a challenging milestone'.

(12)   MM refers to Jesus' teaching that 'Christian suffering is inevitable and productive', yet also expresses the hope that religious freedom will spread

throughout the world. Governments should know that Christians are 'conscientious citizens'; that they renounce 'unworthy witness' in favour of an 'open and honest' statement of the gospel; and that they 'earnestly desire freedom of religion' for all people, not just for themselves.

MM concludes that 'the whole church is called to take the whole gospel to the whole world, proclaiming Christ until he comes, with all necessary urgency, unity and sacrifice'.

The Present and the Future

The purpose of this book is to preserve, and so make available to the Christian public, the main documentation of the Lausanne Movement during the fifteen years between Lausanne I (1974) and Lausanne II in Manila (1989). Lausanne I took place nearly a quarter of a century ago. The Lausanne Covenant is not so well known now as it used to be. A new generation of younger evangelical leaders has arisen who are not familiar with Lausanne or with the basic theological and missiological thinking incorporated in its reports. Ignorance of this groundwork may lead younger missionaries and missionary candidates to re-lay the foundations or re-invent the wheel.

This book is limited to those congresses, conferences and consultations which were officially sponsored by the Lausanne Committee and which produced authorized reports, in the sense that they were substantially endorsed by the participants concerned. Moreover, since all these reports arose out of particular contexts, they have been left alone in their historical integrity; no attempt has been made to modify or update either their language or their content. The reports of the many regional and national Lausanne conferences have not been included. Nor have the reports of those consultations which were not officially sponsored by the Lausanne Committee, even though the evangelical participants were virtually all signatories of the Lausanne Covenant. Examples are ERCDOM, the Evangelical–Roman Catholic Dialogue on Mission (1977–1984)[7] and the Stuttgart Conference of March 1987, sponsored by CWME, which brought twenty evangelical and a number of ecumenical leaders together.[8]

Because this book ends with the Manila Manifesto, it must not be imagined that the Lausanne Movement came to an end at Manila in 1989. For example, a Consultation on Faith and Modernity took place at Uppsala in Sweden in June 1993. See the Appendix on page 251.

What about the 'AD 2000 and Beyond Movement', which has arisen since Lausanne II and has captured the imagination and fired the enthusiasm of

---

[7] The ERCDOM Report, edited by Basil Meeking and John Stott, was published by Eerdmans and Paternoster in 1986.

[8] Arising from this conference was *Proclaiming Christ in Christ's Way*, studies in integral evangelism, edited by Vinay Samuel and Albrecht Hauser (Regnum, 1989).

many? How are the two movements related to one another? Their international directors met in May 1991 to clarify this, and issued a statement that 'the Lausanne Movement (Lausanne) and the AD 2000 and Beyond Movement (AD 2000) share the common commitment to world evangelization. It is the conviction of the leaders that they are complementary to one another'. The text of the AD 2000 and Beyond *Handbook* helps us to express this complementarity more fully. On the one hand, Lausanne has contributed (a) the launching pad of the AD 2000 movement in the Manila plenary and track of this title, (b) the leadership of Dr. Thomas Wang, who was the director of the Lausanne Movement and of the Manila Congress before he became founder and chairman of the AD 2000 movement, and (c) the Lausanne Covenant which AD 2000 has adopted as its basis, together with § 11 of the Manila Manifesto, entitled 'The Challenge of AD 2000 and Beyond'. On the other hand, AD 2000 is contributing further vision and motivation for world evangelization, and likens itself to 'a hot current' within 'the broad flow' of the Lausanne river. It is doing this (a) by popularizing the slogan 'a church for every people and the gospel for every person', (b) by setting the target date of AD 2000 not as having any 'eschatological importance' but 'as a driving force for mobilizing and energizing the church for evangelism', and (c) by urging us to make 'the 10/40 window' the main focus of our prayers, i.e. the rectangular area between 10 and 40 degrees north of the equator, stretching from West Africa to East Asia, where most of the world's unreached and poorest peoples live.[9]

GCOWE in Seoul Korea in July 1995 was deliberately held at the mid point of the decade culminating in AD 2000. It assembled about 4,000 Christians from 186 countries, and in its declaration it reaffirmed (1) the Lausanne Covenant and the Manila Manifesto as its foundation, (2) the 10/40 window as its primary focus, (3) the urgency of the task before the close of the millennium, (4) the need to motivate the church towards both church planting and concern for social justice, and (5) the necessity of developing detailed strategies, while waiting humbly on God.

In February 1994 the Lausanne Committee executive met in Stuttgart, Germany, with the chair persons of the active national, regional and special interest committees. They reaffirmed the mission of Lausanne to further world evangelization by building bridges of understanding and cooperation among Christian leaders everywhere. They noted that the Lausanne Movement is more active today than ever before. For example, during 1993 no fewer than eleven Lausanne consultations and prayer conferences took place in ten countries, while another eleven were planned for 1994. All these, however, were national rather than international meetings. So it was decided at Stuttgart to encourage the decentralization of the Lausanne Movement, and to develop a smaller, more flexible central structure which would be accountable to the national, regional and special interest committees.

[9] *Handbook*, 3rd edition, pp. 8, 9.

The Stuttgart meeting summed up Lausanne's new look in these terms:

'Same mission. New structure. New leaders. An international funding base. Strategic alliances. All of this adds up to a new beginning.'

JOHN STOTT
Easter, 1996

1

— 1974 —

The Lausanne Covenant

With an exposition and commentary
by John Stott

♦♦♦♦♦

The International Congress on World
Evangelization,
Lausanne, Switzerland
16–25 July 1974

— The Lausanne Covenant —
with exposition and commentary

CONTENTS

PREFACE TO THE COMMENTARY

A theologian who teaches in Asia has written about the Lausanne Covenant, 'History may show this Covenant to be the most significant ecumenical confession on evangelism that the church has ever produced.' It is a bold statement. As he says, only history will tell. In the meantime, while we await history's verdict, how did it come to be written?

A first and fairly short statement was produced two or three months before the Congress and submitted by mail to a number of advisers. Already this document may truly be said to have come out of the Congress (although the Congress had not yet assembled), because it reflected the contributions of the main speakers whose papers had been published in advance. The document was revised in the light of the advisers' comments, and this revision was further revised at Lausanne by the drafting committee. So what was submitted to all participants in the middle of the Congress was the third draft. They were invited to send in their contributions, either as individuals or as groups, and they responded with great diligence. Many hundreds of submissions were received (in the official languages), translated into English, sorted and studied. Some proposed amendments cancelled each other out, but the drafting committee incorporated all they could, while at the same time ensuring that the final document was a recognizable revision of the draft submitted to participants. It may truly be said, then, that the Lausanne Covenant expresses a consensus of the mind and mood of the Lausanne Congress.

I would like to express my deep gratitude to Dr. Hudson Armerding and Mr. Samuel Escobar, who were the other members of the drafting committee, and to Dr. Leighton Ford and Dr. Jim Douglas who helped us. They worked hard and conscientiously, and we were all aware of a harmony of mind and spirit which we believe was given to us by God himself.

The word 'covenant' is not used in its technical, biblical sense, but in the ordinary sense of a binding contract. For example, in seventeenth century Scotland there were the famous 'Covenanters' who bound themselves by a 'solemn league and covenant' to maintain the freedom of the church. The reason the expression 'Lausanne Covenant' was chosen in preference to 'Lausanne Declaration' is that we wanted to do more than find an agreed formula of words. We were determined not just to declare something, but to do something, namely to commit ourselves to the task of world evangelization.

The fifteen sections or paragraphs into which the Covenant is divided are all packed fairly tight with content. So the purpose of this exposition and commentary is to help to 'unpack' it, to draw out both the meaning and the implications of what it says. Inevitably this is a personal interpretation, and

5

does not carry the authority of the Congress Planning Committee. Nevertheless, a conscientious attempt has been made to set it in the context of the Congress papers, addresses and discussion, and to let the Covenant speak for itself. It is for this reason that the full text appears twice, first at the head of each section, and secondly broken up into sentences and incorporated into the commentary (in italic type).

The same desire to let the Covenant speak for itself has led to the decision to omit a bibliography and references to other literature. The only quotations are from Congress papers and addresses (which are printed in full in the official Compendium*) and from the Revised Standard Version of the Bible. Biblical references are numerous, for the Covenant will commend itself only in so far as it can show itself to be a true expression of biblical teaching and principles.

Bishop Jack Dain, Chairman of the Congress, has referred to Lausanne as 'a process, not just an event'. One important aspect of the continuing process will be the study of the Covenant both by individuals and by groups. In order to facilitate discussion, a series of questions has been added at the end of each chapter.

JOHN STOTT
September, 1974

---

* *Let The Earth Hear His Voice* ed. J. D. Douglas. For details of this compendium, and for a summary of its contents, see the postscript at the end of this chapter.

INTRODUCTION TO THE COVENANT

The Introduction to the text of the Covenant is not just a formal preamble; it describes the context within which the Covenant must be read and interpreted. It says something important about who the participants were, what the mood of the Congress was and how the Covenant came into being. *We, members of the Church of Jesus Christ, from more than 150 nations, participants in the International Congress on World Evangelization at Lausanne, praise God for his great salvation and rejoice in the fellowship he has given us with himself and with each other. We are deeply stirred by what God is doing in our day, moved to penitence by our failures and challenged by the unfinished task of evangelization. We believe the Gospel is God's good news for the whole world, and we are determined by his grace to obey Christ's commission to proclaim it to all mankind and to make disciples of every nation. We desire, therefore, to affirm our faith and our resolve, and to make public our covenant.*

a. The Lausanne Participants

We who were *participants in the International Congress on World Evangelization at Lausanne, Switzerland* (July 16–25, 1974), identify ourselves in several ways. To begin with, we had come *from more than 150 nations*. TIME magazine referred to the Congress as 'a formidable forum, possibly the widest-ranging meeting of Christians ever held.' Across the wall behind the platform the Congress slogan was displayed in the six official languages: 'Let the Earth Hear His Voice.' Yet we were made aware that the earth had already begun to hear and respond, for the 2,700 participants, with the whole spectrum of skin pigmentation and colorful costume, seemed to have come from every corner of the globe. It was a special joy that 50 percent of the participants, and also of the speakers and the Planning Committee, were from the Third World. One major sorrow was that a few countries, including the USSR and mainland China, were unrepresented.

Despite the diversity of our racial and cultural backgrounds, however, we were conscious of a deep and wonderful unity. For we were all *members of the Church of Jesus Christ*, Christians who take both Christ and Church seriously. We do not confuse the two, imagining that to belong to the visible church necessarily implies that we also belong to Jesus Christ. On the other hand, we acknowledge that we cannot call Jesus Lord and not be responsible members of his new community. In particular, as evangelical Christians, we

7

praise God for his great salvation which he has once for all achieved and now bestows through Jesus Christ.

Aware of our common share in this salvation, we *rejoice in the fellowship he has given us with himself and with each other*.

b.   The Lausanne Spirit

It is always difficult to express a mood in words. Yet 'the spirit of Lausanne' was more tangible than are most spirits. Its first element comes out in the phrase *we are deeply stirred by what God is doing in our day*. For we are convinced that he is on the move, and we have been excited by the evidence laid before us in stories and statistics. Secondly, we are *moved to penitence by our failures*. Several speakers voiced the hope that the Congress would be marked more by evangelical penitence than by evangelical triumphalism. 'Triumphalism' is an attitude of self-confidence and self-congratulation, which is never appropriate in God's children. But the spirit of Lausanne was a spirit of humility and a spirit of penitence. Thirdly, a sense of our past failures and of God's present action leads inevitably to a purposeful look into the future: we are *challenged by the unfinished task of evangelization*, and the challenge has not fallen on deaf ears.

c.   The Lausanne Covenant

It is, then, such people in such a spirit, who felt the need to bind themselves together in a commitment or 'covenant.' *We believe the Gospel is God's good news for the whole world*. Does this talk of world conquest sound presumptuous? If it does, we are content to bear the criticism, for Christians are ambassadors for Jesus Christ, and the world empire we seek (as Jesus told us to, Matt. 6:33) is the kingdom of God. *So we are determined by his grace to obey Christ's commission*. The reference is to the 'great' or 'universal' commission of the risen Lord, which was both *to proclaim* the Gospel *to all mankind* ('the whole creation,' Mark 16:15) and *to make disciples of every nation* (Matt. 28:19).

We desire, therefore, to affirm our faith (our conviction that the Gospel is God's good news for the world) *and our resolve* (our determination to proclaim it to all mankind), and in the light of these things not just to enter into a private commitment ourselves but *to make public our covenant*.

1. THE PURPOSE OF GOD

We affirm our belief in the one eternal God, Creator and Lord of the world, Father, Son and Holy Spirit, who governs all things according to the purpose of his will. He has been calling out from the world a people for himself, and sending his people back into the world to be his servants and his witnesses, for the extension of his kingdom, the building up of Christ's body, and the glory of his name. We confess with shame that we have often denied our calling and failed in our mission, by becoming conformed to the world or by withdrawing from it. Yet we rejoice that even when borne by earthen vessels the Gospel is still a precious treasure. To the task of making that treasure known in the power of the Holy Spirit we desire to dedicate ourselves anew.

Is. 40:28
Mt. 28:19
Eph. 1:11
Ac. 15:14
Jn. 17:6, 18
Eph. 1:12
Eph. 4:12
Ro. 12:2
1 Co. 5:10
2 Co. 4:7

The Covenant opens with a paragraph about God, because God is the beginning of all things. However far back we are able to trace causes and effects, we cannot go further back than God himself. He is the first cause. So Christians want to think theologically, that is, to relate all their thinking to God's who is the ultimate personal Reality behind everything.

In particular, we cannot talk about mission or evangelism without first talking about God. For mission and evangelism are not the novel ideas of modern men, but part of the eternal purpose of God. The paragraph refers briefly to who God is and what he does, goes on to describe his plan for his people, and ends with an assurance of his power even in our human weakness.

a. The Being of God

No attempt is made to give a full statement of biblical teaching about God. We affirm our belief in God and concentrate on a few essentials of our faith in him. It may be helpful to consider these in pairs.

First, God is both eternal and active in time. He is *the . . . eternal God*, existing outside time and before time began. Scripture is clear about this. 'From everlasting to everlasting thou art God' (Psa. 90:2). Nevertheless (to use the terms of classical theology) the God who is 'transcendent' beyond the universe is also 'immanent' within it. He brought it into being and rules all that he has made. He is *Creator and Lord of the world*. The two truths are brought together in Isaiah 40:28, 'The LORD is the everlasting God, the Creator of the ends of the earth.'

9

Secondly, God is both one and three. He is *the one . . . God . . ., Father, Son and Holy Spirit*. There can be no question of his unity. The Christian affirms this as strongly as any Jew or Muslim. 'The LORD our God is one LORD' (Deut. 6:4). He says, 'I am the LORD, and there is no other, beside me there is no God' (Isa. 45:5). The unity of the Godhead is fundamental to all evangelism. It is because 'there is one God' that he demands and deserves the total allegiance of all mankind (Deut. 6:4,5; Mark 12: 29,30; 1 Tim. 2:5). Yet this one God revealed himself in three stages (first as the God of Israel, then as the incarnate Lord, then as the Holy Spirit) in such a way as to show that he exists eternally in these three personal modes of being. So the risen Jesus has commanded us to baptize converts 'in the name (note the singular) of the Father and of the Son and of the Holy Spirit' (Matt. 28:19).

Thirdly, God rules both nature and history. He who is the *Creator and Lord of the world* also *governs all things according to the purpose of his will*. So convinced of this were the apostles that they believed even the hostility of persecutors to be under the control of God. Forbidden to preach, and threatened with severe penalties if they disobeyed, they cried to God as 'Sovereign Lord' and declared that the opposition of men to Christ was part of his predestinating plan (Acts 4:28). This must be so, because God 'accomplishes all things according to the counsel of his will' (Eph. 1:11).

b. The Purpose of God

From the work of God as Lord of nature and history, the Covenant turns to his redeeming purpose, namely to call out *a people for himself*. It began with Abraham, to whom God said, 'I will make of you a great nation . . . and by you all the families of the earth shall bless themselves' (Gen. 12:1–3). It continued with Israel, with whom after the Exodus God renewed his covenant of grace, 'You shall be my own possession among all peoples' (Ex. 19:3–6). It is now finding its completion (through the evangelistic work of the church) in the inclusion of Gentile believers: 'God . . . visited the Gentiles, to take out of them a people for his name' (Acts 15:14). Then in the end there will gather before God's throne a countless, international throng, and his promise to Abraham will be finally fulfilled (Rev. 7:9). This concept of the church as a 'people for God's possession' is taken up in the New Testament (e.g., 1 Pet. 2:9) and indicates that worship is the church's first vocation.

The Lausanne Covenant, in speaking of the people of God, concentrates on the relation of the church to the world, that is, of Christian people to non-Christian people or to secular society. It brings together two complementary aspects of this relation: *He has been calling out from the world a people for himself, and sending his people back into the world.* Jesus himself referred to this double role of the church in his prayer recorded in John 17. He began by describing his own as 'the men whom thou gavest me out of the world' (vv. 6,9). Yet those who in one sense had been taken 'out of' the world in another sense had not, for they were still in it. Jesus could go on to say, 'I am no more in the world, but they are in the world' (v. 11). Moreover, it was not enough for them to reside 'in' the world; he had to send them 'into' the world (v. 18). These prepositions 'out of,' 'in' and 'into' together portray what the Christian's relation to the unbelieving world should be.

When we talk about the church being 'sent into the world' we are talking about its mission, for that is what the word means. And what is the church's mission in the world? Evangelism yes, but not that alone. For God sends his people out *to be his servants and his witnesses*. Not one or the other, but both. Jesus came to serve (Mark 10: 45) and he came to witness (John 18:37). The same two activities constitute the church's mission. They are elaborated later in the Covenant, evangelism in paragraph 4 and Christian social responsibility in paragraph 5. Meanwhile, the objectives of the church's mission are outlined as *the extension of his kingdom* (which Jesus talked about so much, e.g., Matt. 6:10,33; 13:31,32), *the building up of Christ's body* (which Paul wrote about, e.g., Eph. 4:11–16) and *the glory of his name* (which is not only the ultimate aim of mission but also 'the chief end of man') cf. Psa. 115:1; Eph. 1:6,12,14).

This affirmation about God and his high purpose for the church in the world inevitably leads us to *confess with shame that we have often denied our calling and failed in our mission*. For we often tend to go to one or other of two opposite extremes. Either we are so determined to live in the world and maintain contact with non-Christians that we begin to assimilate non-Christian ideas and standards, and are then guilty of *becoming conformed to the world* (Rom. 12:1,2); or we are so determined not to lose our distinctive Christian identity that we begin to shun contact with non-Christians in the world, and then become guilty of *withdrawing from it* (John 17:15; 1 Cor. 5:10). The best way to avoid these two mistakes of conformity and withdrawal is to be engaged in mission. For if we remember that we are sent into the world as Christ's representatives, we can neither conform to it or we cease to represent him, nor withdraw from it or we have no one to represent him to.

c. The Power of God

The consciousness of our failures can be no excuse for opting out of our responsibilities. It is true that we are like *earthen vessels* — frail, weak and fragile. But these vessels carry *a precious treasure, the Gospel*, and it is through our very weakness that the power of God is best exhibited (II Cor. 4:7; cf., I Cor. 2:3–5 and II Cor. 12:9,10). So the Covenant's first paragraph ends with a reference (expanded in paragraph 14) to *the power of the Holy Spirit* for the evangelistic task to which *we desire to dedicate ourselves anew*.

Questions for study:

1. What is the importance of the doctrine of God in connection with evangelism?
2. Read John 17:9–19 and summarize from Christ's teaching there the Christian's relation to the world.
3. Would the attitude of your local church to the world be most accurately described as one of 'conformity,' 'withdrawal' or 'mission'? What steps could be taken to remedy whatever you may find to be wrong?

2. THE AUTHORITY AND POWER OF THE BIBLE

We affirm the divine inspiration, truthfulness and authority of both Old and New Testament Scriptures in their entirety as the only written Word of God, without error in all that it affirms, and the only infallible rule of faith and practice. We also affirm the power of God's Word to accomplish his purpose of salvation. The message of the Bible is addressed to all mankind. For God's revelation in Christ and in Scripture is unchangeable. Through it the Holy Spirit still speaks today. He illumines the minds of God's people in every culture to perceive its truth freshly through their own eyes and thus discloses to the whole church ever more of the many-colored wisdom of God.

2 Ti. 3:16
2 Pe. 1:21

Is. 55:11
Ro. 1:16
1 Co. 1:21

Jn. 10:35
Mt. 5:17, 18
Jude 3

Eph. 1:17, 18;
3:10,18

It may seem strange that the Lausanne Covenant, which is primarily concerned with worldwide evangelization, should include a statement about biblical authority and indeed emphasize it by putting it in such a prominent place, second only to the doctrine of God. But this faithfully reflects the Congress program in which the first biblical foundation paper was entitled 'Biblical Authority and Evangelism.' Dr. Susumu Uda began, 'The problem of authority is the most fundamental problem that the Christian Church always faces.' Both evangelism and the nurture of converts involve teaching and therefore raise the question, 'What shall we teach?' As Dr. Francis Schaeffer wrote in his later paper, 'The Gospel we preach must be rich in content.' And this content must be biblical content. The Covenant concentrates on three features of the Bible — its authority, its power and its interpretation.

a. The Authority of the Bible

What is meant by 'the Bible' is *both Old and New Testament Scriptures in their entirety*, and these are described as *the only written Word of God*. Scripture is 'the Word of God' because God 'spoke' it (Heb. 1:1,2; I Thess. 2:13); it is his 'written Word' for he then caused it to be recorded for the instruction of later generations (Rom. 15:4; I Cor. 10:6, 11; I Tim. 3:14,15); and it is his 'only' written Word, for we cannot accept the so-called sacred scriptures of other religions (e.g., the Koran or the Book of Mormon) as having come out of the mind and mouth of God. Three words are used to define more clearly the divine origin of Scripture — *inspiration, truthfulness and authority*.

13

(i) *Inspiration.* This does not mean that God somehow breathed into words which had already been written, or into the writers who wrote them, but rather that the words themselves were 'God-breathed' (II Tim. 3:16, literally). Of course, they were also the words of men who spoke and wrote freely. Yet these men were 'moved by the Holy Spirit' (II Pet. 1:21) to such an extent that it could be said of their words, 'the mouth of the Lord has spoken it' (Isa. 40:5).

(ii) *Truthfulness.* Since Scripture is God's Word written, it is inevitably true. For 'God is not man that he should lie' (Num. 23:19). On the contrary, as Jesus himself said in prayer to the Father, 'Thy word is truth' (John 17:17). And since it is true, it is *without error in all that it affirms.* Notice the careful qualification. For not everything contained in Scripture is affirmed by Scripture. To take an extreme example, Psalm 14:1 contains the statement, 'There is no God.' This statement is false. But Scripture is not affirming it. What Scripture affirms in that verse is not atheism, but the folly of atheism, 'The fool says in his heart, "There is no God".' It is important, therefore, in all our Bible study to consider the intention of the author, and what is being asserted. It is this, whatever the subject of the assertion may be, which is true and inerrant.

(iii) *Authority.* The order of the three words is logical. It is the divine *inspiration* of Scripture which has secured its *truthfulness,* and it is because Scripture is truth from God that it has *authority* over men. Indeed (echoing the Westminster Confession) it is *the only infallible rule of faith and practice.* Different churches value secondary rules (creeds, confessions and traditions) to govern their faith (what they believe and teach) and their practice (what they do), but Scripture is the only infallible rule, to whose authority therefore all churches should humbly bow. Jesus himself, in his controversy with the Pharisees, made it plain that ecclesiastical traditions must always be subservient to Scripture, because the former are man's words, while the latter is God's (Mark 7: 1–13). Indeed, Jesus' own reverent submission to the Old Testament Scriptures and his provision for the New Testament Scriptures by his appointment of the apostles are together one of the principal reasons for our own acceptance of the authority of Scripture. The disciple is not above his master.

b.   The Power of the Bible

We also affirm the power of God's Word to accomplish his purpose . . . God's words are not like our words. Human words are often as feeble as the breath with which they are spoken. But when God speaks he acts. His Word never returns to him empty, but always accomplishes his purpose (Isa. 55:11). For example, it was by his Word that he created: 'God said . . . and it was so' (Gen. 1:9, and throughout the chapter). 'He spoke, and it came to be' (Psa. 33:6,9).

What is true of creation is equally true of *his purpose of salvation.* The Gospel itself is 'the power of God for salvation to everyone who has faith' (Rom. 1:16).

Man cannot save himself by his own wisdom. Instead, it pleases God 'through the folly of what we preach to save those who believe' (I Cor. 1:21). Not that we should separate the power of God's Word from the power of God's Spirit. The Spirit uses the Word, and speaks and acts through it (e.g., I Cor. 2:1–5; I Thess. 1:5; I Pet. 1:12). Scripture is rich in the metaphors with which it indicates the power of the Word in the hand of the Spirit (e.g., Jer. 23:29 'fire' and 'hammer'; Eph. 6:17 and Heb. 4:12 'sword'; I Pet. 1:23 and Jas. 1:21 'seed,' etc.). This assurance should give great confidence to all Christians who in their preaching and witnessing handle Scripture faithfully and humbly.

c.   The Interpretation of the Bible

The last four sentences of the paragraph touch upon an important paradox regarding our understanding of God's Word.

On the one hand, *the message of the Bible* is exactly the same for all men in all places and at all times. Its relevance is not limited to any particular generation or any particular culture. On the contrary, it is *addressed to all mankind*. This is because *God's revelation in Christ and in Scripture is unchangeable*. As Jesus said, it 'cannot be broken' (John 10:35, cf. Matt. 5:17,18). It has been delivered to us 'once for all' unalterably (Jude 3). And being God's truth it possesses a marvelous universality. As *through it the Holy Spirit still speaks today*, it has a message for everybody everywhere.

On the other hand, its unalterability is not a dead, wooden, colorless uniformity. For as the Holy Spirit used the personality and culture of the writers of his Word in order to convey through each something fresh and appropriate, so today *he illumines the minds of God's people in every culture to perceive its truth freshly through their own eyes*. It is he who opens the eyes of our hearts (Eph. 1:17,18), and these eyes and hearts belong to young and old, Latin and Anglo-Saxon, African, Asian and American, male and female, poetic and prosaic. It is this 'magnificent and intricate mosaic of mankind' (to borrow a phrase of Dr. Donald McGavran's) which the Holy Spirit uses to disclose from Scripture *ever more of the many-colored wisdom of God* (a literal translation of Eph. 3:10). Thus *the whole church* is needed to receive God's whole revelation in all its beauty and richness (cf., Eph. 3:18 'with all the saints').

Questions for study:

1. What relevance to evangelism has the Covenant's strong assertion of the inspiration and authority of the Bible?
2. What difference will it make to our evangelism if we really believe that God's Word has power?
3. The Covenant draws a distinction between the Holy Spirit's work in 'revelation' (the writing of the Bible) and his work in 'illumination' (the reading of the Bible). Why is this important?

3. THE UNIQUENESS AND UNIVERSALITY OF CHRIST

We affirm that there is only one Savior and only one Gospel,   Gal. 1:6–9
although there is a wide diversity of evangelistic approaches. We
recognize that all men have some knowledge of God through his
general revelation in nature. But we deny that this can save, for men   Ro. 1:18–32
suppress the truth by their unrighteousness. We also reject as
derogatory to Christ and the Gospel every kind of syncretism and
dialogue which implies that Christ speaks equally through all relig-
ions and ideologies. Jesus Christ, being himself the only God-man,   1 Tim. 2:5, 6
who gave himself as the only ransom for sinners, is the only mediator
between God and man. There is no other name by which we must be   Ac. 4:12
saved. All men are perishing because of sin, but God loves all men,   Jn. 3:16–19
not wishing that any should perish but that all should repent. Yet   2 Pe. 3:9
those who reject Christ repudiate the joy of salvation and condemn   2 Th. 1:7–9
themselves to eternal separation from God. To proclaim Jesus as   Jn. 4:42
'the Savior of the world' is not to affirm that all men are either
automatically or ultimately saved, still less to affirm that all relig-
ions offer salvation in Christ. Rather it is to proclaim God's love for
a world of sinners and to invite all men to respond to him as Savior   Mt. 11:28–30
and Lord in the wholehearted personal commitment of repentance
and faith. Jesus Christ has been exalted above every other name;   Eph. 1:20, 21
we long for the day when every knee shall bow to him and every   Php. 2:9–11
tongue shall confess him Lord.

This section opens with the strong affirmation that *there is only one Savior and only one Gospel.* Some modern theologians try to prove that even the New Testament itself contains a multiplicity of contradictory gospels. Strange! They cannot have grasped Paul's assertion about the unity of the apostolic message (I Cor. 15:11; NB, the pronouns 'I,' 'they,' 'we' and 'you'), or felt the vehemence with which he anathematizes anybody (including even himself, and even an angel from heaven) who 'should preach . . . a gospel contrary to that which we preached to you . . . contrary to that which you received' (Gal. 1:6–9). Professor Henri Blocher rightly emphasized at Lausanne that what we have in the New Testament is 'diversity without conflict'; not contradictions but 'an unartificial harmony of teachings given so diversely' as to indicate its divine origin.

At the same time, the Covenant immediately guards itself against two misunderstandings. When we assert that there is only one Gospel we are

16

asserting the uniqueness of its content, and neither that there is only one way of presenting it nor that those ignorant of it have no knowledge of truth at all. As to the former, *there is a wide diversity of evangelistic approaches*. Canon Michael Green expressed this well in reference to Paul: 'Great flexibility in presentation, but great firmness on content was his emphasis.' And Dr. George Peters in his wide survey entitled 'Contemporary Practices of Evangelism' emphasized the virtues of 'flexibility, variability and openness.'

What, then, about those ignorant of the Gospel? Are we to say that they are ignorant of God altogether, including those who adhere to non-Christian religions? No. *We recognize that all men have some knowledge of God.* This universal (though partial) knowledge is due to his self-revelation, what theologians call either *his general revelation* because it is made to all men, or his 'natural' revelation because it is made *in nature*, both externally in the universe (Rom. 1:19–21) and internally in the human conscience (Rom. 1:32 and 2:14, 15). Such knowledge of God is not saving knowledge, however. *We deny that this can save*, partly because it is a revelation of God's power, deity and holiness (Rom. 1:20,32) but not of his love for sinners or of his plan of salvation, and partly because men do not live up to the knowledge they have. On the contrary, they *suppress the truth by their unrighteousness* (Rom. 1:18), and their rejection of the truth which they know then leads to idolatry, to immorality and to the judgment of God (Rom. 1:21–32). So, far from saving them, their knowledge actually condemns them. And they are without excuse (Rom. 1:20). Therefore, it is false to suppose that sinners can be saved through other systems, or that *Christ speaks equally through all religions and ideologies*. We firmly repudiate *every kind of syncretism and dialogue* which suggests this, as *derogatory to Christ and the Gospel*. For these are unique, and non-Christian religions know nothing of them.

a. The Uniqueness of Christ: he is the only Savior

The paragraph goes on to define and defend its opening statement that 'there is only one Savior.' It relies first on I Tim. 2:5,6: '. . . there is one mediator between God and men, the man Christ Jesus, who gave himself as a ransom for all . . .' Notice the three nouns which are applied in these verses to Jesus — 'mediator,' 'man' and 'ransom.' 'Man' alludes to his birth of a human mother and 'ransom' to his death on the Cross bearing instead of us the penalty we deserved. Or, theologically speaking, these two words refer to his incarnation and his atonement. Both are unique. Neither has any parallel in other religions. And it is precisely because Jesus Christ is *the only God-man* and *the only ransom for sinners* that he is *the only mediator between God and man*. For nobody else possesses his qualifications or even remotely approaches his competence (on account of his divine-human person and atoning death) to save sinners. Further, with this statement of the apostle Paul the apostle Peter was in complete agreement. He said, 'There is salvation in no one else, for *there is no other name* under heaven given among men *by which we must be saved'* (Acts 4:12).

Such a salvation (a rescue, that is, from the guilt of sin and from the judgment of God upon it) is urgently needed because *all men are perishing because of sin*. 'Perishing' is a terrible word, but Jesus himself used it (e.g., Matt. 18:14; Luke 13: 3,5, cf. John 3:15,16) and so did the apostles (e.g., I Cor. 1:18); therefore we must not shy away from it. *All men* are in this plight until and unless they are saved by Christ. Yet there is something else we know about all men, namely that *God loves all men*. And because of his great love Scripture says that he is forbearing and patient towards sinners, *not wishing that any should perish, but that all should repent* (II Pet. 3:9). Although this is the wish of God (for he says, 'I have no pleasure in the death of any one,' Ezek. 18:32), we have to add that some will refuse to repent and believe, will instead *reject Christ*, and so will *repudiate the joy of salvation and condemn themselves to eternal separation from God* (cf., II Thess. 1: 7–9). The prospect is almost too dreadful to contemplate; we should be able to speak of hell only with tears. Some may ask how these sentences of the Covenant relate to the doctrine of election (which Scripture teaches), and how divine sovereignty in salvation can be reconciled with human responsibility. Theologians have wrestled with this question for centuries. But it should be sufficient for us to accept that the Bible teaches both truths. We could sum it up, however paradoxical it may sound, by saying that those who are saved will ascribe all the credit to God, while those who are lost will accept all the blame themselves.

b. The Universality of Christ: he is the Savior of the world

In the last sentences of this section the subject moves from the uniqueness of Christ to the universality of Christ. Each truth involves the other. It is because Jesus Christ is the only Savior that he must be universally proclaimed. Many Samaritans called him 'the Savior of the world' (John 4:42), and John wrote that 'the Father has sent his Son as the Savior of the world' (I John 4:14). So we too may apply this great and glorious title to Jesus. But we must also be clear what we mean by it.

Negatively, we mean neither *that all men are . . . automatically . . . saved* (for men must believe in the Lord Jesus in order to be saved, Acts 16:31) nor that *all men are . . . ultimately saved* (for, alas, some will reject Christ and perish). *Still less* do we mean that *all religions offer salvation in Christ*, because plainly they do not. All non-Christian religions, if they teach salvation at all, offer it only as a reward for merit which has been accumulated by good works, whereas the Christian message is 'the Gospel of the grace of God' (Acts 20:24), that is, good news of his mercy to sinners who deserve nothing at his hand except judgment.

Positively, to proclaim Jesus Christ as 'the Savior of the world' is *to proclaim God's love for a world of sinners*, a love so great that he gave his only Son even to the death of the Cross (John 3:16; Rom. 5:8; I John 4:9,10). It is also *to invite all men to respond to him*, for the Gospel must be shared with all men without any distinction whatsoever. Perhaps nobody in history has had a clearer understanding or heavier burden regarding the universality of the Gospel than the apostle Paul. It weighed upon him as a debt he must discharge. 'I am under obligation,' he wrote, 'both to Greeks and to barbarians, both to the wise and to the foolish' (Rom. 1:14). That is, neither racial nor social barriers must be raised against the preaching of the Gospel. In particular, the same Gospel must be made known to both Jews and Gentiles, or more accurately 'to the Jew first and also to the Greek' (e.g., Rom. 1:16, 10:12). Some of our Jewish brothers were understandably disappointed that the Covenant contained no reference to them. And with the benefit of hindsight we can now apologize. For God has by no means rejected his ancient people (Rom. 11:1,2), but on the contrary still purposes 'their full inclusion' (Rom. 11:12 ff.). So the invitation goes out to Jew and Gentile alike to *respond* to Christ *as Savior and Lord in the wholehearted personal commitment of repentance and faith*. Paul called it 'the obedience of faith' (Rom. 1:5; 16:26). More is said about this in the next paragraph. The essential fact is that *Jesus Christ has been exalted above every other name*, for God has given him the supreme place at his own right hand, 'far above' every other conceivable competitor (Eph. 1:20–23; Phil. 2:9). God's purpose in thus exalting Jesus was and is 'that at the name of Jesus every knee should bow . . . and every tongue confess that Jesus Christ is Lord . . .' (Phil. 2:10,11). We too should long that the lordship of Jesus Christ should be acknowledged. There is no greater incentive to evangelism than this. Moreover, we know that in the end every knee will be obliged to bow to Christ, for even his enemies will 'be made a stool for his feet' (Heb. 10:12,13; cf. Psa. 110:1). And because our eyes have been opened to see the supremacy of Jesus Christ, *we long for the day when every knee shall bow to him*, some voluntarily, others involuntarily, *and every tongue shall confess him Lord.*

Questions for study:

1. 'Comparative religion' is a popular study today; wherein lies the uniqueness of Christianity?
2. What light does this paragraph throw on the condition of non-Christians?
3. It is sometimes said that we have no right to interfere in another person's religion. How does this paragraph help you to reply?

4.   THE NATURE OF EVANGELISM

To evangelize is to spread the good news that Jesus Christ died for   1 Co. 15:3, 4
our sins and was raised from the dead according to the Scriptures,   Ac. 2:32–39
and that as the reigning Lord he now offers the forgiveness of sins   Jn. 20:21
and the liberating gift of the Spirit to all who repent and believe.
Our Christian presence in the world is indispensable to evangelism,
and so is that kind of dialogue whose purpose is to listen sensitively
in order to understand. But evangelism itself is the proclamation of
the historical, biblical Christ as Savior and Lord, with a view to   1 Co. 1:23
                                                      2 Co. 4:5
persuading people to come to him personally and so be reconciled   2 Co. 5:11, 20
to God. In issuing the Gospel invitation we have no liberty to conceal
the cost of discipleship. Jesus still calls all who would follow him to   Lk. 14:25–33
deny themselves, take up their cross, and identify themselves with   Mk. 8:34
his new community. The results of evangelism include obedience to   Ac. 20:40, 47
Christ, incorporation into his church and responsible service in the   Mk. 10: 43–45
world.

In his opening address at Lausanne, Dr. Billy Graham expressed as his first hope for the Congress that it would 'frame a biblical declaration on evangelism,' and in his final address he declared himself satisfied that it had done so. Indeed, this was the consensus of the whole Congress. Many others shared the same hope and the same satisfaction. The fourth paragraph of the Covenant begins with a definition, and goes on to describe the context of evangelism, namely what must precede and follow it.

a.   The Definition of Evangelism

The English word 'evangelism' is derived from a Greek term meaning literally 'to bring or to spread good news.' It is impossible, therefore, to talk about evangelism without talking about the content of the good news. What is it? At its very simplest, it is *Jesus*. Jesus Christ himself is the essence of the Gospel. If we were to transliterate Acts 8:35, we would say that Philip 'evangelized to him Jesus,' that is, he told him the good news of Jesus (cf. Rom. 1:1,3). But what *is* the good news of Jesus? The Covenant statement attempts to summarize it as it was expounded by the apostle Peter in his early speeches in the Acts (especially 2:22–39) and by the apostle Paul in I Cor. 15:1ff.

20

The first element is those two pivotal events, the death and resurrection of Jesus. The apostles also alluded to his birth and life, his words and works, his reign and return, but they concentrated on *the good news that Jesus Christ died for our sins and was raised from the dead.* His death and resurrection were to them verifiable historical events. And they were significant events, for Christ died *for our sins*, to bear their condemnation and secure our justification, and he *was raised* to prove that his sacrifice for sin had been accepted and that he had not died in vain (Rom. 4:25; I Cor. 15:17–19).

The second element in the early apostolic preaching of the Gospel concerned the witnesses to these events, namely the Old Testament prophets and the apostles' own eyewitness experience. Consequently they kept quoting from the Old Testament and kept adding 'we are witnesses of these things.' In brief, they preached the death and resurrection of Jesus Christ *according to the Scriptures* (1 Cor. 15:3,4). Among several popular reinterpretations of Jesus today are Jesus the violent revolutionary, Jesus the circus clown (of *Godspell*), and Jesus the disillusioned superstar. Over against these fantasies of men's minds we must be faithful to the authentic Jesus, who is *the historical, biblical Christ* (as he is described in the middle of this section), Jesus Christ according to the Scriptures of both Old and New Testaments.

Thirdly, the good news relates not only to what Christ once did (when he died and was raised from death) but to what he *now offers*. For he is now exalted to God's right hand, and from that position of unique authority as *the reigning Lord* he promises to penitent believers two most marvelous gifts: *the forgiveness of sins* (remitting our guilt and instating us in the favor and the family of God), and *the liberating gift of the Spirit* (for the Holy Spirit is given to all who come to Christ, and the Spirit sets us free from self-centeredness to live for God and for others).

Fourthly, in order to receive these free gifts, men must *repent and believe*, turning from their sins, lies and idols (repentance) and trusting in Jesus Christ as the only Savior (faith). The two belong together, for 'faith without repentance is not saving faith but presumptuous believism' (Dr. René Padilla). Perhaps baptism should also be mentioned here, for this is where the apostles put it (e.g., Acts 2:38). Since it is administered 'in the name of Jesus Christ' it at least signifies publicly a penitent faith in the very Lord Jesus who had previously been repudiated.

Here, then, is the irreducible minimum of the apostolic Gospel. We must never stray from these events and their witnesses, from the offer that is based upon the events, or from the conditions on which the offer depends.

b. The Prelude to Evangelism

True evangelism can never take place in a vacuum. It presupposes a context from which it must not be isolated. A certain situation precedes it; certain consequences follow it. In referring to this, the Covenant deliberately uses the words presence, proclamation, persuasion and dialogue which have all figured prominently in recent theological debate. In essence, it insists that *evangelism . . . is the proclamation of the historical, biblical Christ as Savior and Lord.* For the only Jesus there is to proclaim is the Jesus of history, who is the Jesus of Scripture, who is 'our Lord and Savior Jesus Christ' (e.g., II Pet. 3:18). So we have no liberty to preach his salvation without his lordship, or his lordship without his salvation. Listen to Paul, 'We preach Christ crucified' (I Cor. 1:23) and 'we preach . . . Jesus Christ as Lord' (II Cor. 4:5).

Yet the prelude to proclamation is presence. For how can we share Christ with people with whom we have no contact? Hence *our Christian presence in the world is indispensable to evangelism.* The first word of Jesus' Great Commission was not 'preach' but 'go.' For we cannot proclaim Christ from a distance, but only to people to whom we have gone and with whom we have sought to identify. So *presence* is not a substitute for *proclamation* (as some maintain), but rather an indispensable prelude to it. It is in this situation that *dialogue* with non-Christians is not only right but is also (like *presence*) indispensable. *Dialogue* is a much misused word. Some people are using it to describe a situation of compromise in which the Christian renounces his own Christian commitment and regards the Gospel as open to debate! *That* kind of dialogue we have already rejected (in paragraph 3) as 'derogatory to Christ and the Gospel.' But, properly defined, a dialogue is a conversation in which both parties are serious, and each is prepared to listen to the other. Its *purpose is to listen sensitively in order to understand.* Such listening is an essential prelude to evangelism, for how can we share the good news relevantly if we do not understand the other person's position and problems?

c. The Consequences of Evangelism

Although evangelism is itself the spreading of the good news, it is not unconcerned about people's response to the message they hear. On the contrary, evangelism is proclamation with a view to persuasion. The World Congress on Evangelism at Berlin in 1966 declared that 'evangelism is the proclamation of the Gospel . . . with the purpose of persuading condemned and lost sinners to put their trust in God . . .' The Lausanne Covenant similarly asserts that evangelism is the proclamation of Christ *with a view to persuading people to come to him personally and so be reconciled to God.* There can be no doubt that *persuading* figured prominently in the early church's evangelism. Paul summed up his ministry by saying 'we persuade men' (II Cor. 5:11); and in the Acts, Luke describes him doing it (e.g., 17:1–4; 18:4; 19:8–10,26; 28:23,24). Clearly, the apostles did not regard the use of argument as incompatible with trust in the Holy Spirit. We too must not be afraid to expound and argue the Gospel today.

This work of persuasion must be honest and open. We have nothing to hide. For example, *in issuing the Gospel invitation we have no liberty to conceal the cost of discipleship*. Jesus himself, far from concealing anything, urged his would-be followers before committing themselves to him to 'sit down first and count the cost' (Luke 14:28,31). He laid down in the plainest terms the conditions a person must fulfill, without which 'he cannot be my disciple' (Luke 14:26,27,33). And *Jesus still calls all who would follow him today, just as he did during his public ministry, to deny themselves* (putting him before self), *take up their cross* (following him to the place of execution, where self is crucified) *and identify themselves with his new community* (Mark 8:34–38).

The objective of evangelism is conversion, and conversion implies a radical change of lifestyle. It involves the convert in at least three new and conscientious relationships — to Christ, to the church, and to the world. For *the results of evangelism include obedience to Christ* (who is now acknowledged as Lord), *incorporation into his church* (for to belong to Christ is to belong to the people of Christ, Acts 2:40,47), *and responsible service in the world* (for conversion means nothing if it does not result in a change from self-centered living to sacrificial service, Mark 10:43–45).

Questions for study:

1. Using this paragraph as a starting point, summarize (from the New Testament but in your own words) what the good news is.
2. Compare the references to 'dialogue' in paragraph 3 and paragraph 4. What is right and what is wrong about dialogue? Does the right type have a place in your witness?
3. Think of some ways in which you (and your church) could be more faithful in facing people with the cost of discipleship.
4. How would you define the goal of evangelism? Why do we want people to hear the good news?

5. CHRISTIAN SOCIAL RESPONSIBILITY

We affirm that God is both the Creator and the Judge of all men. Ac. 17:26, 31
We therefore should share his concern for justice and reconciliation Ge. 18:25
throughout human society and for the liberation of men from every Ps. 45:7
Is. 1:17
kind of oppression. Because mankind is made in the image of God, Ge. 1:26, 27
every person, regardless of race, religion, color, culture, class, sex Lev. 19:18
Lk. 6:27, 35
or age, has an intrinsic dignity because of which he should be
respected and served, not exploited. Here too we express penitence Jas. 3:9
both for our neglect and for having sometimes regarded evangelism
and social concern as mutually exclusive. Although reconciliation
with man is not reconciliation with God, nor is social action evan-
gelism, nor is political liberation salvation, nevertheless we affirm
that evangelism and socio-political involvement are both part of our
Christian duty. For both are necessary expressions of our doctrines
of God and man, our love for our neighbor and our obedience to
Jesus Christ. The message of salvation implies also a message of
judgment upon every form of alienation, oppression and discrimina-
tion, and we should not be afraid to denounce evil and injustice
wherever they exist. When people receive Christ they are born again Jn. 1:12, 13;
3:3, 5
into his kingdom and must seek not only to exhibit but also to spread
its righteousness in the midst of an unrighteous world. The salvation Mt. 5:20;
6:33
we claim should be transforming us in the totality of our personal 2 Co. 3:18
and social responsibilities. Faith without works is dead. Jas. 2:14–26

In the past, especially perhaps in nineteenth century Britain, evangelical Christians had an outstanding record of social action. In this century, however — partly because of our reaction against the 'social gospel' of liberal optimism — we have tended to divorce evangelism from social concern, and to concentrate almost exclusively on the former. It may be helpful, therefore, to begin this exposition of section 5 with a reference to two sentences, one of confession and the other of affirmation, which occur about halfway through it.

First, *we express penitence both for our neglect of* our Christian social responsibility and for our naive polarization in *having sometimes regarded evangelism and social concern as mutually exclusive.* This confession is mildly worded. A large group at Lausanne, concerned to develop a radical Christian discipleship, expressed themselves more strongly, 'We must repudiate as demonic the attempt to drive a wedge between evangelism and social action.' Secondly, and positively, *we affirm that evangelism and socio-political involvement are both part of our Christian duty.* More will be said about this phrase later.

24

Christian duty arises from Christian doctrine. So this section is not content merely to assert that Christians have social responsibilities: it goes on to outline the four main doctrines out of which our Christian social duty springs, namely the doctrines of God, man, salvation and the kingdom.

a. The Doctrine of God

It is significant that a paragraph which relates entirely to 'Christian social responsibility' should open with an affirmation about God. This is right. For our theology must always govern our conduct. *We affirm that God is both the Creator and the Judge of all men.* Thus the creation and the judgment, the beginning and the end of time, are brought together (cf. Acts 17:26,31). Both concern *all men*, for God is not just interested in the church but in the world. He created all men, and all men will have to give an account to him on the day of judgment. *Therefore* (notice the deduction which is drawn from the universality of creation and judgment) we who claim to be God's people should share the breadth of God's concerns. In particular, *we should share his concern for justice and reconciliation throughout human society and for the liberation of men from every kind of oppression* (see Amos 1 and 2). Justice, reconciliation and freedom — these are more and more the object of human quest in today's world. But they were God's will for society long before they became man's quest. For God loves the good and hates the evil wherever these are found (Psa. 7:9,11; 11:4–7; 33:5). It is written of his King in the Old Testament and applied to the Lord Jesus in the New, 'You love righteousness and hate wickedness' (Psa. 45:7; Heb. 1:9). The same should be true of us all. 'Cease to do evil,' God says, 'learn to do good; seek justice, correct oppression; defend the fatherless, plead for the widow' (Isa. 1:16,17).

b. The Doctrine of Man

Social responsibility and evangelism are together part of our Christian duty, for both are necessary expressions of our doctrines of God and man. Particular reference is made to the great biblical affirmation that *mankind is made in the image of God* (Gen. 1:26,27). It is for this reason that man is unique on earth. There is a similarity between men and animals in that both are God's living creatures dependent on him for their being, but a vast dissimilarity in that man alone is a godlike being with such godlike capacities as rationality, conscience, dominion and love. It is the divine image in man which gives him *an intrinsic dignity* or worth, a worth which belongs to all human beings by creation, *regardless of race, religion, color, culture, class, sex or age.* Because of every person's inherent dignity as a godlike being, he *should be respected and served,* and indeed loved (Lev. 19:18; Luke 6:27,35), *not exploited.* Only when we grasp this foundational biblical doctrine shall we begin to see the evils, for example, of racial discrimination and social prejudice. They are an offense to human dignity and therefore to the God in whose image man is made. It is not exaggerated to say that to insult man in these ways is to blaspheme God (Jas. 3:9,10). Similarly, the reason why murder is such a terrible crime is that 'God made man in his own image' (Gen. 9:5,6).

c. The Doctrine of Salvation

Salvation for many people today is a prohibited word: some are embarrassed by it, others say it is meaningless. Certainly it needs to be interpreted for modern men. So there was a good expectation that the Assembly of the World Council of Churches' Commission on World Mission and Evangelism at Bangkok in January 1973 entitled *Salvation Today* would produce a fresh definition, faithful to Scripture and relevant to today. But Bangkok disappointed us. Although it included some references to personal salvation, its emphasis was to equate salvation with political and economic liberation. The Lausanne Covenant rejects this, for it is not biblical. *Reconciliation with man is not reconciliation with God, nor is social action evangelism, nor is political liberation salvation.* Nevertheless, it is our duty to be involved in socio-political action; that is, both in social action (caring for society's casualties) and in political action (concerned for the structures of society itself). For both active evangelistic and social involvement *are necessary expressions* not only of our doctrines of God and man (as we have seen) but also of *our love for our neighbor and our obedience to Jesus Christ.* Further, although salvation is not to be equated with political liberation, yet *the message of salvation implies also a message of judgment upon every form of alienation, oppression and discrimination.* Salvation is deliverance from evil, and implicit in God's desire to save people from evil is his judgment on the evil from which he saves them. Moreover, this evil is both individual and social. Since God hates evil and injustice, *we should not be afraid to denounce evil and injustice wherever they exist.*

d. The Doctrine of the Kingdom

Section five ends with a challenge to our personal Christian commitment. Christians claim to have received Christ. But do we always remember that *when people receive Christ they are born again into his kingdom* (John 1:12,13; 3:3,5)? To be a citizen of God's kingdom is to be submissive to his righteous rule. As such, we are under obligation *to exhibit* the righteous standards of the kingdom in our own lives. For Jesus taught in the Sermon on the Mount that members of his kingdom must 'hunger and thirst for righteousness' and exhibit a righteousness which exceeds the shallow, formal righteousness of the scribes and Pharisees (Matt. 5:6,20). He also said that we must 'seek first

God's kingdom and his righteousness' (Matt. 6:33); that is, we must set these things before us as the supreme good to which we devote our lives. We must seek not only the spread of the kingdom itself, nor only to exhibit its righteousness ourselves, *but also to spread its righteousness in the midst of an unrighteous world*. How else can we be 'the salt of the earth' (Matt. 5:14)?

The last sentences of this section revert to the terminology of salvation, but we must remember that Jesus drew no distinction between salvation and the kingdom of God (e.g., Mark 10:23–27 and cf. Isa. 52:7). *The salvation* we claim (and Christians do humbly claim to have been saved) *should be transforming us*. 'Be transformed,' Paul commanded the Romans. 'We are being transformed,' he declared to the Corinthians, using the same Greek verb (Rom. 12:2; II Cor. 3:18). And this transformation, if genuine, should touch every part of us, indeed *the totality of our personal and social* responsibilities. If not, how can we claim to be saved? For *faith without works is dead* (Jas. 2:20).

Questions for study:

1. The Covenant relates duty to doctrine. Take the biblical doctrine of either God or man, and think out what effect it should have on our social responsibilities.
2. If your local church takes its social responsibility seriously, how will this affect its program?
3. 'We should not be afraid to denounce evil and injustice . . .' Discuss the implications of this statement.
4. What has salvation got to do with social action?

6. THE CHURCH AND EVANGELISM

We affirm that Christ sends his redeemed people into the world as the Father sent him, and that this calls for a similar deep and costly penetration of the world. We need to break out of our ecclesiastical ghettos and permeate non-Christian society. In the church's mission of sacrificial service evangelism is primary. World evangelization requires the whole church to take the whole Gospel to the whole world. The church is at the very center of God's cosmic purpose and is his appointed means of spreading the Gospel. But a church which preaches the Cross must itself be marked by the Cross. It becomes a stumbling block to evangelism when it betrays the Gospel or lacks a living faith in God, a genuine love for people, or scrupulous honesty in all things including promotion and finance. The church is the community of God's people rather than an institution, and must not be identified with any particular culture, social or political system, or human ideology.

Jn. 17:18; 20:21
Mt. 28:19, 20

Ac. 1:8; 20:27
Eph. 1:9, 10; 3:9–11

Gal. 6:14, 17

2 Co. 6:3, 4
2Ti. 2:19–21
Php. 1:27

7. COOPERATION IN EVANGELISM

We affirm that the church's visible unity in truth is God's purpose. Evangelism also summons us to unity, because our oneness strengthens our witness, just as our disunity undermines our Gospel of reconciliation. We recognize, however, that organizational unity may take many forms and does not necessarily forward evangelism. Yet we who share the same biblical faith should be closely united in fellowship, work and witness. We confess that our testimony has sometimes been marred by sinful individualism and needless duplication. We pledge ourselves to seek a deeper unity in truth, worship, holiness and mission. We urge the development of regional and functional cooperation for the furtherance of the church's mission, for strategic planning, for mutual encouragement, and for the sharing of resources and experience.

Eph. 4:3, 4
Jn. 17:21, 23
Jn. 13:35

Php. 1:27
Jn. 17:11–23

Already in the first paragraph of the Covenant there is a reference to God's purpose for the church. This is now elaborated in two paragraphs which may be studied together. They allude to the church's mission, integrity and unity.

a. The Mission of the Church

The opening affirmation echoes the prayer and the commission of Jesus (John 17:18; 20:21): *we affirm that Christ sends his redeemed people into the world as the Father sent him*. It recognizes that Christ's mission in the world is to be the model of the church's (NB, the "as-so" in both texts), and that *this calls for a similar deep and costly penetration of the world*. For when the Son of God was sent into the world he did not remain aloof from its life or pain. On the contrary, he penetrated deep into our humanity by the incarnation, and by becoming man he became vulnerable to temptation and suffering. Dr. Ralph Winter introduced us at Lausanne to the distinction he draws between three kinds of evangelism — E-1 (within our own culture and language), E-2 (reaching people of a similar culture and language), and E-3 (cross-cultural evangelism). In all three kinds, the Christian must identify with those he is seeking to reach, striving to enter their thought world. But E-3 evangelism is likely to be the most costly because the gulf to be crossed is deeper and wider. All of us *need to break out of our ecclesiastical ghettos and permeate non-Christian society*. This is part and parcel of *the church's mission of sacrificial service*. As we have seen, it includes both evangelistic and social action, so that normally the church will not have to choose between them.

But if a choice has to be made, then *evangelism is primary*. Two reasons are given. The first is the immensity of the task: *world evangelization requires the whole church to take the whole Gospel to the whole world*. Unless the whole church is mobilized, the whole world is not likely to be reached. The second is the biblical truth that the church is not a man-made society but, on the contrary, *is at the very center of God's cosmic purpose*. This phrase comes from the Rev. Howard Snyder's paper entitled 'The Church as God's Agent of Evangelism.' He adds, 'Paul was concerned to speak of the church as the result of, and within the context of, the plan of God for his whole creation (Eph. 1:9,10,20–23; 3:10; 6:12).' In addition, the church is God's *appointed means of spreading the Gospel*. Thus, God's purpose and the world's need together bring to the church an insistent call to evangelize.

b. The Integrity of the Church

Halfway through paragraph six comes a significant *but*. It introduces the uncomfortable question of the church's credibility. The church may evangelize (preach the Gospel); but will the world hear and heed its message? Not unless the church retains its own integrity, the Covenant insists. If we hope to be listened to, we must practice what we preach. Our behavior must be 'worthy of the Gospel' (Phil. 1:27). And not our individual behavior only. For the Gospel is proclaimed by the church. And, as Samuel Escobar insisted in his address at Lausanne, the church must demonstrate that it is a 'radically different community,' with new standards, a new view of money and property, a new attitude to secular power and a new power of its own (the Holy Spirit), and an altogether new quality of love and brotherhood.

In particular, the Cross must be as central to our lives as it is to our message. Do we preach Christ crucified (I Cor. 1:23)? Then let us remember that *a church which preaches the Cross must itself be marked by the Cross* (Gal. 6:14,17), that is, by self-denial, self-humbling, and self-giving. This striking reference to the Cross is taken from the *Response to Lausanne* composed by the 'radical discipleship' group. They interpret what they mean by adding that the church must 'identify and agonize with men, renounce status and demonic power, and give itself in selfless service of others for God.' Otherwise the very church which is intended to be the agent of evangelism *becomes a stumbling block to evangelism* (cf., II Cor. 6:3). Four 'scandals' (the Greek word for stumbling blocks) are singled out, namely when the church *betrays the Gospel* (distorting its content in any way), *or lacks a living faith in God* (by putting its confidence elsewhere), *a genuine love for people* (by any failure in Christian caring), *or scrupulous honesty in all things — including promotion and finance.* It may well be as evil in God's sight to falsify facts in our statistical reports, or to falsify our accounts, as it is to falsify our message.

It is all the more important for the church to retain its own integrity because of what it is. It is not primarily *an institution*; nor must it be *identified with any particular culture, social or political system, or human ideology.* The church is above and beyond all these organizations of man. It is *the community of God's people.* It bears God's name and so puts God's name at risk.

c.   The Unity of the Church

Paragraph seven broaches the difficult subjects of unity and cooperation. It begins with two reasons why we should be concerned for the unity of the church, the first theological and the second pragmatic. Theologically, *we affirm that the church's visible unity in truth is God's purpose.* Of course, in one sense the church's unity already exists and can no more be destroyed than the unity of the Godhead (Eph. 4:4–6), but this invisible, indestructible unity still needs to become a *visible unity* (Eph. 4:3). It must also be *a unity in truth* (Eph. 4:13). This is the kind of unity for which Jesus prayed. It would come about only through the revelation of the Father which he had given to the apostles (John 17:11,20–23).

The second and pragmatic reason for this quest is that *evangelism . . . summons us to unity.* Our message is one of love and peace, but it always rings hollow when we are not living in love and peace ourselves (John 13: 35; 17:21).

Therefore, *our oneness strengthens our witness, just as our disunity undermines our Gospel of reconciliation.*

At the same time, we have to admit two facts about *organizational unity.* The first is that *it may take many forms.* For about fifty years following World War I it was generally assumed that 'organic union' or the total merger of churches was the right way forward. But now rigid structures are everywhere being questioned, and people are not so sure. Visible unity should certainly be characterized by a common confession of truth, but in other matters by diversity and flexibility. The second fact about organizational unity is that it *does not necessarily forward evangelism.* Leaders of some united churches have admitted with sorrow that union has not brought that impetus to evangelize which they had expected.

Since the only unity pleasing to God is unity in truth, surely *we who share the same biblical faith should be closely united in fellowship, work and witness.* For though we still disagree with one another on some secondary issues, we stand firm and stand together on the great fundamentals of the biblical revelation. Yet we have to admit our frequent failures in this area. *We confess that our testimony has sometimes been marred by sinful individualism* (we evangelicals are often rugged individualists), and by *needless duplication* (at times we appear to prefer to build our own little empire rather than to allow our distinctive work to be absorbed in common action for the common good). After this statement of what we ought to be (closely united) and this confession of what we sometimes are (sinful individualists), the paragraph ends with a pledge and a plea.

First, *we pledge ourselves to seek a deeper unity in truth, worship, holiness and mission.* That is, we who are one in truth undertake by God's grace to seek to worship God together, to grow together in Christ-likeness, and together to share in the mission of the church. Then the plea: *we urge the development of regional and functional cooperation.* A questionnaire was submitted to the Lausanne Congress participants, asking whether they would favor any kind of post-Congress organization. In reply, quite strong opposition was expressed to the notion of a centralized evangelical world structure, but a comparably strong desire was voiced for evangelical cooperation regionally and functionally. The Lausanne Continuation Committee,* which has been formed from names chosen by Congress participants, will seek to implement this desire, and will no doubt bear in mind the purposes of cooperation with which this paragraph of the Covenant concludes, namely, *for the furtherance of the church's mission, for strategic planning, for mutual encouragement, and for the sharing of resources and experience.* In other words, we must learn to plan and work together, and also to give to one another and receive from one another whatever good gifts God has given us.

---

* Its name was later changed to the Lausanne Committee for World Evangelization.

Questions for study:

1. *Penetrate* and *permeate* are two verbs used in paragraph six to describe the church's mission. What will this mean in practice?
2. The second part of paragraph six is outspoken in saying what makes the church a stumbling block to evangelism. Examine your life and your church's life in the light of this analysis.
3. Paragraph seven is about unity and cooperation. Can you apply it to your local situation?

8. CHURCHES IN EVANGELISTIC PARTNERSHIP

We rejoice that a new missionary era has dawned. The dominant role of western missions is fast disappearing. God is raising up from the younger churches a great new resource for world evangelization, and is thus demonstrating that the responsibility to evangelize belongs to the whole body of Christ. All churches should therefore be asking God and themselves what they should be doing both to reach their own area and to send missionaries to other parts of the world. A re-evaluation of our missionary responsibility and role should be continuous. Thus a growing partnership of churches will develop and the universal character of Christ's church will be more clearly exhibited. We also thank God for agencies which labor in Bible translation, theological education, the mass media, Christian literature, evangelism, missions, church renewal and other specialist fields. They too should engage in constant self-examination to evaluate their effectiveness as part of the church's mission.

Ro. 1:8
Php. 1:5;
4:15

Ac. 13:1–3
1Th. 1:6–8

9. THE URGENCY OF THE EVANGELISTIC TASK

More than 2,700 million people, which is more than two-thirds of mankind, have yet to be evangelized. We are ashamed that so many have been neglected; it is a standing rebuke to us and to the whole church. There is now, however, in many parts of the world an unprecedented receptivity to the Lord Jesus Christ. We are convinced that this is the time for churches and parachurch agencies to pray earnestly for the salvation of the unreached and to launch new efforts to achieve world evangelization. A reduction of foreign missionaries and money in an evangelized country may sometimes be necessary to facilitate the national church's growth in self-reliance and to release resources for unevangelized areas. Missionaries should flow ever more freely from and to all six continents in a spirit of humble service. The goal should be, by all available means and at the earliest possible time, that every person will have the opportunity to hear, understand, and receive the good news. We cannot hope to attain this goal without sacrifice. All of us are

Mk. 16:15

Jn. 9:4

Mt. 9:35–38

33

shocked by the poverty of millions and disturbed by the injustices Is. 58:6, 7
Jas. 2:1–9
which cause it. Those of us who live in affluent circumstances accept 1 Co. 9:19–23
Jas 1:27
our duty to develop a simple lifestyle in order to contribute more Mt. 25:31–46
Ac. 2:44, 45
generously to both relief and evangelism. 4:34, 35

It may be said that paragraphs eight and nine bring us to the heart of the Covenant because they relate to world evangelization, which was the main theme of the International Congress at Lausanne. In these paragraphs, five segments of the human community are mentioned — churches, parachurch agencies (i.e., independent agencies working alongside the church), unevangelized people, foreign missionaries, and the deprived, impoverished millions.

a. Churches

For about 150 years, since the dawn of the modern missionary movement at the beginning of the 19th century, Christendom was neatly divided between 'sending churches' and 'receiving churches.' The sending churches were the older churches of the West (especially Europe and North America). And it was their missions which, under God, led to the birth and growth of younger churches who were at the receiving end. But now these distinctions are rapidly breaking down. *We rejoice that a new missionary era has dawned*, whose chief characteristic is what paragraph eight later calls a *growing partnership of churches*. On the one hand, *the dominant role of western missions is fast disappearing*, and with it the notion that missions anywhere in the world can be directed from some remote mission control in Europe, North America or elsewhere. On the other hand, *God is raising up from the younger churches a great new resource for world evangelization*. This phrase comes from Dr. Donald McGavran's paper. In it, he gave the startling figure of 200 Third World missionary societies with 3,400 missionaries reported in 1972 and more today. The All-Asia Mission Consultation's continuation committee have pledged to send out 10,000 Asian missionaries by the end of this century.

By this new missionary impetus from Asia, Africa and Latin America, God is *demonstrating that the responsibility to evangelize belongs to the whole body of Christ*. This plain biblical truth, which is beginning to be witnessed today, leads to a practical and demanding conclusion: *All churches* (whether young or old, whether large or small, whether in a developed or a developing country) *should therefore be asking God and themselves* a searching question, namely *what they should be doing both to reach their own area and to send missionaries to other parts of the world*. Some of the churches planted by the apostles seem almost immediately to have become centers of evangelistic witness (e.g., Rom. 1:8; Phil. 1:5; 4:15; 1 Thess. 1:6–8; cf., Acts 13:1–3). Moreover, it is not enough for a church to ask itself this question once, and then conveniently forget about it. No, a reevaluation of our missionary *responsibility and role should be continuous*. Only then, when all churches conscientiously accept their God-given vocation, will *a growing partnership of churches* come to maturity, and *the universal character of Christ's church will be more clearly exhibited.*

b. Parachurch Agencies

Although paragraph six has stated that God's 'appointed means of spreading the Gospel' is the church, yet the Congress recognized the valid existence of parachurch agencies. These do not (or should not) work in competition with the churches, but rather, being (in most cases) interdenominational in personnel and specialist in function, enable the churches to diversify their outreach. So *we thank God* for them. Some are seeking to extend the church by *evangelism and missions*, while others are seeking to deepen it by *theological education* and *church renewal*. Yet others concentrate on a particular means of communicating the Gospel like *Bible translation* (and distribution), *the mass media* (radio, television, journalism, etc.) and *Christian literature*. Even this is only a selection, for there are *other specialist fields* which are not mentioned. Although the right of such agencies to exist is agreed, and God is thanked for their work, yet the wisdom of their indefinite survival is not taken for granted. Like churches, parachurch agencies should also *engage in constant self-examination* — in particular *to evaluate their effectiveness as part of the church's mission.* Howard Snyder urged that 'a clear distinction should be made between the church as the community of God's people and man-made structures.' The Church is God's creation, essential and eternal; denominational and parachurch agencies, however, being man's creation and expendable, cannot claim the same immortality. Some outlive their usefulness. In such cases voluntary termination is to be recommended. But this drastic action will not be necessary if the agency concerned is sensitive and flexible enough to keep adjusting itself to contemporary needs.

c. Unevangelized people

Paragraph nine ('The Urgency of the Evangelistic Task') begins with the appalling statistic that *more than 2,700 million people,* representing *more than two-thirds of mankind, have yet to be evangelized.* That is, they have not yet heard the good news of Jesus Christ. And this number keeps growing. The 'population clock,' started at the beginning of the Congress and stopped at its end, registered a world population increase of about one-and-a-half million people during those 10 days. The huge number of the unevangelized is more than a cold fact; it points the finger of accusation at us and forces us to acknowledge our guilty failure. *We are ashamed that so many have been neglected; it is a standing rebuke to us and to the whole church.* Such words can be written and spoken with comparative ease. But not until we get the

unevangelized millions on our conscience, and take them to our heart in deep
compassion, will we stir ourselves to action.

Then another fact is stated, not to shame us but to encourage us, namely,
that now in many parts of the world there is *an unprecedented receptivity to the
Lord Jesus Christ.* Nobody has brought this fact to the church's attention
more forcefully than Dr. Donald McGavran. In his paper at Lausanne he
gave a few sample figures; e.g., the church in Taiwan had (by 1971) multiplied
20 times in 25 years, and in Africa south of the Sahara (according to Dr.
David Barrett) there may well be 357 million Christians by the year 2000.
Although in some parts of the world the door is still closed, in many parts of
the world it is open, and the Holy Spirit is making millions receptive to Christ.
We cannot be pessimistic. On the contrary, *we are convinced that this is the
time for churches and parachurch agencies to pray earnestly for the salvation
of the unreached, and to launch new efforts to achieve world evangelization.* The
great need is for Christians with the vision, the courage and the commitment
to respond to this challenge and opportunity.

d.   Foreign Missionaries

The Bangkok Conference, already mentioned in the commentary on paragraph five, gave currency to the idea of a moratorium (or suspension) of
missionary funds and personnel. The call was not altogether understood, and
the word has become emotive. So the Covenant avoids the word, but clarifies
the concept. It agrees that *a reduction of foreign missionaries and money . . .
may sometimes be necessary.* But it qualifies this statement in three important
ways.

First, such a situation is likely to arise only *in an evangelized country,* that
is, when the primary, pioneer task of making the Gospel known has been
done. Secondly, the purpose of such a reduction would be *to facilitate the
national church's growth in self-reliance.* For it must be frankly acknowledged
that foreign missionaries have sometimes stayed on too long in leadership
roles in the national church, and in consequence have impeded the development of the church's own leaders, while the continued supply of foreign
money has sometimes perpetuated in the national church a certain immature
dependence. Thirdly, the ultimate objective of such a reduction of men and
money would not be to reduce overall missionary advance, but to further it,
for it would *release resources for unevangelized areas.* Our desire should be to
increase the availability and mobility of missionaries, for *missionaries should
flow ever more freely from and to all six continents.* We dare not impose any
limit on the number of missionaries while so much of the world remains
unevangelized — unless it be to exclude the wrong sort of missionaries. There
is no room in today's church for the proud and the dominant, but only for
those who will offer themselves *in a spirit of humble service.*

What, then, is our *goal?* It *should be, by all available means and at the earliest possible time* (no date is given), *that every person will have the opportunity to hear*, and not only to hear in some casual or superficial way, but so to hear as to *understand and*, by God's grace, *receive the good news*.

e. The Impoverished Millions

The deprived, impoverished, undernourished people of the world are introduced in the context of evangelism. For the Covenant declares that *we cannot hope to attain this goal* (of world evangelization) *without sacrifice*. But it goes on to speak of both the plight of the poor and the duty of the affluent. *All of us are shocked by the poverty of millions and disturbed by the injustices which cause it*. We may not all give an identical definition of justice and injustice, or share the same economic theories and remedies, or believe that God's will is an egalitarian society in which even the slightest differences of income and possessions are not tolerated. But we are all appalled by poverty, that is, by the immense numbers of people who do not have enough to eat, whose shelter and clothing are woefully inadequate, and whose opportunities for education, employment and medical care are minimal. Every sensitive Christian should be shocked by this situation and never grow so accustomed to it as to be unmoved by it (Isa. 58:6,7).

Moreover, *those of us who live in affluent circumstances accept* that we have a particular *duty*. This includes most people in the West, where the average income is nearly 15 times more than the average in the developing world, but also includes a small minority of rich Third World citizens. Our duty is *to develop a simple lifestyle*. Perhaps no expression in the Covenant caused more anxious thought in would-be signatories at Lausanne than this. What does it mean for the affluent to develop a simple style of living? Some have wished that the adjective were a comparative and read 'a simpler lifestyle.' But even this would pose problems for us: how much simpler? and, in any case, simpler than what? The truth is that concepts like 'poverty,' 'simplicity' and 'generosity' are all relative and are bound to mean different things to different people. For example, running water, let alone constant hot water, is regarded as a wonderful luxury by those who have to queue for water at the village well, which sometimes dries up. But in other parts of the world it can hardly be regarded as incompatible with 'a simple lifestyle.' Scripture lays down no absolute standards. On the one hand, it gives no encouragement to an austere and negative asceticism, for it does not forbid the possession of private property (Acts 5:4), and it commands us to enjoy with gratitude the good gifts of our Creator (e.g., I Tim. 4:1–5; 6:17). On the other hand, it implies that some measure of equality is more pleasing to God than disparity, and its appeal to believers to be generous is based on the grace of our Lord Jesus Christ, because grace means generosity (II Cor. 8:8–15).

Every Christian should be content with the necessities of life (I Tim. 6:6–8), but every Christian must make his own conscientious decision before God where he draws the line between necessities and luxuries. It is certainly a sin to eat too much, and to waste food, especially when so many are starving. As for possessions, one way to decide whether we need something is to consider whether we use it, for we evidently do not need what we do not use. It would be at least a start if all of us went through our belongings (including our clothes) annually, in order to give away what we do not use. The paragraph concludes that the development of a simple lifestyle will not only be right in itself out of a caring solidarity with the poor, but will also enable us *to contribute more generously to both relief and evangelism,* for these good works are almost everywhere hampered by a shortage of money.

Questions for study:

1. 'All churches should be asking God and themselves what they should be doing . . .' Complete the question from paragraph eight and then put it to your own church.
2. If you share in, or support, a parachurch agency, can you evaluate its effectiveness?
3. Paragraph nine sets a goal. What is it? Can you make any personal contribution to its attainment?
4. 'A simple lifestyle.' What might it mean for you to develop a 'simple' or 'simpler' lifestyle?

10. EVANGELISM AND CULTURE

The development of strategies for world evangelization calls for imaginative pioneering methods. Under God, the result will be the rise of churches deeply rooted in Christ and closely related to their culture. Culture must always be tested and judged by Scripture. Because man is God's creature, some of his culture is rich in beauty and goodness. Because he is fallen, all of it is tainted with sin and some of it is demonic. The Gospel does not pre-suppose the superiority of any culture to another, but evaluates all cultures according to its own criteria of truth and righteousness, and insists on moral absolutes in every culture. Missions have all too frequently exported with the Gospel an alien culture, and churches have sometimes been in bondage to culture rather than to Scripture. Christ's evangelists must humbly seek to empty themselves of all but their personal authenticity in order to become the servants of others, and churches must seek to transform and enrich culture, all for the glory of God.

Mk. 7:8, 9, 13
Ge. 4:21, 23

1 Co. 9:19–23

Php. 2:5–7
2 Co. 4:5

11. EDUCATION AND LEADERSHIP

We confess that we have sometimes pursued church growth at the expense of church depth, and divorced evangelism from Christian nurture. We also acknowledge that some of our missions have been too slow to equip and encourage national leaders to assume their rightful responsibilities. Yet we are committed to indigenous principles, and long that every church will have national leaders who manifest a Christian style of leadership in terms not of domination but of service. We recognize that there is a great need to improve theological education, especially for church leaders. In every nation and culture there should be an effective training program for pastors and laymen in doctrine, discipleship, evangelism, nurture and service. Such training programs should not rely on any stereotyped methodology but should be developed by creative local initiatives according to biblical standards.

Col. 1:27, 28

Ac. 14:23

Tit. 1:5, 9
Mk. 10:42–45

Eph. 4:11, 12

39

Paragraphs ten and eleven handle two related subjects, culture and leadership. Both have to do with churches which come into being as the fruit of missionary labor. For *the development of strategies for world evangelization*, calling for *imaginative pioneering methods, will under God . . . result . . . in the rise of churches*. What should be the relation of these churches to culture? What kind of leadership should they have?

a.   Culture

Culture was a major topic of thought and discussion at Lausanne. But the word is difficult to define. Culture may be likened to a tapestry, intricate and often beautiful, which is woven by a given society to express its corporate identity. The colors and patterns of the tapestry are the community's common beliefs and common customs, inherited from the past, enriched by contemporary art and binding the community together. Each of us, without exception, has been born and bred in a particular culture. Being part of our upbringing and environment, it is also part of ourselves, and we find it very difficult to stand outside it and evaluate it Christianly. Yet this we must learn to do. For if Jesus Christ is to be Lord of all, our cultural heritage cannot be excluded from his lordship. And this applies to churches as well as individuals.

The churches which arise in every place are bound to have a double orientation, towards Christ and towards culture. They cannot escape the responsibility to develop an attitude to both. What should it be? An earlier draft of the Covenant described churches as 'rooted in Christ and in culture.' But it was correctly pointed out that the roots of a church are in Christ alone. So the draft was amended to portray churches as *rooted in Christ and closely related to their culture*. Now Christ and culture are sometimes in conflict. What does the Covenant have to say about this? First, it insists on the proper evaluation of culture. Secondly, it gives examples of the dangerous influence of culture when it is not properly evaluated.

(i)   *The evaluation of culture Culture must always be tested and judged by Scripture*. This is because culture is the product of human society, whereas Scripture is the product of divine revelation; and Jesus was emphatic that God's Word must always take precedence over man's traditions (Mark 7: 8,9,13). Not that all culture is bad. Culture is ambiguous because man is ambiguous. Man is both noble (because made in God's image) and ignoble (because fallen and sinful). And his culture faithfully reflects these two aspects of man. *Because man is God's creature, some of his culture is rich in beauty and goodness*. Man's total depravity means that every part of him has been affected by the fall; it does not mean that he is incapable of anything good, beautiful or true. On the contrary, Jesus himself said that evil men can do good things (Matt. 7:11; cf. Luke 6:32). And the beauty of man's artistic achievement bears witness to the creativity with which his Creator has endowed him (Gen. 4:21,22). On the other hand, because man *has fallen, all his* culture is *tainted with sin and some of it is demonic*, that is, actually inspired by the devil and the powers of darkness.

So then, because of its ambiguous nature, all culture must be tested. *The Gospel does not presuppose the superiority of any culture to another.* In matters which are morally neutral, cultures are simply different from one another, rather than superior or inferior to each other. When we travel, for example, we have no liberty to assume that our way of doing things (the way we talk, dress, eat, greet people, organize our program, etc.) is necessarily better than other people's. 'According to the Bible,' said Dr. McGavran at Lausanne, 'God has no favorite among cultures. He accepts them all' (Rev. 21:26, but cf. v. 27).

What, then, is the relation of the Gospel to culture? It *evaluates all cultures according to its own criteria of truth and righteousness.* It rejects, for example, any idolatry which denies the uniqueness of God, any merit-system which denies the need of grace, and any oppression which denies the dignity of man. And it insists *on moral absolutes in every culture.* For although human customs are relative in value, God's moral law is absolute and invariable.

(ii) *The influence of culture.* Having insisted that all culture must be tested by Scripture, paragraph ten goes on to give some examples of our failure to do this. The principle is applied to missions, churches and evangelists. *Missions have all too frequently exported with the Gospel an alien culture.* That is, their message and manner of life have been partly biblical, partly cultural. Dr. René Padilla was particularly outspoken in his paper on the harmfulness of what he called 'culture Christianity,' namely, 'the identification of Christianity with culture or a cultural expression.' He referred both to European colonialism and to the American way of life, but was careful to point out that other examples could be given. Certainly, the younger churches of the Third World know the painful trauma which some missions have caused by their failure to distinguish between their Gospel and their culture. The apostle Paul, far from imposing an alien culture on others, adapted himself to their culture, becoming 'all things to all men' (I Cor. 9:19–23).

If younger churches have been confused by the importation of an alien culture, they have a second problem in knowing how to relate to their own national or tribal culture. Here the truth is that not only missions but also *churches have sometimes been in bondage to culture rather than to Scripture.* Yet if some have been too subservient to their local culture, others have been too critical of it, and have failed to develop any music, liturgy, art, architecture or literature in their own national idiom. Churches should even go beyond reacting to the culture that is already there, and should take initiatives to influence it. *Churches must seek to transform and enrich culture, all for the glory of God.*

The third example concerns *Christ's evangelists*, especially those called to cross-cultural missionary work, who find it hard to renounce their own culture and adapt themselves to the culture of those among whom they live and labor. Yet, following the example of the Son of God who 'emptied himself' of his glory in order to serve (Phil. 2:5–7), Christ's evangelists are called *humbly to seek to empty themselves* of their cultural status, power, privileges and prejudices, indeed *of all but their personal authenticity*. Such self-humbling, self-emptying and self-giving will be *in order to become the servants of others* (II Cor. 4:5).

b. Leadership

Paragraph eleven, 'Education and Leadership,' opens with a frank double confession. First, *we confess that we have sometimes pursued church growth at the expense of church depth, and divorced evangelism from Christian nurture.* As a result, it is not an exaggeration to say that Christian superficiality has become a worldwide phenomenon. Many converts never grow up in Christ. Secondly, *we acknowledge that some of our missions have been too slow to equip and encourage national leaders to assume their rightful responsibilities.* This, too, is a fact of missionary history. The transition from a mission situation to a church situation has too often been marred by a reluctance to hand over the leadership to nationals.

It is significant that the apostle Paul, who might be described as the greatest Christian missionary of all time, made neither of these two mistakes. His great ambition, he wrote, was not just to win converts but to 'present every man mature in Christ' (Col. 1:28,29), and it was his practice from the first missionary journey onwards to appoint local leaders as elders in every church (Acts 14:23).

(i) *Principles of leadership.* The Covenant mentions two essential principles of Christian leadership. First, *we are committed to indigenous principles*, that is, to the vision of an autonomous church with national (as opposed to foreign) leadership, and *we long that every church will have national leaders*. Paul instructed Titus to 'appoint elders in every town' (Tit.1:5), and presumably they were local men. The second principle concerns the kind of leadership which nationals will give. Being equally the children of Adam, national leaders are no more immune than missionaries to the sins of pride, power-hunger, and pomposity. So our longing is for national leaders *who manifest a Christian style of leadership*, drawing their inspiration not from secular government but from Christ's teaching and example, a leadership *in terms not of domination but of service* (Mark 10: 42–45; cf. II Cor. 4:5; I Pet. 5:3).

(ii) *Training for leadership. There is a great need to improve theological education, especially for church leaders.* The problems facing the church are always basically theological. Therefore, the church needs leaders who have learned to think theologically, so that they can apply Christian principles to every situation. This is also true of pastors who as the church's teachers not only need to be 'apt teachers' (I Tim. 3:2) but 'must hold firm to the sure word as taught' so that they may be able 'to give instruction in sound doctrine, and also to confute those who contradict it' (Tit. 1:9). So there was much discussion at Lausanne about the strategic need to develop, especially but not exclusively in the Third World, evangelical seminaries, theological education by extension, research centers, regional and national theological fellowships, and the exchange of theological teachers.

Church leaders include lay leaders. Clericalism (the suppression of the laity by the clergy) is not only incompatible with the biblical doctrine of the church as the people of God but hinders the work of the church by denying it gifted leadership which God has provided. Yet lay leaders also need training (Eph. 4:11,12). So one of the most urgent needs of the day is the availability *in every nation and culture* of a really *effective training program for pastors and laymen*.

Such a program will have at least two characteristics. First, it will be thorough, and should include in its syllabus not only *doctrine* (biblical theology) but also the outworking of doctrine in *discipleship, evangelism, nurture and service*. Secondly, it will be indigenous, like the leadership being trained by it. It should not be imposed from outside but *developed by . . . local initiatives*. Nor should it *rely on any stereotyped methodology*, since the local initiatives should be *creative*. When such initiatives, besides being local and creative, are also truly submissive to *biblical standards*, the result should be a training program of enormous benefit to the church.

Questions for study:

1. What are some of the major ingredients of your local culture? Isolate those parts of it which you think should be (a) accepted, (b) judged, (c) transformed and enriched.
2. Paragraph ten talks about evangelists as 'servants of others' and paragraph eleven about leadership in terms of 'service.' Discuss the relation between authority and service in a leadership role.
3. 'Christian nurture.' What steps does your church take to nurture new converts?
4. 'An effective training program for . . . laymen.' Supposing you had the responsibility to arrange one, what would it be like?

12. SPIRITUAL CONFLICT

We believe that we are engaged in constant spiritual warfare with the   Eph. 6:12
principalities and powers of evil, who are seeking to overthrow the   2 Co. 4:3, 4
church and frustrate its task of world evangelization. We know our
need to equip ourselves with God's armor and to fight this battle with   Eph. 6:11, 13–18
  2 Co. 10:3–5
the spiritual weapons of truth and prayer. For we detect the activity of
our enemy, not only in false ideologies outside the church, but also
inside it in false gospels which twist Scripture and put man in the place   1 Jn. 2:18–26;
  4:1–3
of God. We need both watchfulness and discernment to safeguard the
biblical Gospel. We acknowledge that we ourselves are not immune to   Gal. 1:6–19
worldliness of thought and action, that is, to a surrender to secularism.   2 Co. 2:17;
  4:2
For example, although careful studies of church growth, both numeri-
cal and spiritual, are right and valuable, we have sometimes neglected
them. At other times, desirous to ensure a response to the Gospel, we
have compromised our message, manipulated our hearers through
pressure techniques, and become unduly preoccupied with statistics or
even dishonest in our use of them. All this is worldly. The church must   Jn. 17:15
be in the world; the world must not be in the church.

13. FREEDOM AND PERSECUTION

It is the God-appointed duty of every government to secure conditions   1 Tim. 2:1–4
of peace, justice and liberty in which the church may obey God, serve   Col. 3:24
the Lord Christ, and preach the Gospel without interference. We   Ac. 4:19;
  5:29
therefore pray for the leaders of the nations and call upon them to
guarantee freedom of thought and conscience, and freedom to practice
and propagate religion in accordance with the will of God and as set
forth in The Universal Declaration of Human Rights. We also express
our deep concern for all who have been unjustly imprisoned, and   Heb. 13:1–3
especially for our brethren who are suffering for their testimony to the   Lk. 4:18
Lord Jesus. We promise to pray and work for their freedom. At the
same time we refuse to be intimidated by their fate. God helping us, we
too will seek to stand against injustice and to remain faithful to the   Gal. 5:11;
  6:12
Gospel, whatever the cost. We do not forget the warnings of Jesus that   Mt. 5:10–12
  Jn. 15:18–21
persecution is inevitable.

44

Paragraphs 12 and 13 introduce into the Covenant a somber note, namely, that the church must expect fierce opposition. True, Jesus promised that he would build his church on the rock and that not even the powers of hades (death) would be able to overcome it (Matt. 16:18). The church has an eternal destiny, and even in time is secure in the hand of its sovereign Lord (Acts 4:24–28). Yet Jesus also warned us that we would encounter much hostility (e.g., John 15:18; 16:4), which would be stirred up by that wicked spirit he called 'the ruler of this world' (John 12:31; 14:30; 16:11).

So paragraph 12, 'Spiritual Conflict,' begins with the statement of two facts, first about the battle we have to fight, and secondly about the armor we need to wear. First, *we believe that we are engaged in constant spiritual warfare with the principalities and powers of evil.* The church has human enemies, but behind them lurk 'spiritual hosts of wickedness' (Eph. 6:12), as subtle as they are unscrupulous, and with them our warfare must be unremitting. For they are *seeking to overthrow the church and frustrate its task of world evangelization* (II Cor. 4:3,4). Yet we could never hope to resist them, let alone defeat them, in our puny human strength. The church is no match for the devil. So *we know our need to equip ourselves with God's armor* (Eph. 6:10–17) *and to fight this battle with . . . spiritual weapons* (II Cor. 10:3–5), especially the mighty weapons *of truth and prayer.* As for the power of truth, we need to remember Paul's conviction that 'we cannot do anything against the truth, but only for the truth' (II Cor. 13:8). As for the power of prayer, Jesus said that he himself used this weapon against Satan (Luke 22:31,32).

After this general introduction to *spiritual warfare* and *spiritual weapons*, the paragraph goes on to particularize. It dares to state that we are able to *detect the activity of our enemy.* Although he is himself invisible, his tactics are not, and so we are 'not ignorant of his designs' (II Cor. 2:11). We know from Scripture what weapons he used in his attack upon the early church, and we know from history and experience that his methods have not changed. The three chief weapons of his armory are still error, worldliness and persecution.

a. Error

Jesus called the devil 'a liar and the father of lies' (John 8:44). He hates the truth and is constantly seeking to deceive men into error. Thus, we do not hesitate to attribute to his malevolent work *false ideologies outside the church.* Indeed, it would be impossible to understand how intelligent, educated people can believe some of the nonsense taught by non-Christian systems and cults if it were not for the work of deceiving spirits (I John 2:18–26; 4:1–3). But the devil does not limit his activity to the sphere outside the church. It is grievous to have to add that he is also responsible for *false gospels . . . inside it.* Paul rejected the message of the Judaizers as a false gospel (Gal. 1:6–9), and there are false teachers who trouble the church with false gospels today. How may they be recognized?

In two main ways. First, they *twist Scripture* (cf., II Cor. 2:17; 4:2 and II Pet. 3:15–16). Far from desiring to be submissive to its authority and its message, they presume to stand in judgment on it and distort its plain meaning to favor their own unbiblical presuppositions. The second of their characteristics is such an unbounded confidence in man and his abilities as virtually to *put man in the place of God.* 'Godliness,' or a due reverence for God, is always a mark of true religion (I Tim. 4:7; II Tim. 2:16; Tit. 1:1), whereas the attempted deification of man was the essence of the first sin ('you will be like God' Gen. 3:5) and remains the essence of all sin today.

It is true that man has unique dignity as the only creature made in God's image, but he is still a creature, and a sinner too, dependent on God's grace. A good test of every ideology is whether it exalts God and humbles man, or whether it exalts man and dethrones God. *We need both watchfulness* ('be watchful, stand firm in your faith!' I Cor. 16:13) *and discernment* ('test the spirits to see whether they are of God,' I John 4:1) if we are *to safeguard the biblical Gospel.* Christ and his apostles regularly warned us of false teachers (e.g., Matt. 7:15 ff; Acts 20:29 ff; II Pet. 2; I John 2: 18 ff): we need to be constantly on our guard.

b. Worldliness

The devil uses moral as well as intellectual weapons. If he cannot deceive the church into error, he will attempt to corrupt it with sin and worldliness. This part of the paragraph has a particular application to us as evangelical Christians. We may by God's grace be kept faithful to the biblical Gospel; yet *we acknowledge that we ourselves are not immune* to the onslaught of Satan, especially *to worldliness of thought and action.* Worldliness has often been defined in our evangelical circles in relation to questionable habits like smoking, drinking, dancing, and going to the movies. And indeed all of us have to make up our mind conscientiously about these and similar practices. But worldliness is something far more subtle. 'The world' means secular or Christless society, and 'worldliness' is its outlook, *a surrender to secularism* in either our thinking or our behavior.

The paragraph goes on to cite as an example of worldliness our attitude to *careful studies of church growth, both numerical and spiritual. We have sometimes neglected them,* it says, as if we really did not care whether our church was growing in either size or depth. Such indifference and neglect are signs of worldliness, for these studies *are right and valuable. At other times,* we have made the opposite mistake. The numerical growth of the church has become almost an obsession with us. And therefore, *desirous* (even determined) *to ensure a response to the Gospel,* we have resorted to doubtful methods, which Paul would almost certainly have included in the 'disgraceful underhanded ways' which he said he had renounced (II Cor. 4:2). Either *we have compromised our message* ('tampered with God's Word' II Cor. 4:2), eliminating such unfashionable elements as self-denial and judgment in order to make it more palatable to modern man; or we have *manipulated our hearers through pressure techniques*, which is to treat human beings as less than human; or we have *become unduly preoccupied with statistics* (as if the work of the Holy Spirit of God could ever be reduced to mere statistics!), or *even dishonest in our use of them* (publishing reports which are not strictly true). It is an ugly list of misdemeanors. *All this is worldly.* Wherever it is found, it indicates that somehow the devil has insinuated a worldly perspective into the church, and so has succeeded in getting things the wrong way round. *The church must be in the world; the world must not be in the church* (John 17:15).

c. Persecution

Not content with his attempts to introduce sin and error into the church, the devil also attacks the church from outside, seeking either by physical persecution or by restrictive legislation to hinder the church's work. So paragraph 13, 'Freedom and Persecution,' boldly grasps the thorny issue of relations between church and state. It recognizes that each has a duty to the other, and it expounds these duties with special reference to I Tim. 2:1–4.

It is the God-appointed duty of every government to secure conditions of peace, justice and liberty. For then 'we may lead a quiet and peaceable life, godly and respectful in every way' (v.2). In such conditions *the church may obey God* ('godly'), *serve the Lord Christ* (Col. 3:24; no Christian who has confessed, 'Jesus is Lord' can also declare, 'Caesar is Lord,' cf. Mark 12:17) *and preach the Gospel without interference* (implied in verses 3 and 4, cf. Acts 4:19; 5:29).

The church also has a responsibility to the state, and in particular *to pray for the leaders of the nations* (verses 1 and 2a). The church cannot stop with prayer, however. In addition it has a duty, insofar as it is able, to be the nation's conscience, and to remind leaders of their God-ordained role. Therefore, we not only call upon God for our leaders, but *we call upon* our leaders themselves *to guarantee freedom of thought and conscience, and freedom to practice and propagate religion.* These freedoms have been *set forth in The Universal Declaration of Human Rights*, which was unanimously adopted by the General Assembly of the United Nations in December, 1948, with eight abstentions.

Article 18 reads, 'Everyone has the right to freedom of thought, conscience and religion; this right includes freedom to change his religion or belief; and freedom, either alone or in community with others, and in public or private, to manifest his religion or belief in teaching, practice, worship or observance.'

More important still, the guarantee of these freedoms is *in accordance with the will of God*, for he has instituted 'governing authorities' to punish criminals and reward good citizens, not to curtail legitimate freedoms, still less to tyrannize the innocent (Rom. 13:1 ff).

Having outlined the reciprocal duties of church and state, the paragraph turns its attention to the victims of oppression. *We also express our deep concern for all who have been unjustly imprisoned.* We do not call them 'prisoners of conscience,' for some men's conscience is too perverted to be a reliable guide. We are thinking rather of those victims of tyranny who have neither done nor plotted any harm, but have been imprisoned either merely for their opinions, or for actions within the freedoms mentioned above. Among such we mention *especially our brethren who are suffering for their testimony to the Lord Jesus* (Rev. 1:9). We have been commanded to remember them and even to feel for them 'as though in prison with them' (Heb. 13:3). Sympathy, however, is not enough; *we promise to pray and work for their freedom* (cf. Luke 4:18).

There is one thing more to say, and this is that *we refuse to be intimidated by their fate.* Oppressors have always imagined that they could use violence to assert their will and crush the church. They have never been able to, and they never will. Although we know our human frailty, yet, *God helping us, we too will seek to stand against injustice and to remain faithful to the Gospel, whatever the cost.* No doubt it costs most of us nothing to say this, but at least we recognize the real possibility of tyranny and persecution spreading into countries which at present are free. For *we do not forget the warnings of Jesus that persecution is inevitable* (e.g., Matt. 5:10–12).

Questions for study:

1. Read Ephesians 6: 10–20. What does this teach about Christian warfare and Christian weapons?
2. 'We detect the activity of our enemy.' Do you? Where does he seem to you to be most active today?
3. Some examples are given at the end of paragraph 12 of the worldliness of the church. Do any of them fit your situation? Can you add to the list?
4. Can you think of any practical action you or your church could take (a) in appealing to national leaders, and (b) in working for the release of prisoners?

14. THE POWER OF THE HOLY SPIRIT

We believe in the power of the Holy Spirit. The Father sent his Spirit to bear witness to his Son; without his witness ours is futile. Conviction of sin, faith in Christ, new birth and Christian growth are all his work. Further, the Holy Spirit is a missionary Spirit; thus evangelism should arise spontaneously from a Spirit-filled church. A church that is not a missionary church is contradicting itself and quenching the Spirit. Worldwide evangelization will become a realistic possibility only when the Spirit renews the church in truth and wisdom, faith, holiness, love and power. We therefore call upon all Christians to pray for such a visitation of the sovereign Spirit of God that all his fruit may appear in all his people and that all his gifts may enrich the body of Christ. Only then will the whole church become a fit instrument in his hands, that the whole earth may hear his voice.

Ac. 1:8
1 Co. 2:4
Jn. 15:26, 27
Jn. 16:8–11
1 Co. 12:3
Jn. 3:6–8
2 Co. 3:18
Jn. 7:37–39
1 Th. 5:19
Ps. 85:4–7
Gal. 5:22, 23
Ro. 12:3–8
1 Co. 12:4–31
Ps. 67:1–3

15. THE RETURN OF CHRIST

We believe that Jesus Christ will return personally and visibly, in power and glory, to consummate his salvation and his judgment. This promise of his coming is a further spur to our evangelism, for we remember his words that the Gospel must first be preached to all nations. We believe that the interim period between Christ's ascension and return is to be filled with the mission of the people of God, who have no liberty to stop before the End. We also remember his warning that false Christs and false prophets will arise as precursors of the final Antichrist. We therefore reject as a proud, self-confident dream the notion that man can ever build a utopia on earth. Our Christian confidence is that God will perfect his kingdom, and we look forward with eager anticipation to that day, and to the new heaven and earth in which righteousness will dwell and God will reign forever. Meanwhile, we rededicate ourselves to the service of Christ and of men in joyful submission to his authority over the whole of our lives.

Mk. 14:62
Heb. 9:28
Mk. 13:10
Mt. 28:20
Ac. 1:8–11
Mk. 13:21–23
1 Jn. 2:18;
4:1–3
2 Th. 2:1–12
Lk. 12:32
Rev. 21:1–5
2 Pe. 3:13
Mt. 28:18

The last two paragraphs of the Covenant emphasize two neglected dimensions of evangelism. One is the only ground on which we can hope for results (the power of the Holy Spirit); the other is the ultimate goal to which we look (the return of Jesus Christ). These are great Christian doctrines concerning the second and third persons of the Trinity; so each paragraph begins with an affirmation of faith: *We believe in the power of the Holy Spirit . . . We believe that Jesus Christ will return . . .* Happy is the church which is fortified by these assurances; wretched indeed are those who lack them!

a.   The Power of the Holy Spirit

After a reminder of the malicious, destructive power of the devil (paragraph 12), it is an appropriate relief to turn our thoughts to the gracious and constructive power of the Holy Spirit. Again and again Scripture links the Spirit with power. In the Old Testament, it is 'not by might, nor by power, but by my Spirit, says the Lord of hosts' (Zech. 4:6). In the New Testament Jesus himself spoke of the power of the Spirit for witness (Acts 1:8) and the apostle Paul wrote that, conscious of his own weakness, he relied in his ministry on the 'demonstration of the Spirit and power' (I Cor. 2:3–5, cf. I Thess. 1:5). We must do the same.

The particular spheres mentioned in which the Holy Spirit's power is needed are: first, the witness of the church; and, secondly, the renewal of the church.

(i)   ***The witness of the church.*** We are reminded that *the Father sent his Spirit to bear witness to his Son.* This is an echo of the Trinitarian teaching of Jesus in the Upper Room. He emphasized that the distinctive work of the Spirit whom the Father was going to send would be in relation to himself, the Son; that the Spirit would delight above all else to glorify or manifest the Son (John 16:14); and that therefore in the spread of the Gospel the Holy Spirit would be the chief witness. 'He will bear witness to me.' Only after saying this did Jesus add to his apostles, 'and you also are witnesses' (John 15:26,27). Once we have grasped the significance of this order, we shall have no difficulty in agreeing that *without his witness ours is futile.*

All four main stages in the great event we call conversion are the work of the Holy Spirit. First, *conviction of sin.* It is the Spirit, Jesus said, who would 'convince the world of sin and of righteousness and of judgment' (John 16:8–11). Next, *faith in Christ.* It is the Spirit who opens the eyes of convicted sinners to see in Jesus their Savior and Lord, and to believe in him, for 'no one can say "Jesus is Lord" except by the Holy Spirit' (I Cor. 12:3). Thirdly, the *new birth* is a birth 'of the Spirit' (John 3:6–8). Fourthly, *Christian growth* or sanctification is his work too (II Cor. 3:18). So the power of the Holy Spirit in evangelism is not optional, but indispensable.

The work of the Spirit arises from his nature. *The Holy Spirit is a missionary Spirit*, and this is the reason why *evangelism*, instead of being imposed by constraint, *should arise spontaneously from a Spirit-filled church*. Since the Spirit is a missionary Spirit, it follows that a Spirit-filled church becomes a missionary church, as we see clearly in the book of Acts. *A church that is not a missionary church*, but instead is preoccupied with its own affairs, *is contradicting itself*, contradicting its very nature as an outward-looking missionary community, and is also *quenching the Spirit* who longs to flow forth from his people into the world like 'rivers of living water' into a desert (John 7:37–39; I Thess. 5:19). Only the Spirit can turn introverted churches inside out.

   (ii)   *The renewal of the church.* What has been said so far about the church's witness, evangelism and missionary zeal is in many parts of the world more a theory than a reality. So it is recognized that *worldwide evangelization will become a realistic possibility only when the Spirit renews the church.* There is a lot of talk about the renewal of the church today. But some who broach the subject have a rather restricted aspiration. They concentrate their concern on the renewal of the church's unity, or the church's structures, or the church's experience of spiritual gifts. The Covenant paints on a broader canvas, however, and longs for the Spirit to renew the church in every way, *in truth* (as at the Reformation) *and wisdom*, in *faith, holiness, love, and power.* For such a total and wholesome renewal we need to pray. True, the Holy Spirit is a sovereign Spirit and cannot be commanded or organized. Nevertheless, God graciously hears his people's prayers. *So we call upon all Christians to pray for . . . a visitation of the sovereign Spirit of God. The word* 'visitation' is used here as Scripture sometimes uses it, to indicate special manifestations of God's presence and special activities of God's power. For example, although God is constantly present and active in his world, he is said to 'visit' the earth when he enriches it with rain and prepares it for the harvest (Psa. 65:9). So too we may say that the Holy Spirit, who indwells and never forsakes his people, yet 'visits' them whenever he puts forth his power on their behalf. And our confidence is that when he visits the church in power he will both bear his fruit (the nine Christian graces listed in Gal. 5:22,23) and bestow his gifts (some 20 of which are mentioned in Rom. 12:3–8, I Cor. 12:4–31, and Eph. 4:11). So we pray for *such a visitation* of the Spirit that *all his fruit may appear in all his people* (since all nine qualities are to characterize us) and that *all his gifts may enrich the body of Christ* (since they are service gifts bestowed 'for the common good' and distributed to different believers 'as he wills' I Cor. 12:7,11).

   The paragraph ends with the conviction that *only then*, when the Holy Spirit is free to move with power, *will the whole church become a fit instrument in his hands*, so that, in words which take up the Congress theme, *the whole earth may hear his voice* (Psa. 67:1–3).

b.   The Return of Jesus Christ

For many centuries the universal church believed in the second advent, and all Christians could recite the relevant clause of the Nicene Creed ('And he shall come again with glory to judge both the quick and the dead') without any mental reservations or any need surreptitiously to cross their fingers. But now scientific secularism has eroded the historic faith of the church, and the cry has arisen to demythologize this article of the creed. Against this background of unbelief, the biblical faith of the Congress participants stands out in bold relief: *We believe that Jesus Christ will return.* And although evangelical Christians, anxious not to go beyond the plain assertions of the Bible, retain a humble agnosticism about some of the details of the Lord's return, we are able to affirm at least four truths about it.

First, he will return *personally*, for the one who is coming is 'this Jesus' whom the apostles saw ascend into heaven (Acts 1:11). Secondly, he will return *visibly*, so that 'every eye will see him' (Rev. 1:7). Thirdly, in striking contrast to the manner of his first coming, he will return *in power and glory*. The very words are borrowed from Jesus who said, 'They will see the Son of man coming in clouds with great power and glory' (Mark 13:26). Fourthly, he will return *to consummate his salvation and judgment*, for both processes began with his first coming and both will be completed at his second (John 5:21–29; Heb. 9:27,28). All Christians should be looking and longing for Christ to come, and should share this great confidence that his coming will be personal, visible, glorious and final.

This promise of his coming is not a piece of unpractical theologizing. On the contrary, Christ and his apostles never spoke of it to satisfy idle curiosity, but always to stimulate practical action. In particular, it is *a further spur to our evangelism*. For he himself forged a link between our proclamation and his return, and *we remember his words that the Gospel must first be preached to all nations* 'and then the end will come' (Matt. 24:14). So *the interim period* between his two comings, *between Christ's ascension and return*, is by his own appointment *to be filled with the mission of the people of God.* 'Go . . . and make disciples of all nations . . .,' he said, 'and lo I am with you always, to the close of the age' (Matt. 28:19,20; Acts 1:8–11). Thus, *we have no liberty to stop before the End.*

There follows a clarification. What exactly is the church's expectation or hope? Some speak nowadays as if we should expect the world to get better and better, and as if to secure conditions of material prosperity, international peace, social justice, political freedom and personal fulfillment is equivalent to establishing the kingdom of God. Certainly, it is our duty to work for justice and freedom, as was stated in paragraph five. And certainly too, in God's providence and common grace we can expect some success. But Jesus gave us no expectation that everything would get steadily better. On the contrary, *we remember his warning* that the coming of Christ will be preceded by the coming of Antichrist, and *that false Christs and false prophets will arise as precursors of the final Antichrist* (Mark 13:21–23; I John 2:18; 4:1–3). *We therefore reject as a proud, self-confident dream*, and as entirely at variance with the teaching of Jesus, *the notion that man can ever build a utopia on earth.* This is simply not the Christian hope according to Scripture. *Our Christian confidence is that God will perfect his kingdom,* for Jesus always spoke of the kingdom as God's gift, not man's achievement (Luke 12:32).

Professor Peter Beyerhaus distinguished clearly in his paper on 'World Evangelization and the Kingdom of God' between two stages of the kingdom, and argued that evangelization is both 'inviting into the kingdom of grace' now and 'preparing for the kingdom of glory' to come. Men enter the kingdom of grace today by spiritual regeneration and should become 'convincing models of social and political involvement.' But the total redemption of man, society and creation awaits the kingdom of glory. This eschatological vision 'has inspired many missionaries with a holy restlessness' as they long for Christ's promise to be fulfilled. And although we may differ from one another in the precise form we expect his kingdom to take, yet all of us *look forward with eager anticipation to that day, and to the new heaven and earth,* which are clearly promised, *in which righteousness will dwell and God will reign forever* (Rev. 21:1–5; II Pet. 3:13).

From this glorious vision of the future we turn back to the concrete realities of the present. Indeed, it is our Christian hope which inspires us always to abound in the work of the Lord, because we know that our labor will not be in vain (I Cor. 15:58). So *meanwhile,* as we patiently await the consummation, *we rededicate ourselves to the service of Christ and of men in joyful submission to his authority over the whole of our lives* (Matt. 28:18).

Questions for study:

1. It is easy to talk about the power of the Holy Spirit in evangelism. But what does it mean in practice to rely on his power rather than our own?
2. The renewal of the church is much discussed today. What is it? How will it happen?
3. Does the promise of Christ's return make any difference to your life?
4. What is the kingdom of God? How does it spread? How will it be consummated?

CONCLUSION

Therefore, in the light of this our faith and our resolve, we enter into a solemn covenant with God and with each other, to pray, to plan and to work together for the evangelization of the whole world. We call upon others to join us. May God help us by his grace and for his glory to be faithful to this our covenant! Amen, Alleluia!

The declaration so far made has consisted partly of affirmation (what we believe) and partly of determination (what we intend to do); in other words, partly of faith, partly of resolve. *Therefore,* we conclude, it is *in the light of this our faith and our resolve* that we frame our Covenant or binding promise. *We enter into a solemn Covenant with God and with each other,* first *to pray* together, secondly *to plan* together, and thirdly *to work together* (in that order of priority) *for the evangelization of the whole world,* that is to say, to bring the good news within meaningful reach of the whole population of the earth. It is a colossal undertaking. Indeed, without the mobilization of the church, and especially without the grace of God, it is a hopeless undertaking. So *we call upon others to join us,* hoping that many besides the original signatories at Lausanne will thoughtfully consider and sign the Covenant. Above all, we pray that God will enable us to be faithful. We know our weakness, and put no confidence in ourselves. Our only hope of remaining faithful lies in his grace, and our supreme motivation is his greater glory. Therefore our prayer is that God will *help us by his grace and for his glory to be faithful to this our Covenant. Amen. Alleluia!*

POSTSCRIPT

Let the Earth Hear His Voice, 'a comprehensive reference volume on World Evangelization', edited by J. D. Douglas, was published by World Wide Publications, Minneapolis, in 1975. This is a massive compendium of 1471 pages, which preserves the full documentation of Lausanne I. It therefore contains the following: the introductory speeches; the text of the Covenant; the eight devotional Bible studies; the fifteen plenary papers submitted in advance of the Congress, together with the speeches delivered by the authors in response to comments sent in by participants; the message on Psalm 23 given by Billy Graham in the Laustade (stadium), and the three supporting testimonies; the six evening presentations; the thirty-four 'Evangelistic

54

Strategy' papers and the group reports; the twenty-five 'Theology of Evangelism' papers and the group reports; the statement on 'radical discipleship' produced by an *ad hoc* group; eight 'Functional Reports'; eight regional and fifty-two national strategy reports; and Billy Graham's closing address entitled 'The King is Coming'.

This compendium of Lausanne I material remains an invaluable resource on all aspects of world evangelization.

2

— 1977 —

The Pasadena Statement on the Homogeneous Unit Principle

◆◆◆◆◆

A Colloquium on the Homogeneous Unit Principle,
Pasadena, S. California, 31 May–2 June 1977

EXPLANATORY PREFACE

The Lausanne Theology and Education group (LTEG) was set up by the Executive of the Lausanne Committee for World Evangelization during its meeting in Berlin in September 1976. Its task is to promote theological reflection on issues related to world evangelization and, in particular, to explore the implications of the Lausanne Covenant.

Charged with this responsibility, LTEG chose as the first topic for discussion the controversial 'homogeneous unit principle,' which has been developed by Fuller Seminary's School of World Mission. The School of World Mission has had a very wide influence in recent years. Large numbers of mission theorists, mission executives, missionaries, pastors, and lay leaders have been challenged and stimulated by its philosophy of church growth. At the same time, some aspects of this philosophy have not escaped criticism. So during the present decade a number of books and articles have appeared, expounding and defending different points of view. The most important of them are listed in the bibliography. This interchange, however, somewhat resembled the lobbing of hand grenades across no-man's-land from the trenches on either side. Not until June 1977 did representatives of both viewpoints meet face to face in a spirit of Christian brotherhood. The colloquium was set up as a common exploration rather than as a confrontation, and as a result we grew in mutual understanding and respect.

This first Lausanne Occasional Paper contains the agreed statement which we were able to issue on 2nd June 1977.

JOHN STOTT
(Chairman: Lausanne Theology and Education Group)

—The Pasadena Statement—

(A colloquium on the Homogeneous Unit Principle)

CONTENTS

1. INTRODUCTION: THE SETTING

A discussion of the 'homogeneous unit principle' of Church Growth theory was held under the auspices of the Lausanne Theology and Education Group from May 31 to June 2, 1977, in Pasadena, California. Five faculty members of the Fuller Theological Seminary School of World Mission had prepared advance papers on the methodological, anthropological, historical, ethical, and theological implications of the homogeneous unit principle (HUP). Five discussants had prepared papers in response to these. The ten of us then debated the issues raised, with the help of about 25 consultants. We are grateful to Fuller Seminary for their generous hospitality.

This consultation was the first to be held under Lausanne's sponsorship since the International Congress on World Evangelization took place in July 1974. We desire to express our heartfelt thanks to God that the so-called 'spirit of Lausanne' has characterized our conversation, in that we have been able to discuss controversial issues face-to-face with openness, honesty, and love.

We have found ourselves to be entirely united in our commitment to the Lord Jesus Christ, the supreme authority of the Bible, and the task of worldwide evangelization. We have not polarized into two groups who are respectively 'for' and 'against' the HUP or HU churches. Our discussion has been much more subtle than that. We have striven to listen to each other and to understand not only each other's arguments but the concerns which lie behind the arguments. And we bear witness to the help which God has given us.

Now we desire to make public both the substantial areas of agreement which we have discovered and the points of tension and disagreement which still remain. We earnestly hope that the former will contribute to the spread of the Gospel, and that the latter will stimulate us all to further study and discussion.

2. DEFINITION OF TERMS

Dr. Donald McGavran's definition of a HU is 'a section of society in which all members have some characteristic in common.' Used in this way, the term is broad and elastic. To be more precise, the common bond may be geographical, ethnic, linguistic, social, educational, vocational, or economic, or a combination of several of these and other factors. Whether or not members of the group can readily articulate it, the common characteristic makes them feel at home with each other and aware of their identity as 'we' in distinction to 'they.'

We are agreed that everybody belongs to at least one such homogeneous unit. This is an observable fact which all of us recognize. Not all of us, however, consider that it is the best term to use. Some of us prefer 'sub-culture,' while others of us would like to explore further the biblical concept of *ethnos* (usually translated 'nation' or 'people') as enjoying a 'solidarity in covenant' by creation, although in rebellion against its Creator. Nevertheless, for the purposes of this statement we shall retain the more familiar expression 'homogeneous unit.'

3.   THE HOMOGENEOUS UNIT PRINCIPLE AND EVANGELISM

What we have been specially concerned to discuss is the relation of HUs to the evangelistic task laid upon the church by the Great Commission of our Lord, and the propriety of using them as a means to world evangelization. Dr. McGavran's well-known statement is that people 'like to become Christians without crossing racial, linguistic or class barriers.' That is, the barriers to the acceptance of the Gospel are often more sociological than theological; people reject the Gospel not because they think it is false but because it strikes them as alien. They imagine that in order to become Christians they must renounce their own culture, lose their own identity, and betray their own people.

Therefore, in order to reach them, not only should the evangelist be able to identify with them, and they with the evangelist; not only must the Gospel be contextualized in such a way that it communicates with them; but the church into which they are invited must itself belong to their culture sufficiently for them to feel at home in it. It is when these conditions are fulfilled that men and women are won to Jesus Christ, and subsequently that churches grow.

4.   THE RICHES OF CULTURAL DIVERSITY

The arguments advanced to support the concept of the importance of culture are not only pragmatic ('churches grow fastest that way') but biblical ('God desires it that way'). We leave aside for the moment the question whether the best way to express the diversity of human cultures is to encourage a diversity of homogeneous unit churches. At this point we are unanimous in celebrating the colorful mosaic of the human race that God has created. This rich variety should be preserved, not destroyed, by the Gospel. The attempt to impose another culture on people who have their own is cultural imperialism. The attempt to level all cultures into a colorless uniformity is a denial of the Creator and an affront to his creation. The preservation of cultural diversity honors God, respects man, enriches life, and promotes evangelization. Each church, if it is to be truly indigenous, should be rooted in the soil of its local culture.

5. THE CHURCH, THE CHURCHES AND THE HOMOGENEOUS UNIT PRINCIPLE

We are all agreed that, as there is one God and Father, one Lord Jesus, and one Holy Spirit, so he has only one church. The unity of the church is a given fact (Ephesians 4:4–6). At the same time, we have the responsibility to maintain this unity (v.3), to make it visible, and to grow up into the fullness of unity in Christ (vv. 13–16).

How then can the unity of the church (to which we are committed) and the diversity of cultures (to which we are also committed) be reconciled with one another? More particularly, how can separate HU churches express the unity of the Body of Christ?

We are all agreed that the dividing wall which Jesus Christ abolished by his death was *echthra*, 'enmity' or 'hostility.' All forms of hatred, scorn, and disrespect between Christians of different backgrounds are forbidden, being totally incompatible with Christ's reconciling work. But we must go further than this. The wall dividing Jew from Gentile was not only their active reciprocal hatred; it was also their racial and religious alienation symbolized by 'the law of commandments and ordinances.' This, too, Jesus abolished, in order to 'create in himself one new man in place of two, so making peace' (Eph. 2:15).

This did not mean that Jews ceased to be Jews, or Gentiles to be Gentiles. It did mean, however, that their racial differences were no barrier to their fellowship, for through their union with Jesus Christ both groups were now 'joint heirs, joint members of the same body and joint partakers of the promise' (Eph. 3:6 literally). The union of Jews and Gentiles in Christ was the 'mystery' which was revealed to Paul and which he proclaimed to all (Ephesians 3:3–6,9,10). Thus the church as the single new humanity or God's new society is central to the Gospel. Our responsibility is both to preach it and to exhibit it before the watching world.

What did this mean in practice in the early church? It seems probable that, although there were mixed Jewish-Gentile congregations, there were also homogeneous Jewish congregations (who still observed Jewish customs) and homogeneous Gentile congregations (who observed no Jewish customs). Nevertheless, Paul clearly taught them that they belonged to each other in Christ, that they must welcome one another as Christ had welcomed them (compare Romans 15:7), and that they must respect one another's consciences, and not offend one another. He publicly rebuked Peter in Antioch for withdrawing from table fellowship with Gentile believers, and argued that his action was a denial of the truth of the Gospel, that is, of the justification of all believers (whether Jews or Gentiles) by grace through faith (compare Galatians 2:11–16). This incident and teaching should be taken as a warning to all of us of the seriousness of permitting any kind of apartheid in the Christian fellowship. And it should go without saying that no one visiting a church or requesting membership in it should ever be turned away on merely cultural grounds. On the contrary, visitors and members should be welcomed from all cultures.

All of us are agreed that in many situations a homogeneous unit church can be a legitimate and authentic church. Yet we are also agreed that it can never be complete in itself. Indeed, if it remains in isolation, it cannot reflect the universality and diversity of the Body of Christ. Nor can it grow into maturity. Therefore, every HU church must take active steps to broaden its fellowship in order to demonstrate visibly the unity and the variety of Christ's church. This will mean forging with other and different churches creative relationships which express the reality of Christian love, brotherhood, and interdependence.

During our consultation we have shared several possible ways of developing such relationships. They will range from occasional united evangelistic crusades, Christian concerts, conferences, conventions and annual festivals, through a variety of voluntary associations and interchurch federations to the regular enjoying of intercultural fellowship. One model of this we have looked at is the large city church (or congregation) with several HU sub-churches (or subcongregations) which normally worship separately but sometimes together. On these occasions their common celebration is enriched by the dress, music, and liturgy of different traditions. Another model is a multicultural Sunday congregation which divides into mid-week HU house churches, while a third and more radical way is to work towards integration, although without cultural assimilation.

In our commitment to evangelism, we all understand the reasons why homogeneous unit churches usually grow faster than heterogeneous or multicultural ones. Some of us, however, do not agree that the rapidity with which churches grow is the only or even always the most important Christian priority. We know that an alien culture is a barrier to faith. But we also know that segregation and strife in the church are barriers to faith. If, then, we have to choose between apparent acquiescence in segregation for the sake of numerical church growth and the struggle for reconciliation at the expense of numerical church growth, we find ourselves in a painful dilemma. Some of us have had personal experience of the evils of tribalism in Africa, racism in America, caste in India, and economic injustice in Latin America and elsewhere, and all of us are opposed to these things. In such situations none of us could with a good conscience continue to develop HU churches which seem to ignore the social problems and even tolerate them in the church, while some of us believe that the development of HU churches can often contribute to their solution.

We recognize that both positions can be defended in terms of obedience — obedience to Christ's commission to evangelize on the one hand, and obedience to the commands to live in love and justice on the other. The synthesis between these two still eludes us, although we all accept our Lord's own words that it is through the brotherly love and unity of Christians that the world will come to believe in him (John 13:35; 17:21,23).

6. CULTURE, EVIL AND PROCESS OF CHANGE

We have tried to consider carefully what our attitude to peoples' different cultures should be. At Lausanne we affirmed that 'culture must always be tested and judged by Scripture. Because man is God's creature, some of his culture is rich in beauty and goodness. Because he has fallen, all of it is tainted with sin and some of it is demonic.' We do not forget the Scripture which declares that 'the whole world is in the power of the evil one' (1 John 5:19).

So some of us are more positive and others more negative towards culture. In our discussions, however, we have concentrated particularly on the negative or demonic elements in human culture. We recognize that in all human groupings there is a latent tendency either to claim from their members too high a loyalty (and so become idolatrous), or to shun outsiders (and so become self-centered).

Further, in some groups the common trait of homogeneity which binds them together is itself evil. This might, for example, be cannibalism, racism, or (if we may cite opposite ends of the social scale) crime and prostitution in the slums or oppressive wealth in the suburbs. In such cases, what constitutes the homogeneous unit must be opposed rather than affirmed. The church should not be planted in it without making its opposition plain, nor without seeking to overcome the evil principle and/or uncover and change its underlying causes. The church should never avoid this prophetic and social ministry. Belonging to Jesus Christ involves enmity with the world.

We have found considerable help in the concept of change. To acknowledge the fact of HUs is not to acquiesce in the characteristics they possess which are displeasing to Christ. The Christian attitude to HUs is often called the 'realist attitude,' because it realistically accepts that HUs exist and will always exist. We would prefer, however, to call this an attitude of 'dynamic realism' because we wish also to affirm that HUs can change and must always change. For Christ the Lord gives to his people new standards. They also receive a new homogeneity which transcends all others, for now they find their essential unity in Christ, rather than in culture.

Not that change can be taken for granted, for it does not always happen automatically. It needs to be actively sought, beginning with the first acknowledgement of Jesus as Lord, and then steadily growing through a process of continuous re-evaluation according to Scripture. When this happens, sometimes a HU church replaces its principle of cohesion with another and better one, while at other times it disbands altogether, its members gravitating to other churches.

7. THE LORDSHIP OF CHRIST AND REPENTANCE

In connection with the concept of 'people movements', the distinction has been drawn between 'discipling' (becoming a Christian and being baptized) and 'perfecting' (the process of growth into maturity). We have had a full discussion of the issues which this distinction raises, and in particular whether it involves some kind of 'postponement of ethical awareness' in enquirers, and what form or degree of repentance is implicit in conversion and baptism. Here we have thankfully discovered a wide area of agreement.

We agree that to preach the Gospel is to proclaim Jesus Christ in the fullness of his person and work; that this is to 'preach the kingdom' which embraces both the total salvation and the total submission implicit in the gracious rule of God; and that it is always wrong to preach Jesus as Savior without presenting him also as Lord, since it is precisely because he is the supreme Lord exalted to the Father's right hand that he has the authority to bestow salvation and the power to rescue sinners from sin, fear, evil, the thraldom of spirits, and death. We agree that in what has been called 'lordship evangelism' we must not isolate from one another the separate parts of Christ's commission, namely to 'make disciples,' to 'baptize,' and to 'teach'; that the Christian nurture of converts is indispensable because Christian growth is not automatic; and that daily repentance and daily obedience are necessary parts of Christian discipleship. We agree that the call to repentance must always be faithfully sounded; that there can be no repentance without ethical content; and that the precise ethical issues will vary according to each situation and HU. We also agree that the evangelist must pay attention to a community's or individual's sense of guilt, although, because this is not always a reliable guide, he must also draw attention to sins which the Bible clearly condemns; and that no evangelist has the right to conceal either the offence *(skandalon)* of the Gospel which is Jesus Christ and his cross, or any ethical implication of the Gospel which is relevant to the particular situation in which he is preaching it.

At the same time, we recognize the dangers to which any unbalance in these matters would expose us. If we underemphasize repentance, we offer sinners what Bonhoeffer called 'cheap grace,' but if we overemphasize it we may be preaching the law rather than the Gospel, a code rather than Christ, and salvation by works rather than by grace through faith. Secondly, if we do nothing to identify what is meant by 'sin,' we are asking for repentance in a vacuum, which is an impossibility, whereas if we become too specific in naming sins, we either try to do the Holy Spirit's convicting work for him or we may forget the complex cultural factors (e.g., in the case of polygamy) which should make us tentative in our teaching rather than dogmatic. Thirdly, it is possible to imply that conversion involves no radical change, while it is equally possible to expect too much of enquirers and new converts. Perfection is indeed the goal to be set before them, but we must not require maturity of understanding or behavior from a newborn babe in Christ.

8. CONCLUSION: OUR ESCHATOLOGICAL HOPE

The vision of the end which God has given us in Scripture contains several references to the nations. We are allowed to glimpse 'a great multitude which no man could number, from every nation, from all tribes and peoples and tongues' standing before God's throne and celebrating his salvation (Rev. 7: 9,10). We also see the new Jerusalem which will be enriched by 'the glory and honor of the nations', and whose tree of life will be 'for the healing of the nations' (Rev. 21:26; 22:2). These biblical phrases seem to us to warrant the conviction that heaven will be adorned by the best products of God-given human creativity, that heavenly fellowship will be harmonious and heterogeneous, and that the diversity of languages and cultures will not inhibit but rather ennoble the fellowship of the redeemed.

Now the church is an eschatological community. Already it is the new society of the new age. Already it has tasted the powers of the age to come (Hebrews 6:5). Already it has received the great promise for the end-time, the Holy Spirit himself (Acts 2:17). Therefore it is called to anticipate on earth the life of heaven, and thus to develop both cultural richness and heterogeneous fellowship.

In particular, we should seek to express and experience these things at the Lord's supper, which God intends to be a foretaste of the messianic banquet in his kingdom, which Jesus has promised to grace with his presence, and from which he sends us back into the world as his servants and his witnesses.

APPENDICES

(1) Position Papers

1. *Methodology: The Genesis and Strategy of the Homogeneous Unit*
   Principle
   Proposer: Donald A. McGavran
   Discussant: Harvie M. Conn
2. *Anthropology: The HUP and our Understanding of Culture*
   Proposer: Charles H. Kraft
   Discussant: Robert L. Ramseyer
3. *History: The HUP and the Record of Worldwide Missionary*
   Expansion
   Proposer: Ralph D. Winter
   Discussant: Victor E. W. Hayward
4. *Ethics: The Ethical Implications of the HUP*
   Proposer: C. Peter Wagner
   Discussant: John H. Yoder
5. *Theology: The Unity of the Church and the HUP*
   Proposer: Arthur F. Glasser
   Discussant: C. René Padilla

(2) Bibliography

A small selection of books on church growth is detailed below. Those by Dr. McGavran and Dr. Wagner advocate the homogeneous unit principle; the others raise questions about it.

1970 *Understanding Church Growth*, by Donald A. McGavran (Grand Rapids: Eerdmans)

1973 *The Challenge of Church Growth*, edited by Wilbert R. Shenk (Elkhart, Indiana: Institute of Mennonite Studies)

1974 *The Church and Its Mission: A Shattering Critique from the Third World*, by Orlando E. Costas (Wheaton, Illinois: Tyndale House)

1976 *Theological Perspectives on Church Growth*, edited by Harvie M. Conn (Nutley, NJ: Presbyterian and Reformed Publishing Co.)

1978 *Our Kind of People: The Ethical Dimension of Church Growth in America*, by C. Peter Wagner (Atlanta: John Knox Press)

(3) Participants

Speakers
Dr. Harvie M. Conn
Associate Professor of Missions and Apologetics
Westminster Theological Seminary

Dr. Arthur F. Glasser
Dean and Associate Professor of Theology of Mission and East Asian
Studies, School of World Mission, Fuller Theological Seminary

Rev. Dr. Victor E. W. Hayward
at one time Research Secretary, International Missionary Council

Dr. Charles H. Kraft
Professor of Anthropology and African Studies, School of World Mission,
Fuller Theological Seminary

Dr. Donald Anderson McGavran
Dean Emeritus and Senior Professor of Missions, Church Growth and South Asian
Studies, School of World Mission
Fuller Theological Seminary

Dr. C. René Padilla
Director of *Ediciones Certeza*

Dr. Robert L. Ramseyer
Director, Overseas Mission Training Center, Professor of Missions and
Anthropology, Associated Mennonite Biblical Seminaries

Dr. C. Peter Wagner
Associate Professor of Church Growth and Latin American Studies, School of World
Mission, Fuller Theological Seminary

Dr. Ralph D. Winter
General Director, United States Center for World Mission

Prof. John H. Yoder
Professor of Theology, University of Notre Dame, South Bend, Indiana and also at
the Associated Mennonite Biblical Seminaries, Elkhart, Indiana

Moderator
Rev. John R. W. Stott
Rector Emeritus, All Souls Church, Langham Place, London

Consultants
Prof. R. Pierce Beaver
Professor Emeritus, the University of Chicago, and Visiting Professor in
Historiography and American Mission History, School of World Mission, Fuller
Theological Seminary

Prof. J. Ronald Blue
Chairman, Department of World Missions, Dallas Theological Seminary

Dr. Clyde Cook
Director of Intercultural Studies, Biola College
and Talbot Theological Seminary

Dr. Ralph R. Covell
Professor of World Missions, Conservative Baptist Seminary,
Denver, Colorado

Prof. Phillip W. Elkins
Ph.D. candidate and Adjunct Professor, Fuller Theological Seminary

Rev. Leighton Ford
Chairman, Lausanne Committee for World Evangelization

Mr. David A. Fraser
Research Associate, MARC, World Vision International

Dr. P. G. Hiebert
Associate Professor of Anthropology and Indian Studies, School of World Mission,
Fuller Theological Seminary

Rev. Fred Holland
Adjunct Instructor of Theological Education by Extension, School of World Mission,
Fuller Theological Seminary

Dr. David Allan Hubbard
President, Fuller Theological Seminary

Dr. Hans Kasdorf
Associate Professor of Missions and Languages, Pacific College, and Lecturer in
Missions, Mennonite Brethren Biblical Seminary

Dr. Lloyd E. Kwast
Associate Professor of Missions, Talbot Theological Seminary

Dr. Alvin Martin
Director of In-Service Program, School of World Mission, Fuller Theological
Seminary

Rev. Don M. McCurry
Research Fellow, MARC, World Vision International, and Adjunct Professor of
Islamics, School of World Mission, Fuller Theological Seminary

Rev. Juan Carlos Miranda
Director of Hispanic Ministries, Church Growth Department, Fuller Evangelistic
Association

Dr. Edward F. Murphy
Special Assistant to the President of Overseas Crusades and Associate Professor of
Missions, Biola College and Talbot Theological Seminary

Dr. J. Edwin Orr
Part-time Professor of History of Awakenings and Dynamic of Missions, School of
World Mission, Fuller Theological Seminary

Rev. Gottfried Osei-Mensah
Executive Secretary, Lausanne Committee for World Evangelization

Dr. William E. Pannell
Assistant Professor of Evangelism, Fuller Theological Seminary

Rev. Raymond W. Schenk, Jr.
Director of Extension, Christian and Missionary Alliance

Rev. Glenn J. Schwartz
Assistant to the Dean and International Student Advisor, School of World Mission, Fuller Theological Seminary

Dr. Ronald J. Sider
Convenor of the Unit on Ethics and Society of the World Evangelical Fellowship's Theological Commission

Dr. James C. Smith
General Director, Christian Missionary Fellowship, Indianapolis, Indiana

Dr. Alan R. Tippett
Senior Professor of Anthropology and Oceanic Studies, School of World Mission, Fuller Theological Seminary

Rev. Edward L. Wheeler
Associate Director, Department of Cooperative Ministries, Southern Baptist Home Mission Board

Dr. J. Christy Wilson, Jr.
Professor of Missions and Evangelism, Gordon-Conwell Theological Seminary

Dr. Tetsunao Yamamori
Dean of the College, Northwest Christian College, Eugene, Oregon

POSTSCRIPT

Dr. Peter Wagner's paper was published in the January 1978 issue of the *Occasional Bulletin of Missionary Research*. Dr. Charles Kraft's substantially re-written paper appeared in the October 1978 issue. The other papers were not published at the time.

In 1996, however, Dr. Wilbert Shenk gathered all the papers together into book form under the title *Homogeneous Unit Principle Consultation* (Pasadena, California, January 1977). This has been deposited in the library of Fuller Theological Seminary (135 North Oakland Avenue, Pasadena, California 91182), where copies may be obtained.

3

— 1978 —

The Willowbank Report on Gospel and Culture

◆◆◆◆◆

An International Consultation on
'Gospel and Culture', Willowbank, Bermuda,
7–12 January 1978

—The Willowbank Report—

CONTENTS

INTRODUCTION

The process of communicating the Gospel cannot be isolated from the human culture from which it comes, or from that in which it is to be proclaimed. This fact constituted one of the preoccupations of the Lausanne Congress on World Evangelization in July 1974. So the Lausanne Committee's Theology and Education Group convened a consultation on this topic to meet in January 1978. It met from 6th to 13th January 1978 at Willowbank, Somerset Bridge, Bermuda. It brought 33 theologians, anthropologists, linguists, missionaries and pastors together from all six continents to study 'Gospel and Culture.' Co-sponsored by the Lausanne Committee's Strategy Working Group, it had four goals:

1. To develop our understanding of the interrelation of the Gospel and culture with special reference to God's revelation, to our interpretation and communication of it, and to the response of the hearers in their conversion, their churches and their lifestyle.
2. To reflect critically on the implications of the communication of the Gospel cross-culturally.
3. To identify the tools required for more adequate communication of the Gospel.
4. To share the fruits of the consultation with Christian leaders in church and mission.

This report reflects the content of 17 written papers circulated in advance, summaries of them and reactions to them made during the Consultation, and many viewpoints expressed in the plenary and group discussions.

Our programme for six days was very full, and we worked at high pressure. In consequence, basic methodological questions about the presuppositions and procedures of theology and the social sciences, and about the proper way to relate them to each other, could not be explored; and there were points at which our discussions clearly reflected this fact. Also, many questions which were raised had to be left on one side, and many particular debates had to be foreclosed as we went along. We are conscious, therefore, that what we say is to some extent provisional, and may need to be sharpened and deepened at various points in the light of future work. In addition, we resort to a number of generalizations; more case-studies are needed to see how these relate to specific situations.

Before the consultation ended, we spent time together working through the draft report and revising it. The final document is a report, not a statement or declaration; so none of us has signed it. But we send it out as a summary of what took place at Willowbank, and we commend it to our fellow Christians throughout the world for study and appropriate action.

1. The Biblical Basis of Culture

'Because man is God's creature, some of his culture is rich in beauty and goodness. Because he is fallen, all of it is tainted with sin and some of it is demonic.' (Lausanne Covenant, para. 10)

God created mankind male and female in his own likeness by endowing them with distinctive human faculties — rational, moral, social, creative and spiritual. He also told them to have children, to fill the earth and to subdue it (Gen. 1: 26–28). These divine commands are the origin of human culture. For basic to culture are our control of nature (that is, of our environment) and our development of forms of social organization. Insofar as we use our creative powers to obey God's commands, we glorify God, serve others and fulfill an important part of our destiny on earth.

Now, however, we are fallen. All our work is accompanied by sweat and struggle (Gen. 3:17–19), and is disfigured by selfishness. So none of our culture is perfect in truth, beauty or goodness. At the heart of every culture — whether we identify this heart as religion or world-view — is an element of self-centredness, of man's worship of himself. Therefore a culture cannot be brought under the lordship of Christ without a radical change of allegiance.

For all that, the affirmation that we are made in God's image still stands (Gen. 9:6; James 3:9), though the divine likeness has been distorted by sin. And still God expects us to exercise stewardship of the earth and of its creatures (Gen. 9:1–3, 7), and in his common grace makes all persons inventive, resourceful and fruitful in their endeavours. Thus, although Genesis 3 records the fall of humanity, and Genesis 4 Cain's murder of Abel, it is Cain's descendants who are described as the cultural innovators, building cities, breeding livestock, and making musical instruments and metal tools (Gen. 4:17–22).

Many of us evangelical Christians have in the past been too negative towards culture. We do not forget the human fallenness and lostness which call for salvation in Christ. Yet we wish to begin this report with a positive affirmation of human dignity and human cultural achievement. Wherever human beings develop their social organization, art and science, agriculture and technology, their creativity reflects that of their Creator.

2. A Definition of Culture

Culture is a term which is not easily susceptible of definition. In the broadest sense, it means simply the patterned way in which people do things together. If there is to be any common life and corporate action, there must be agreement, spoken or unspoken, about a great many things. But the term 'culture' is not generally used unless the unit concerned is larger than the family, unitary or extended.

Culture implies a measure of homogeneity. But, if the unit is larger than the clan or small tribe, a culture will include within itself a number of subcultures, and subcultures of subcultures, within which a wide variety and diversity is possible. If the variations go beyond a certain limit, a counter-culture will have come into being, and this may prove a destructive process.

Culture holds people together over a span of time. It is received from the past, but not by any process of natural inheritance. It has to be learned afresh by each generation. This takes place broadly by a process of absorption from the social environment, especially in the home. In many societies certain elements of the culture are communicated directly in rites of initiation, and by many other forms of deliberate instruction. Action in accordance with the culture is generally at the subconscious level.

This means that an accepted culture covers everything in human life.

At its centre is a world-view, that is, a general understanding of the nature of the universe and of one's place in it. This may be 'religious' (concerning God, or gods and spirits, and our relation to them), or it may express a 'secular' concept of reality, as in a Marxist society.

From this basic world-view flow both standards of judgement or values (of what is good in the sense of desirable, of what is acceptable as in accordance with the general will of the community, and of the contraries) and standards of conduct (concerning relations between individuals, between the sexes and the generations, with the community and with those outside the community).

Culture is closely bound up with language, and is expressed in proverbs, myths, folk tales, and various art forms, which become part of the mental furniture of all members of the group. It governs actions undertaken in community — acts of worship or of general welfare; laws and the administration of law; social activities such as dances and games; smaller units of action such as clubs and societies, associations for an immense variety of common purposes.

Cultures are never static; there is a continuous process of change. But this should be so gradual as to take place within the accepted norms; otherwise the culture is disrupted. The worst penalty that can be inflicted on the rebel is exclusion from the culturally defined social community.

Men and women need a unified existence. Participation in a culture is one of the factors which provide them with a sense of belonging. It gives a sense of security, of identity, of dignity, of being part of a larger whole, and of sharing both in the life of past generations and in the expectancy of society for its own future.

Biblical clues to the understanding of the human culture are found in the threefold dimension of people, land and history, on which the Old Testament focuses attention. The ethnic, the territorial, and the historical (who, where and whence we are) appear there as the triple source of economic, ecological, social and artistic forms of human life in Israel, of the forms of labour and production, and so of wealth and well-being. This model provides a perspective for interpreting all cultures.

Perhaps we may try to condense these various meanings as follows: Culture is an integrated system of beliefs (about God or reality or ultimate meaning), of values (about what is true, good, beautiful and normative), of customs (how to behave, relate to others, talk, pray, dress, work, play, trade, farm, eat, etc.), and of institutions which express these beliefs, values and customs (government, law courts, temples or churches, family, schools, hospitals, factories, shops, unions, clubs, etc.), which binds a society together and gives it a sense of identity, dignity, security, and continuity.

3.   Culture in the Biblical Revelation

God's personal self-disclosure in the Bible was given in terms of the hearers' own culture. So we have asked ourselves what light it throws on our task of cross-cultural communication today.

The biblical writers made critical use of whatever cultural material was available to them for the expression of their message. For example, the Old Testament refers several times to the Babylonian sea monster named 'Leviathan,' while the form of God's 'covenant' with his people resembles the ancient Hittite suzerain's 'treaty' with his vassals. The writers also made incidental use of the conceptual imagery of the 'three-tiered' universe, though they did not thereby affirm a pre-Copernican cosmology. We do something similar when we talk about the sun 'rising' and 'setting.'

Similarly, New Testament language and thought-forms are steeped in both Jewish and Hellenistic cultures, and Paul seems to have drawn from the vocabulary of Greek philosophy. But the process by which the biblical authors borrowed words and images from their cultural milieu, and used them creatively, was controlled by the Holy Spirit so that they purged them of false or evil implications and thus transformed them into vehicles of truth and goodness.

These undoubted facts raise a number of questions with which we have wrestled. We mention five:

(a)   The nature of biblical inspiration
Is the biblical authors' use of the words and ideas of their own culture incompatible with divine inspiration? No. We have taken note of the different literary genres of Scripture, and of the different forms of the process of inspiration which they imply. For instance, there is a broad distinction in form between the work of the prophets, receiving visions and words of the Lord, and historians and writers of letters. Yet the same Spirit uniquely inspired them all. God used the knowledge, experience and cultural background of the authors (though his revelation constantly transcended these),

and in each case the result was the same, namely God's word through human words.

(b) Form and meaning

Every communication has both a meaning (what we want to say) and a form (how we say it). The two — form and meaning — always belong together, in the Bible as well as in other books and utterances. How then should a message be translated from one language into another?

A literal translation of the form ('formal correspondence') may conceal or distort the meaning. In such cases, the better way is to find in the other language an expression which makes an equivalent impact on the hearers now as did the original. This may involve changing the form in order to preserve the meaning. This is called 'dynamic equivalence.' Consider, for example, the RSV translation of Rom. 1:17, which states that in the Gospel 'the righteousness of God is revealed through faith for faith.' This gives a word-for-word rendering of the original Greek, that is, a 'formal correspondence' translation. But it leaves the meaning of the Greek words 'righteousness' and 'from faith to faith' unclear. A translation such as TEV — 'the gospel reveals how God puts people right with himself: it is through faith from beginning to end' — abandons the principle of one-to-one correspondence between Greek and English words; but it expresses the meaning of the original sentence more adequately. The attempt to produce such a 'dynamic equivalence' translation may well bring the translator to a deeper understanding of Scripture, as well as make the text more meaningful to people of another language.

Some of the biblical forms (words, images, metaphors) should be retained, however, because they are important recurring symbols in Scripture (e.g., cross, lamb, or cup). While retaining the form, the translators will try to bring out the meaning. For example, in the TEV rendering of Mark 14:36 — 'take this cup of suffering away from me' — the form (i.e., the 'cup' image) is retained, but the words 'of suffering' are added to clarify the meaning.

Writing in Greek, the New Testament authors used words that had a long history in the secular world, but they invested them with Christian meanings, as when John referred to Jesus as 'the Logos.' It was a perilous procedure, because 'logos' had a wide variety of meanings in Greek literature and philosophy, and non-Christian associations doubtless clung to the word. So John set the title within a teaching context, affirming that the Logos was in the beginning, was with God, was God, was the agent of creation, was the light and life of men, and became a human being (John 1:1–14). Similarly, some Indian Christians have taken the risk of borrowing the Sanskrit word 'avatar' (descent), used in Hinduism for the so-called 'incarnations' of Vishnu, and applied it, with careful explanatory safeguards, to the unique incarnation of God in Jesus Christ. But others have refused to do so, on the ground that no safeguards are adequate to prevent misinterpretation.

(c)   The normative nature of Scripture

The Lausanne Covenant declares that Scripture is 'without error in all that it affirms' (para. 2). This lays upon us the serious exegetical task of discerning exactly what Scripture is affirming. The essential meaning of the biblical message must at all costs be retained. Though some of the original forms in which this meaning was expressed may be changed for the sake of cross-cultural communication, we believe that they too have a certain normative quality. For God himself chose them as wholly appropriate vehicles of his revelation. So each fresh formulation and explanation in every generation and culture must be checked for faithfulness by referring back to the original.

(d)   The cultural conditioning of Scripture

We have not been able to devote as much time as we would have liked to the problem of the cultural conditioning of Scripture. We are agreed that some biblical commands (e.g., regarding the veiling of women in public and washing one another's feet) refer to cultural customs now obsolete in many parts of the world. Faced by such texts, we believe the right response is neither a slavishly literal obedience nor an irresponsible disregard, but rather first a critical discernment of the text's inner meaning and then a translation of it into our own culture. For example, the inner meaning of the command to wash each other's feet is that mutual love must express itself in humble service. So in some cultures we may clean each other's shoes instead. We are clear that the purpose of such 'cultural transposition' is not to avoid obedience but rather to make it contemporary and authentic.

The controversial question of the status of women was not debated at our consultation. But we acknowledge the need to search for an understanding which attempts with integrity to do justice to all the biblical teaching, and which sees the relations between men and women as being both rooted in the created order and at the same time wonderfully transformed by the new order which Jesus introduced.

(e)   The continuing work of the Holy Spirit

Does our emphasis on the finality and permanent normativeness of Scripture mean that we think the Holy Spirit has now ceased to operate? No, indeed not. But the nature of his teaching ministry has changed. We believe that his work of 'inspiration' is done, in the sense that the canon of Scripture is closed, but that his work of 'illumination' continues both in every conversion (e.g., 2 Cor. 4:6) and in the life of the Christian and the church. So we need constantly to pray that he will enlighten the eyes of our hearts so that we may know the fullness of God's purpose for us (Eph. 1:17ff) and may be not timorous but courageous in making decisions and undertaking fresh tasks today.

We have been made aware that the experience of the Holy Spirit revealing the application of God's truth to personal and church life is often less vivid than it should be; we all need a more sensitive openness at this point.

Questions for Discussion
1. The commands of Genesis 1:26–28 are sometimes referred to as 'the cultural mandate' which God gave to mankind. How responsibly is it being fulfilled today?
2. In the light of the definition of culture in Section 2, what are the main distinctive elements of your own culture?
3. If you know two languages, make up a sentence in one and then try to find a 'dynamic equivalence' translation of it into the other.
4. Give other examples of 'cultural transposition' (see 3d), which preserve the biblical text's 'inner meaning' but transpose it into your own culture.

4. Understanding God's Word Today

The cultural factor is present not only in God's self-revelation in Scripture, but also in our interpretation of it. To this subject we now turn. All Christians are concerned to understand God's Word, but there are different ways of trying to do so.

(a) Traditional approaches

The commonest way is to come straight to the words of the biblical text, and to study them without any awareness that the writer's cultural context differs from the reader's. The reader interprets the text as if it had been written in his own language, culture and time.

We recognize that much Scripture can be read and understood in this way, especially if the translation is good. For God intended his word for ordinary people; it is not to be regarded as the preserve of scholars; the central truths of salvation are plain for all to see; Scripture is 'useful for teaching the truth, rebuking error, correcting faults, and giving instruction for right living' (2 Tim. 3:16 TEV); and the Holy Spirit has been given to be our teacher.

The weakness of this 'popular' approach, however, is that it does not seek first to understand the text in its original context; and, therefore, it runs the risk of missing the real meaning God intends and of substituting another.

A second approach takes with due seriousness the original historical and cultural context. It seeks also to discover what the text meant in its original language, and how it relates to the rest of Scripture. All this is an essential discipline because God spoke his word to a particular people in a particular context and time. So our understanding of God's message will grow when we probe deeply into these matters.

The weakness of this 'historical' approach, however, is that it fails to consider what Scripture may be saying to the contemporary reader. It stops short at the meaning of the Bible in its own time and culture. It is thus liable to analyse the text without applying it, and to acquire academic knowledge without obedience. The interpreter may also tend to exaggerate the possibility of complete objectivity and ignore his or her own cultural presuppositions.

(b) The contextual approach

A third approach begins by combining the positive elements of both the 'popular' and the 'historical' approaches. From the 'historical' it takes the necessity of studying the original context and language, and from the 'popular' the necessity of listening to God's word and obeying it. But it goes further than this. It takes seriously the cultural context of the contemporary readers as well as of the biblical text, and recognizes that a dialogue must develop between the two.

It is the need for this dynamic interplay between text and interpreters which we wish to emphasize. Today's readers cannot come to the text in a personal vacuum, and should not try to. Instead, they should come with an awareness of concerns stemming from their cultural background, personal situation, and responsibility to others. These concerns will influence the questions which are put to the Scriptures. What is received back, however, will not be answers only, but more questions. As we address Scripture, Scripture addresses us. We find that our culturally conditioned presuppositions are being challenged and our questions corrected. In fact, we are compelled to reformulate our previous questions and to ask fresh ones. So the living interaction proceeds.

In this process of interaction our knowledge of God and our response to his will are continuously being deepened. The more we come to know him, the greater our responsibility becomes to obey him in our own situation, and the more we respond obediently, the more he makes himself known.

It is this continuous growth in knowledge, love and obedience which is the purpose and profit of the 'contextual' approach. Out of the context in which his word was originally given, we hear God speaking to us in our contemporary context, and we find it a transforming experience. This process is a kind of upward spiral in which Scripture remains always central and normative.

(c) The learning community

We wish to emphasize that the task of understanding the Scriptures belongs not just to individuals but to the whole Christian community, seen as both a contemporary and a historical fellowship.

There are many ways in which the local or regional church can come to discern God's will in its own culture today. Christ still appoints pastors and teachers in his church. And in answer to expectant prayer he speaks to his people, especially through the preaching of his word in the context of worship. In addition, there is a place for 'teaching and admonishing one another' (Col. 3:16) both in group Bible studies and in consulting sister churches, as well as for the quiet listening to the voice of God in the Scriptures, which is an indispensable element in the believer's Christian life.

The church is also a historical fellowship and has received from the past a rich inheritance of Christian theology, liturgy and devotion. No group of believers can disregard this heritage without risking spiritual impoverishment. At the same time, this tradition must not be received uncritically, whether it comes in the form of a set of denominational distinctives or in any other way, but rather be tested by the Scripture it claims to expound. Nor must it be imposed on any church, but rather be made available to those who can use it as a valuable resource material, as a counterbalance to the spirit of independence, and as a link with the universal church.

Thus the Holy Spirit instructs his people through a variety of teachers of both the past and the present. We need each other. It is only 'with all the saints' that we can begin to comprehend the full dimensions of God's love (Eph. 3:18,19). The Spirit 'illumines the minds of God's people in every culture to perceive its [i.e., the Scripture's] truth freshly through their own eyes and thus discloses to the whole church ever more of the many-colored wisdom of God' (Lausanne Covenant, para. 2, echoing Eph. 3:10).

(d)   The silences of Scripture
We have also considered the problem of Scripture silences, that is, those areas of doctrine and ethics on which the Bible has nothing explicit to say. Written in the ancient Jewish and Graeco-Roman world, Scripture does not address itself directly, for example, to Hinduism, Buddhism, or Islam today, or to Marxist socio-economic theory, or modern technology. Nevertheless, we believe it is right for the church guided by the Holy Spirit to search the Scriptures for precedents and principles which will enable it to develop the mind of the Lord Christ and so be able to make authentically Christian decisions. This process will go on most fruitfully within the believing community as it worships God and engages in active obedience in the world. We repeat that Christian obedience is as much a prelude to understanding as a consequence of it.

Questions for Discussion
1. Can you recall any examples of how either of the two 'traditional approaches' to Bible reading had led you astray?
2. Choose a well-known text like Matthew 6:24–34 (anxiety and ambition) or Luke 10:25–38 (the Good Samaritan) and use the 'contextual approach' in studying it. Let a dialogue develop between you and the text, as you question it and it questions you. Write down the stages of the interaction.
3. Read Sections 3e and 4c, and then discuss practical ways of seeking the guidance of the Holy Spirit today.

5.   The Content and Communication of the Gospel

Having thought about God's communication of the Gospel to us in Scripture, we now come to the very heart of our concern, our responsibility to communicate it to others, that is, to evangelize. But before we consider the communication of the Gospel, we have to consider the content of the Gospel which

is to be communicated. For 'to evangelize is to spread the good news.'
(Lausanne Covenant, para. 4). Therefore there can be no evangelism without
the evangel.

(a)   The Bible and the Gospel

The Gospel is to be found in the Bible. In fact, there is a sense in which the
whole Bible is Gospel, from Genesis to Revelation. For its overriding purpose
throughout is to bear witness to Christ, to proclaim the good news that he is
lifegiver and Lord, and to persuade people to trust in him (e.g., John 5:39,40;
20: 31; 2 Tim. 3:15).

The Bible proclaims the gospel story in many forms. The Gospel is like a
multi-faceted diamond, with different aspects that appeal to different people
in different cultures. It has depths we have not fathomed. It defies every
attempt to reduce it to a neat formulation.

(b)   The heart of the Gospel

Nevertheless, it is important to identify what is at the heart of the Gospel. We
recognize as central the themes of God as Creator, the universality of sin,
Jesus Christ as Son of God, Lord of all, and Savior through his atoning death
and risen life, the necessity of conversion, the coming of the Holy Spirit and
his transforming power, the fellowship and mission of the Christian church,
and the hope of Christ's return.

While these are basic elements of the Gospel, it is necessary to add that no
theological statement is culture-free. Therefore, all theological formulations
must be judged by the Bible itself, which stands above them all. Their value
must be judged by their faithfulness to it as well as by the relevance with which
they apply its message to their own culture.

In our desire to communicate the Gospel effectively, we are often made
aware of those elements in it which people dislike. For example, the Cross
has always been both an offense to the proud and folly to the wise. But Paul
did not on that account eliminate it from his message. On the contrary, he
continued to proclaim it, with faithfulness and at the risk of persecution,
confident that Christ crucified is the wisdom and the power of God. We too,
although concerned to contextualize our message and remove from it all
unnecessary offense, must resist the temptation to accommodate it to human
pride or prejudice. It has been given to us. Our responsibility is not to edit it
but to proclaim it.

(c)   Cultural barriers to the communication of the Gospel

No Christian witness can hope to communicate the Gospel if he or she ignores
the cultural factor. This is particularly true in the case of missionaries. For
they are themselves the product of one culture and go to people who are the
products of another. So inevitably they are involved in cross-cultural communication, with all its exciting challenge and exacting demand. Two main
problems face them.

Sometimes people resist the Gospel not because they think it false but because they perceive it as a threat to their culture, especially the fabric of their society, and their national or tribal solidarity. To some extent this cannot be avoided. Jesus Christ is a disturber as well as a peacemaker. He is Lord, and demands our total allegiance. Thus, some first-century Jews saw the Gospel as undermining Judaism and accused Paul of 'teaching men everywhere against the people, the law, and this place,' i.e., the temple (Acts 21:28). Similarly, some first-century Romans feared for the stability of the state, since in their view the Christian missionaries, by saying that 'there is another king, Jesus,' were being disloyal to Caesar and advocating customs which it was not lawful for Romans to practise (Acts 16:21; 17:7). Still today Jesus challenges many of the cherished beliefs and customs of every culture and society.

At the same time, there are features of every culture which are not incompatible with the lordship of Christ, and which therefore need not be threatened or discarded, but rather preserved and transformed. Messengers of the Gospel need to develop a deep understanding of the local culture, and a genuine appreciation of it. Only then will they be able to perceive whether the resistance is to some unavoidable challenge of Jesus Christ or to some threat to the culture which, whether imaginary or real, is not necessary.

The other problem is that the Gospel is often presented to people in alien cultural forms. Then the missionaries are resented and their message rejected because their work is seen not as an attempt to evangelize but as an attempt to impose their own customs and way of life. Where missionaries bring with them foreign ways of thinking and behaving, or attitudes of racial superiority, paternalism, or preoccupation with material things, effective communication will be precluded.

Sometimes these two cultural blunders are committed together, and messengers of the Gospel are guilty of a cultural imperialism which both undermines the local culture unnecessarily and seeks to impose an alien culture instead. Some of the missionaries who accompanied the Catholic *conquistadores* of Latin America and the Protestant colonizers of Africa and Asia are historical examples of this double mistake. By contrast, the apostle Paul remains the supreme example of one whom Jesus Christ first stripped of pride in his own cultural privileges (Phil. 3:4–9) and then taught to adapt to the cultures of others, making himself their slave and becoming 'all things to all men' in order by all means to save some (1 Cor. 9:19–23).

(d)   Cultural sensitivity in communicating the Gospel
Sensitive cross-cultural witnesses will not arrive at their sphere of service with a pre-packaged Gospel. They must have a clear grasp of the 'given' truth of the Gospel. But they will fail to communicate successfully if they try to impose this on people without reference to their own cultural situation and that of the people to whom they go. It is only by active, loving engagement with the local people, thinking in their thought patterns, understanding their world-view, listening to

their questions, and feeling their burdens, that the whole believing community (of which the missionary is a part) will be able to respond to their need. By common prayer, thought and heart-searching, in dependence on the Holy Spirit, expatriate and local believers may learn together how to present Christ and contextualize the Gospel with an equal degree of faithfulness and relevance. We are not claiming that it will be easy, although some Third World cultures have a natural affinity to biblical culture. But we believe that fresh creative understandings do emerge when the Spirit-led believing community is listening and reacting sensitively to both the truth of Scripture and the needs of the world.

(e)   Christian witness in the Islamic world

Concern was expressed that insufficient attention had been given at our consultation to the distinctive problems of the Christian mission in the Islamic world, though there are approximately 600 million Muslims today. On the one hand, a resurgence of Islamic faith and mission is taking place in many lands; on the other hand, there is a new openness to the Gospel in a number of communities which are weakening their ties to traditional Islamic culture.

There is a need to recognize the distinctive features of Islam which provide a unique opportunity for Christian witness. Although there are in Islam elements which are incompatible with the Gospel, there are also elements with a degree of what has been called 'convertibility.' For instance, our Christian understanding of God, expressed in Luther's great cry related to justification, 'Let God be God,' might well serve as an inclusive definition of Islam. The Islamic faith in divine unity, the emphasis on man's obligation to render God a right worship, and the utter rejection of idolatry could also be regarded as being in line with God's purpose for human life as revealed in Jesus Christ. Contemporary Christian witnesses should learn humbly and expectantly to identify, appreciate and illuminate these and other values. They should also wrestle for the transformation — and, where possible, integration — of all that is relevant in Islamic worship, prayer, fasting, art, architecture, and calligraphy.

All this proceeds only within a realistic appreciation of the present situation of the Islamic countries characterized by technological development and secularization. The social liabilities of new wealth and traditional poverty, the tensions of political independence, and the tragic Palestinian dispersion and frustration — all of these afford areas of relevant Christian witness. The last has given birth to much passionate poetry, one note in which is the paradigm of the suffering Jesus. These and other elements call for a new Christian sensitivity and a real awareness of the habits of introversion under which the church has for so long laboured in the Middle East. Elsewhere, not least in sub-Sahara Africa, attitudes are more flexible and possibilities more fluid.

In order to fulfill more adequately the missionary challenge, fresh attempts are needed to develop ways of association of believers and seekers, if need be outside the traditional church forms. The crux of a lively, evangelizing sense of responsibility towards Muslims will always be the quality of Christian personal and corporate discipleship and the constraining love of Christ.

(f)   An expectation of results

Messengers of the Gospel who have proved in their own experience that it is 'the power of God for salvation' (Rom. 1:16) rightly expect it to be so in the experience of others also. We confess that sometimes, just as a Gentile centurion's faith put to shame the unbelief of Israel in Jesus' day (Matt. 8:10), so today the believing expectancy of Christians in other cultures sometimes shows up the missionary's lack of faith. So we remind ourselves of God's promises through Abraham's posterity to bless all the families of the earth and through the Gospel to save those who believe (Gen. 12:1–4; 1 Cor. 1:21). It is on the basis of these and many other promises that we remind all messengers of the Gospel, including ourselves, to look to God to save people and to build his church.

At the same time, we do not forget our Lord's warnings of opposition and suffering. Human hearts are hard. People do not always embrace the Gospel, even when the communication is blameless in technique and the communicator in character. Our Lord himself was fully at home in the culture in which he preached, yet he and his message were despised and rejected, and his Parable of the Sower seems to warn us that most of the good seed we sow will not bear fruit. There is a mystery here we cannot fathom. 'The Spirit blows where he wills' (John 3:8). While seeking to communicate the Gospel with care, faithfulness and zeal, we leave the results to God in humility.

Questions for Discussion

1.   In Section 5 a and b the Report refuses to give a 'neat formulation' of the Gospel, but identifies its 'heart.' Would you want to add to these 'central themes,' or subtract from them, or amplify them?

2.   Clarify the 'two cultural blunders' of 5 c. Can you think of examples? How can such mistakes be avoided?

3.   Think of the cultural situation of the people you are wanting to win for Christ. What would 'cultural sensitivity' mean in your case?

6.   Wanted: Humble Messengers of the Gospel!

We believe that the principal key to persuasive Christian communication is to be found in the communicators themselves and what kind of people they are. It should go without saying that they need to be people of Christian faith, love, and holiness. That is, they must have a personal and growing experience of the transforming power of the Holy Spirit, so that the image of Jesus Christ is ever more clearly seen in their character and attitudes.

Above all else we desire to see in them, and specially in ourselves, 'the meekness and gentleness of Christ' (2 Cor. 10:1), in other words, the humble sensitivity of Christ's love. So important do we believe this to be that we are devoting the whole of this section of our report to it. Moreover, since we have no wish to point the finger at anybody but ourselves, we shall use the first person plural throughout. First, we give an analysis of Christian humility in a missionary situation, and secondly, we turn to the incarnation of God in Jesus Christ as the model we desire by his grace to follow.

(a)   An analysis of missionary humility
First, there is the humility to acknowledge the problem which culture presents, and not to avoid or over-simplify it. As we have seen, different cultures have strongly influenced the biblical revelation, ourselves, and the people to whom we go. As a result, we have several personal limitations in communicating the Gospel. For we are prisoners (consciously or unconsciously) of our own culture, and our grasp of the cultures both of the Bible and of the country in which we serve is very imperfect. It is the interaction between all these cultures which constitutes the problem of communication; it humbles all who wrestle with it.

Secondly, there is the humility to take the trouble to understand and appreciate the culture of those to whom we go. It is this desire which leads naturally into that true dialogue 'whose purpose is to listen sensitively in order to understand' (Lausanne Covenant, para. 4). We repent of the ignorance which assumes that we have all the answers and that our only role is to teach. We have very much to learn. We repent also of judgemental attitudes. We know we should never condemn or despise another culture, but rather respect it. We advocate neither the arrogance which imposes our culture on others, nor the syncretism which mixes the Gospel with cultural elements incompatible with it, but rather a humble sharing of the good news — made possible by the mutual respect of a genuine friendship.

Thirdly, there is the humility to begin our communication where people actually are and not where we would like them to be. This is what we see Jesus doing, and we desire to follow his example. Too often we have ignored people's fears and frustrations, their pains and preoccupations, and their hunger, poverty, deprivation or oppression, in fact their 'felt needs,' and have been too slow to rejoice or to weep with them. We acknowledge that these 'felt needs' may sometimes be symptoms of deeper needs which are not immediately felt or recognized by the people. A doctor does not necessarily accept a patient's self-diagnosis. Nevertheless, we see the need to begin where people are, but not to stop there. We accept our responsibility gently and patiently to lead them on to see themselves, as we see ourselves, as rebels to whom the Gospel directly speaks with a message of pardon and hope. To begin where people are not is to share an irrelevant message; to stay where people are and never lead them on to the fullness of God's good news, is to share a truncated Gospel. The humble sensitivity of love will avoid both errors.

Fourthly, there is the humility to recognize that even the most gifted, dedicated and experienced missionary can seldom communicate the Gospel in another language or culture as effectively as a trained local Christian. This fact has been acknowledged in recent years by the Bible Societies, whose policy has changed from publishing translations by missionaries (with help from local people) to training mother-tongue specialists to do the translating. Only local Christians can answer the questions, 'God, how would you say this in our language?' and 'God, what will obedience to you mean in our culture?' Therefore, whether we are translating the Bible or communicating the Gospel, local Christians are indispensable. It is they who must assume the responsibility to contextualize the Gospel in their own languages and cultures. Would-be cross-cultural witnesses are not on that account necessarily superfluous; but we shall be welcome only if we are humble enough to see good communication as a team enterprise, in which all believers collaborate as partners.

Fifthly, there is the humility to trust in the Holy Spirit of God, who is always the chief communicator, who alone opens the eyes of the blind and brings people to new birth. 'Without his witness, ours is futile' (Lausanne Convenant, para. 14).

(b)   The Incarnation as a model for Christian witness

We have met for our consultation within a few days of Christmas, which might be called the most spectacular instance of cultural identification in the history of mankind, since by his incarnation the Son became a first-century Galilean Jew.

We have also remembered that Jesus intended his people's mission in the world to be modelled on his own. 'As the Father has sent me, even so I send you,' he said (John 20:21; cf. 17:18). We have asked ourselves, therefore, about the implications of the Incarnation for all of us. The question is of special concern to cross-cultural witnesses, whatever country they go to, although we have thought particularly of those from the West who serve in the Third World.

Meditating on Philippians 2, we have seen that the self-humbling of Christ began in his mind: 'he did not count equality with God a thing to be grasped.' So we are commanded to let his mind be in us, and in humility of mind to 'count' others better or more important than ourselves. This 'mind' or 'perspective' of Christ is a recognition of the infinite worth of human beings and of the privilege it is to serve them. Those witnesses who have the mind of Christ will have a profound respect for the people they serve, and for their cultures.

Two verbs then indicate the action to which the mind of Christ led him: 'he emptied himself . . . he humbled himself . . .' The first speaks of sacrifice (what he renounced) and the second of service, even slavery (how he identified himself with us and put himself at our disposal). We have tried to think what these two actions meant for him, and might mean for cross-cultural witnesses.

We began with his *renunciation*. First, the renunciation of status. 'Mild he lays his glory by,' we have been singing at Christmas. Because we cannot conceive what his eternal glory was like, it is impossible to grasp the greatness of his self-emptying. But certainly he surrendered the rights, privileges, and powers which he enjoyed as God's Son. 'Status' and 'status symbols' mean much in the modern world, but are incongruous in missionaries. We believe that wherever missionaries are they should not be in control or work alone, but always with — and preferably under — local Christians who can advise and even direct them. And whatever the missionaries' responsibility may be they should express attitudes 'not of domination but of service' (Lausanne Covenant, para. 11).

Next the renunciation of independence. We have looked at Jesus — asking a Samaritan woman for water, living in other people's homes and on other people's money because he had none of his own, being lent a boat, a donkey, an upper room, and even being buried in a borrowed tomb. Similarly, cross-cultural messengers, especially during their first years of service, need to learn dependence on others.

Thirdly, the renunciation of immunity. Jesus exposed himself to temptation, sorrow, limitation, economic need, and pain. So the missionary should expect to become vulnerable to new temptations, dangers and diseases, a strange climate, an unaccustomed loneliness, and possibly death.

Turning from the theme of renunciation to that of *identification*, we have marvelled afresh at the completeness of our Saviour's identification with us, particularly as this is taught in the Letter to the Hebrews. He shared our 'flesh and blood,' was tempted as we are, learned obedience through his sufferings and tasted death for us (Heb. 2:14–18; 4:15; 5:8). During his public ministry Jesus befriended the poor and the powerless, healed the sick, fed the hungry, touched untouchables, and risked his reputation by associating with those whom society rejected.

The extent to which we identify ourselves with the people to whom we go is a matter of controversy. Certainly it must include mastering their language, immersing ourselves in their culture, learning to think as they think, feel as they feel, do as they do. At the socio-economic level we do not believe that we should 'go native,' principally because a foreigner's attempt to do this may not be seen as authentic but as play-acting. But neither do we think there should be a conspicuous disparity between our lifestyle and that of the people around us. In between these extremes, we see the possibility of developing a standard of living which expresses the kind of love which cares and shares, and which finds it natural to exchange hospitality with others on a basis of reciprocity, without embarrassment. A searching test of identification is how far we feel that we belong to the people, and — still more — how far they feel that we belong to them. Do we participate naturally in days of national or tribal thanksgiving or sorrow? Do we groan with them in the oppression which they suffer and join them in their quest for justice and freedom? If the country is struck by earthquake or engulfed in civil war, is our instinct to stay and suffer with the people we love, or to fly home?

Although Jesus identified himself completely with us, he did not lose his own identity. He remained himself. 'He came down from heaven . . . and was made man' (Nicene Creed); yet in becoming one of us he did not cease to be God. Just so, 'Christ's evangelists must humbly seek to empty themselves of all but their personal authenticity' (Lausanne Covenant, para. 10). The Incarnation teaches identification without loss of identity. We believe that true self-sacrifice leads to true self-discovery. In humble service there is abundant joy.

Questions for Discussion
1. If the main key to communication lies in the communicators, what sort of people should they be?
2. Give your own analysis of the humility which all Christian witnesses should have. Where would you put your emphasis?
3. Since the Incarnation involved both 'renunciation' and 'identification,' it was obviously very costly for Jesus. What would be the cost of 'incarnational evangelism' today?

7. Conversion and Culture

We have thought of the relations between conversion and culture in two ways. First, what effect does conversion have on the cultural situation of converts, the ways they think and act, and their attitudes to their social environment? Secondly, what effect has our culture had on our own understanding of conversion? Both questions are important. But we want to say at once that elements in our traditional evangelical view of conversion are more cultural than biblical and need to be challenged. Too often we have thought of conversion as a crisis, instead of as a process as well; or we have viewed conversion as a largely private experience, forgetting its consequent public and social responsibilities.

(a)   The radical nature of conversion
We are convinced that the radical nature of conversion to Jesus Christ needs to be reaffirmed in the contemporary church. For we are always in danger of trivializing it, as if it were no more than a surface change, and a self-reformation at that. But the New Testament authors write of it as the outward expression of a regeneration or new birth by God's Spirit, a recreation, and resurrection from spiritual death. The concept of resurrection seems to be particularly important. For the resurrection of Jesus Christ from the dead was the beginning of the new creation of God, and by God's grace through union with Christ we have shared in this resurrection. We have therefore entered the new age and have already tasted its powers and its joys. This is the eschatological dimension of Christian conversion. Conversion is an integral part of the Great Renewal

which God has begun, and which will be brought to a triumphant climax when Christ comes in his glory.

Conversion involves as well a break with the past so complete that it is spoken of in terms of death. We have been crucified with Christ. Through his cross we have died to the godless world, its outlook, and its standards. We have also 'put off' like a soiled garment the old Adam, our former and fallen humanity. And Jesus warned us that this turning away from the past may involve painful sacrifices, even the loss of family and possessions (e.g., Lk. 14:25ff).

It is vital to keep together these negative and positive aspects of conversion, the death and the resurrection, the putting off of the old and the putting on of the new. For we who died are alive again, but alive now with a new life lived in, for, and under Christ.

(b)   The lordship of Jesus Christ

We are clear that the fundamental meaning of conversion is a change of allegiance. Other gods and lords — idolatries every one — previously ruled over us. But now Jesus Christ is Lord. The governing principle of the converted life is that it is lived under the lordship of Christ or (for it comes to the same thing) in the kingdom of God. His authority over us is total. So this new and liberating allegiance leads inevitably to a reappraisal of every aspect of our lives and in particular of our world-view, our behaviour, and our relationships.

First, our world-view. We are agreed that the heart of every culture is a 'religion' of some kind, even if it is an irreligious religion like Marxism. 'Culture is religion made visible' (J. H. Bavinck). And 'religion' is a whole cluster of basic beliefs and values, which is the reason why for our purposes we are using 'world-view' as an equivalent expression. True conversion to Christ is bound, therefore, to strike at the heart of our cultural inheritance. Jesus Christ insists on dislodging from the centre of our world whatever idol previously reigned there, and occupying the throne himself. This is the radical change of allegiance which constitutes conversion, or at least its beginning. Then once Christ has taken his rightful place, everything else starts shifting. The shock waves flow from the centre to the circumference. The convert has to rethink his or her fundamental convictions. This is *metanoia*, 'repentance' viewed as a change of mind, the replacement of 'the mind of the flesh' by 'the mind of Christ.' Of course, the development of an integrated Christian world-view may take a lifetime, but it is there in essence from the start. If it does grow, the explosive consequences cannot be predicted.

Secondly, our behaviour. The lordship of Jesus challenges our moral standards and whole ethical lifestyle. Strictly speaking, this is not 'repentance' but rather the 'fruit that befits repentance' (Matt. 3.8), the change of conduct which issues from a change of outlook. Both our minds and our wills must submit to the obedience of Christ (cf. 2 Cor. 10:5; Matt. 11:29,30; John 13:13).

Listening to case-studies of conversion, we have been impressed by the primacy of love in the new convert's experience. Conversion delivers both from the inversion which is too preoccupied with self to bother about other people and from the fatalism which considers it impossible to help them. Conversion is spurious if it does not liberate us to love.

Thirdly, our relationships. Although the convert should do his utmost to avoid a break with nation, tribe and family, sometimes painful conflicts arise. It is clear also that conversion involves a transfer from one community to another, that is, from fallen humanity to God's new humanity. It happened from the very beginning on the Day of Pentecost: 'Save yourselves from this crooked generation,' Peter appealed. So those who received his message were baptized into the new society, devoted themselves to the new fellowship, and found that the Lord continued to add to their numbers daily (Acts 2:40–47). At the same time, their 'transfer' from one group to another meant rather that they were spiritually distinct than that they were socially segregated. They did not abandon the world. On the contrary, they gained a new commitment to it, and went out into it to witness and to serve.

All of us should cherish great expectations of such radical conversions in our day, involving converts in a new mind, a new way of life, a new community, and a new mission, all under the lordship of Christ. Yet now we feel the need to make several qualifications.

(c) The convert and his culture

Conversion should not 'de-culturize' a convert. True, as we have seen, the Lord Jesus now holds his or her allegiance, and everything in the cultural context must come under their Lord's scrutiny. This applies to every culture, not just to those of Hindu, Buddhist, Muslim, or animistic cultures but also to the increasingly materialistic culture of the West. The critique may lead to a collision, as elements of the culture come under the judgement of Christ and have to be rejected. At this point, on the rebound, the convert may try to adopt the evangelist's culture instead; the attempt should be firmly but gently resisted.

The convert should be encouraged to see his or her relation to the past as a combination of rupture and continuity. However much new converts feel they need to renounce for the sake of Christ, they are still the same people with the same heritage and the same family. 'Conversion does not unmake; it remakes.' It is always tragic, though in some situations it is unavoidable, when a person's conversion to Christ is interpreted by others as treachery to his or her own cultural origins. If possible, in spite of the conflicts with their own culture, new converts should seek to identify with their culture's joys, hopes, pains and struggles.

Case histories show that converts often pass through three stages: (1) 'rejection' (when they see themselves as 'new persons in Christ' and repudiate everything associated with their past); (2) 'accommodation' (when they discover their ethnic and cultural heritage, with the temptation to compromise the new-found Christian faith in relation to their heritage); and (3) 'the re-establishment of identity' (when either the rejection of the past or the accommodation to it may increase, or preferably, they may grow into a balanced self-awareness in Christ and in culture).

(d)   The power encounter

'Jesus is Lord' means more than that he is Lord of the individual convert's world-view, standards and relationships, and more even than that he is Lord of culture. It means that he is Lord of the powers, having been exalted by the Father to universal sovereignty, principalities and powers having been made subject to him (1 Peter 3:22). A number of us, especially those from Asia, Africa, and Latin America, have spoken both of the reality of evil powers and of the necessity to demonstrate the supremacy of Jesus over them. For conversion involves a power encounter. People give their allegiance to Christ when they see that his power is superior to magic and voodoo, the curses and blessings of witch doctors, and the malevolence of evil spirits, and that his salvation is a real liberation from the power of evil and death.

Of course, some are questioning today whether a belief in spirits is compatible with our modern scientific understanding of the universe. We wish to affirm, therefore, against the mechanistic myth on which the typical western world-view rests, the reality of demonic intelligences which are concerned by all means, overt and covert, to discredit Jesus Christ and keep people from coming to him. We think it vital in evangelism in all cultures to teach the reality and hostility of demonic powers, and to proclaim that God has exalted Christ as Lord of all and that Christ, who really does possess all power, however we may fail to acknowledge this, can (as we proclaim him) break through any world-view in any mind to make his lordship known and bring about a radical change of heart and outlook.

We wish to emphasize that the power belongs to Christ. Power in human hands is always dangerous. We have called to mind the recurring theme of Paul's two letters to the Corinthians — that God's power, which is clearly seen in the cross of Christ, operates through human weakness (e.g., 1 Cor. 1. 18–2:5; 2 Cor. 4:7; 12:9,10). Worldly people worship power; Christians who have it know its perils. It is better to be weak, for then we are strong. We specially honour the Christian martyrs of recent days (e.g., in East Africa) who have renounced the way of power, and followed the way of the cross.

(e)   Individual and group conversions

Conversion should not be conceived as being invariably and only an individual experience, although that has been the pattern of western expectation for many years. On the contrary, the covenant theme of the Old Testament and the household baptisms of the New should lead us to desire, work for, and expect both family and group conversions. Much important research has been undertaken in recent years into 'people movements' from both theological and sociological perspectives. Theologically, we recognize the biblical emphasis on the solidarity of each *ethnos*, i.e., nation or people. Sociologically, we recognize that each society is composed of a variety of subgroups, subcultures or homogeneous units. It is evident that people receive the Gospel most readily when it is presented to them in a manner which is appropriate — and not alien — to their culture, and when they can respond to it with and among their own people. Different societies have different procedures for making group decisions, e.g., by consensus, by the head of the family, or by a group of elders. We recognize the validity of the corporate dimension of conversion as part of the total process, as well as the necessity for each member of the group ultimately to share in it personally.

(f)   Is conversion sudden or gradual?
Conversion is often more gradual than traditional evangelical teaching has allowed. True, this may be only a dispute about words. Justification and regeneration, the one conveying a new status and the other a new life, are works of God and instantaneous, although we are not necessarily aware when they take place. Conversion, on the other hand, is our own action (moved by God's grace) of turning to God in penitence and faith. Although it may include a conscious crisis, it is often slow and sometimes laborious. Seen against the background of the Hebrew and Greek vocabulary, conversion is in essence a turning to God, which continues as all areas of life are brought in increasingly radical ways under the lordship of Christ. Conversion involves the Christian's complete transformation and total renewal in mind and character according to the likeness of Christ (Rom. 12:1,2).

This progress does not always take place, however. We have given some thought to the sad phenomena called 'backsliding' (a quiet slipping away from Christ) and 'apostasy' (an open repudiation of him). These have a variety of causes. Some people turn away from Christ when they become disenchanted with the church; others capitulate to the pressures of secularism or of their former culture. These facts challenge us both to proclaim a full Gospel and to be more conscientious in nurturing converts in the faith and in training them for service.

One member of our consultation has described his experience in terms of turning first to Christ (receiving his salvation and acknowledging his lordship), secondly to culture (rediscovering his natural origins and identity), and thirdly to the world (accepting the mission on which Christ sends him). We agree that conversion is often a complex experience, and that the biblical language of 'turning' is used in different ways and contexts. At the same time, we all emphasize that personal commitment to Jesus Christ is foundational. In him alone we find salvation, new life, and personal identity. Conversion must also result in new attitudes and relationships, and lead to a responsible involvement in our church, our culture, and our world. Finally, conversion is a journey, a pilgrimage, with ever-new challenges, decisions, and returnings to the Lord as the constant point of reference, until he comes.

Questions for Discussion
1. Distinguish between 'regeneration' and 'conversion' according to the New Testament.
2. 'Jesus is Lord.' What does this mean for you in your own culture? See Section 7 b and d. What are the elements of your cultural heritage which you feel (a) you must, and (b) you need not, renounce for the sake of Christ?
3. What is sudden and what is (or may be) gradual in Christian conversion?

8.   Church and Culture

In the process of church formation, as in the communication and reception of the Gospel, the question of culture is vital. If the Gospel must be contextualized, so must the church. Indeed, the sub-title of our consultation has been 'the contextualization of world and church in a missionary situation.'

(a)   Older, traditional approaches
During the missionary expansion of the early part of the 19th century, it was generally assumed that churches 'on the mission field' would be modelled on churches 'at home.' The tendency was to produce almost exact replicas. Gothic architecture, prayer book liturgies, clerical dress, musical instruments, hymns and tunes, decision-making processes, synods and committees, superintendents and archdeacons — all were exported and unimaginatively introduced into the new mission-founded churches. It should be added that these patterns were also eagerly adopted by the new Christians, determined not to be at any point behind their western friends, whose habits and ways of worship they had been attentively watching. But all this was based on the false assumptions that the Bible gave specific instructions about such matters and that the home churches' pattern of government, worship, ministry and life were themselves exemplary.

In reaction to this monocultural export system, pioneer missionary thinkers like Henry Venn and Rufus Anderson in the middle of the last century and Roland Allen earlier in this century popularized the concept of 'indigenous' churches, which would be 'self-governing, self-supporting and self-propagating.' They argued their case well. They pointed out that the policy of the apostle Paul was to plant churches, not to found mission stations. They also added pragmatic arguments to biblical ones, namely that indigeneity was indispensable to the church's growth in maturity and mission. Henry Venn confidently looked forward to the day when missions would hand over all responsibility to national churches, and then what he called 'the euthanasia of the mission' would take place. These views gained wide acceptance and were immensely influential.

In our day, however, they are being criticized, not because of the ideal itself, but because of the way it has often been applied. Some missions, for example, have accepted the need for indigenous leadership and have then gone on to recruit and train local leaders, indoctrinating them (the word is harsh but not unfair) in western ways of thought and procedure. These westernized local leaders have then preserved a very western-looking church, and the foreign orientation has persisted, only lightly cloaked by the appearance of indigeneity.

Now, therefore, a more radical concept of indigenous church life needs to be developed, by which each church may discover and express its selfhood as the body of Christ within its own culture.

(b) The dynamic equivalence model

Using the distinctions between 'form' and 'meaning,' and between 'formal correspondence' and 'dynamic equivalence,' which have been developed in translation theory and on which we have commented in Section 3, it is being suggested that an analogy may be drawn between Bible translation and church formation. 'Formal correspondence' speaks of a slavish imitation, whether in translating a word into another language or exporting a church model to another culture. Just as a 'dynamic equivalence' translation, however, seeks to convey to contemporary readers meanings equivalent to those conveyed to the original readers, by using appropriate cultural forms, so would a 'dynamic equivalence' church. It would look in its culture as a good Bible translation looks in its language. It would preserve the essential meanings and functions which the New Testament predicates of the church, but would seek to express these in forms equivalent to the originals but appropriate to the local culture.

We have all found this model helpful and suggestive, and we strongly affirm the ideals it seeks to express. It rightly rejects foreign imports and imitations, and rigid structures. It rightly looks to the New Testament for the principles of church formation, rather than to either tradition or culture, and it equally rightly looks to the local culture for the appropriate forms in which these principles should be expressed. All of us (even those who see limitations in the model) share the vision which it is trying to describe.

Thus, the New Testament indicates that the church is always a worshiping community, 'a holy priesthood to offer spiritual sacrifices to God through Jesus Christ' (1 Pet. 2:5), but forms of worship (including the presence or absence of different kinds of liturgy, ceremony, music, colour, drama, etc.) will be developed by the church in keeping with indigenous culture. Similarly, the church is always a witnessing and a serving community, but its methods of evangelism and its program of social involvement will vary. Again, God desires all churches to have pastoral oversight (*episkopē*), but forms of government and ministry may differ widely, and the selection, training, ordination, service, dress, payment and accountability of pastors will be determined by the church to accord with biblical principles and to suit the local culture.

The questions which are being asked about the 'dynamic equivalence' model are whether by itself it is large enough and dynamic enough to provide all the guidance which is needed. The analogy between Bible translation and church formation is not exact. In the former the translator controls the work, and when the task is complete it is possible to make a comparison of the two texts. In the latter, however, the original to which an equivalent is being sought is not a detailed text but a series of glimpses of the early church in operation, making the comparison more difficult, and instead of a controlling translator the whole community of faith must be involved. Further, a translator aims at personal objectivity, but when the local church is seeking to relate itself appropriately to the local culture, it finds objectivity almost impossible. In many situations it is caught in 'an encounter between two civilizations' (that of its own society and that of the missionaries'). Furthermore, it may have great difficulty in responding to the conflicting voices of the local community. Some clamour for change (in terms of literacy, education, technology, modern medicine, industrialization, etc.), while others insist on the conservation of the old culture and resist the arrival of a new day. It is asked whether the 'dynamic equivalence' model is dynamic enough to face this kind of challenge.

The test of this or any other model for helping churches develop appropriately, is whether it can enable God's people to capture in their hearts and minds the grand design of which their church is to be the local expression. Every model presents only a partial picture. Local churches need to rely ultimately on the dynamic pressure of the living Lord of history. For it is he who will guide his people in every age to develop their church life in such a way as both to obey the instructions he has given in Scripture and to reflect the good elements of their local culture.

(c)   The freedom of the church

If each church is to develop creatively in such a way as to find and express itself, it must be free to do so. This is its inalienable right. For each church is God's church. United to Christ, it is a dwelling place of God through his Spirit (Eph. 2: 22). Some missions and missionaries have been slow to recognize this, and to accept its implications in the direction of indigenous forms and an every-member ministry. This is one of the many causes which have led to the formation of independent churches, notably in Africa, which are seeking new ways of self-expression in terms of local culture.

Although local church leaders have also sometimes impeded indigenous development, the chief blame lies elsewhere. It would not be fair to generalize. The situation has always been diverse. In earlier generations there were missions which never manifested a spirit of domination. In this century some churches have sprung up which have never been under missionary control, having enjoyed self-government from the start. In other cases missions have entirely surrendered their former power, so that some mission-founded churches are now fully autonomous, and many missions now work in genuine partnership with churches.

Yet this is not the whole picture. Other churches are still almost completely inhibited from developing their own identity and programme by policies laid down from afar, by the introduction and continuation of foreign traditions, by the use of expatriate leadership, by alien decision-making processes, and especially by the manipulative use of money. Those who maintain such control may be genuinely unaware of the way in which their actions are regarded and experienced at the other end. They may be felt by the churches concerned to be a tyranny. The fact that this is neither intended nor realized illustrates perfectly how all of us (whether we know it or not) are involved in the culture which has made us what we are. We strongly oppose such 'foreignness,' wherever it exists, as a serious obstacle to maturity and mission, and a quenching of the Holy Spirit of God.

It was in protest against the continuance of foreign control that a few years ago the call was made to withdraw all missionaries. In this debate some of us want to avoid the word 'moratorium', because it has become an emotive term and sometimes betrays a resentment against the very concept of 'missionaries.' Others of us wish to retain the word in order to emphasize the truth it expresses. To us it means not a rejection of missionary personnel and money in themselves, but only of their misuse in such a way as to suffocate local initiative. We all agree with the statement of the Lausanne Covenant that 'a reduction of foreign missionaries and money . . . may sometimes be necessary to facilitate the national church's growth in self-reliance . . .' (para. 9).

(d)   Power structures and mission

What we have just written is part of a much wider problem, which we have not felt able to ignore. The contemporary world does not consist of isolated atomistic societies, but is an interrelated global system of economic, political, technological and ideological macro-structures, which undoubtedly results in much exploitation and oppression.

What has this got to do with mission? And why do we raise it here? Partly because it is the context within which the Gospel must be preached to all nations today. Partly also because nearly all of us either belong to the Third World, or live and work there, or have done so, or have visited some countries in it. So we have seen with our own eyes the poverty of the masses, we feel for them and with them, and we have some understanding that their plight is due in part to an economic system which is controlled mostly by the North Atlantic countries (although others are now also involved). Those of us who are citizens of North American or European countries cannot avoid some feeling of embarrassment and shame, by reason of the oppression in which our countries in various degrees have been involved. Of course, we know that there is oppression in many countries today, and we oppose it everywhere. But now we are talking about ourselves, our own countries, and our responsibility as Christians. Most of the world's missionaries and missionary money come from these countries, often at great personal sacrifice. Yet we have to confess that some missionaries themselves reflect a neo-colonial attitude and even defend it, together with outposts of western power and exploitation such as Southern Africa.

So what should we do? The only honest response is to say that we do not know. Armchair criticism smacks of hypocrisy. We have no ready-made solutions to offer to this worldwide problem. Indeed, we feel victims of the system ourselves. And yet we are also part of it. So we feel able to make only these comments.

First, Jesus himself constantly identified with the poor and weak. We accept the obligation to follow in his footsteps in this matter as in all others. At least by the love which prays and gives we mean to strengthen our solidarity with them.

Jesus did more than identify, however. In his teaching and that of the apostles the corollary of good news to the oppressed was a word of judgement to the oppressor (e.g., Luke 6:24–26; Jas. 5:1–6). We confess that in complex economic situations it is not easy to identify oppressors in order to denounce them without resorting to a shrill rhetoric which neither costs nor accomplishes anything. Nevertheless, we accept that there will be occasions when it is our Christian duty to speak out against injustice in the name of the Lord who is the God of justice as well as of justification. We shall seek from him the courage and wisdom to do so.

Thirdly, this Consultation has expressed its concern about syncretism in Third World churches. But we have not forgotten that western churches fall prey to the same sin. Indeed, perhaps the most insidious form of syncretism in the world today is the attempt to mix a privatized gospel of personal forgiveness with a worldly (even demonic) attitude to wealth and power. We are not guiltless in this matter ourselves. Yet we desire to be integrated Christians for whom Jesus is truly Lord of all. So we who belong to, or come from, the West will examine ourselves and seek to purge ourselves of western-style syncretism. We agree that 'the salvation we claim should be transforming us in the totality of our personal and social responsibilities. Faith without works is dead' (Lausanne Covenant, para. 5).

(e)   The danger of provincialism

We have emphasized that the church must be allowed to indigenize itself, and to 'celebrate, sing and dance' the Gospel in its own cultural medium. At the same time, we wish to be alert to the dangers of this process. Some churches in all six continents go beyond a joyful and thankful discovery of their local cultural heritage, and either become boastful and assertive about it (a form of chauvinism) or even absolutize it (a form of idolatry). More common than either of these extremes, however, is 'provincialism,' that is, such a retreat into their own culture as cuts them adrift from the rest of the church and from the wider world. This is a frequent stance in western churches as well as in the Third World. It denies the God of creation and redemption. It is to proclaim one's freedom, only to enter another bondage. We draw attention to the three major reasons why we think this attitude should be avoided.

First, each church is part of the universal church. The people of God are by his grace a unique multi-racial, multi-national, multi-cultural community. This community is God's new creation, his new humanity, in which Christ has abolished all barriers (see Ephesians 2 and 3). There is therefore no room for racism in the Christian society, or for tribalism — whether in its African form, or in the form of European social classes, or of the Indian caste system. Despite the church's failures, this vision of a supra-ethnic community of love is not a romantic ideal, but a command of the Lord. Therefore, while rejoicing in our cultural inheritance and developing our own indigenous forms, we must always remember that our primary identity as Christians is not in our particular culture but in the one Lord and his one body (Eph. 4:3–6).

Secondly, each church worships the living God of cultural diversity. If we thank him for our cultural heritage, we should thank him for others' also. Our church should never become so culture-bound that visitors from another culture do not feel welcome. Indeed, we believe it is enriching for Christians, if they have the opportunity, to develop a bi-cultural and even a multi-cultural existence, like the apostle Paul who was a Hebrew of the Hebrews, a master of the Greek language, and a Roman citizen.

Thirdly, each church should enter into a 'partnership . . . in giving and receiving' (Phil. 4:15). No church is, or should try to become, self-sufficient. So churches should develop with each other relationships of prayer, fellowship, interchange of ministry and cooperation. Provided that we share the same central truths (including the supreme lordship of Christ, the authority of the Scriptures, the necessity of conversion, confidence in the power of the Holy Spirit, and the obligations of holiness and witness), we should be outgoing and not timid in seeking fellowship; and we should share our spiritual gifts and ministries, knowledge, skills, experience and financial resources. The same principle applies to cultures. A church must be free to reject alien cultural forms and develop its own; it should also feel free to borrow from others. This way lies maturity.

One example of this concerns theology. Cross-cultural witnesses must not attempt to impose a ready-made theological tradition on the church in which they serve, either by personal teaching or by literature or by controlling seminary and Bible college curricula. For every theological tradition both contains elements which are biblically questionable and have been ecclesiastically divisive, and omits elements which, while they might be of no great consequence in the country where it originated, may be of immense importance in other contexts. At the same time, although missionaries ought not to impose their own tradition on others, they also ought not to deny them access to it (in the form of books, confessions, catechism, liturgies and hymns), since it doubtless represents a rich heritage of faith. Moreover, although the theological controversies of the older churches should not be exported to the younger churches, yet an understanding of the issues, and of the work of the Holy Spirit in the unfolding history of Christian doctrine, should help to protect them from unprofitable repetition of the same battles.

Thus we should seek with equal care to avoid theological imperialism and theological provincialism. A church's theology should be developed by the community of faith out of the Scripture in interaction with other theologies of the past and present, and with the local culture and its needs.

(f)   The danger of syncretism

As the church seeks to express its life in local cultural forms, it soon has to face the problem of cultural elements which either are evil or have evil associations. How should the church react to these? Elements which are intrinsically false or evil clearly cannot be assimilated into Christianity without a lapse into syncretism. This is a danger for all churches in all cultures. If the evil is in the association only, however, we believe it is right to seek to 'baptize' it into Christ. It is the principle on which William Booth operated when he set Christian words to popular music, asking why the devil should have all the best tunes. Thus many African churches now use drums to summon people to worship, although previously they were unacceptable, as being associated with war dances and mediumistic rites.

Yet this principle raises problems. In a proper reaction against foreigners, an improper flirtation with the demonic element of local culture sometimes takes place. So the church, being first and foremost a servant of Jesus Christ, must learn to scrutinize all culture, both foreign and local, in the light of his lordship and God's revelation. By what guidelines, therefore, does a church accept or reject culture traits in the process of contextualization? How does it prevent or detect and eliminate heresy (wrong teaching) and syncretism (harmful carry-overs from the old way of life)? How does it protect itself from becoming a 'folk church' in which church and society are virtually synonymous?

One particular model we have studied is that of the church in Bali, Indonesia, which is now about 40 years old. Its experience has provided the following guidelines:

The believing community first searched the Scriptures and learned from them many important biblical truths. They then observed that other churches (e.g., round the Mediterranean) used architecture to symbolize Christian truth. This was important because the Balinese are very 'visual' people and value visible signs. So it was decided, for example, to express their affirmation of faith in the Trinity in a Balinese-style three-tiered roof for their church buildings. The symbol was first considered by the council of elders who, after studying both biblical and cultural factors, recommended it to local congregations.

The detection and elimination of heresy followed a similar pattern. When believers suspected an error in life or teaching, they would report it to an elder, who would take it to the council of elders. Having considered the matter, they in their turn passed their recommendations to the local churches who had the final word.

What was the most important safeguard of the church? To this question the answer was: 'We believe that Jesus Christ is Lord and Master of all powers.' By preaching his power, 'the same yesterday and today and for ever,' by insisting at all times on the normative nature of the Scriptures, by entrusting elders with the obligation to reflect on Scripture and culture, by breaking down all barriers to fellowship, and by building into structures, catechism, art forms, drama, etc., constant reminders of the exalted position of Jesus Christ, his church has been preserved in truth and holiness.

Sometimes, in different parts of the world, a cultural element may be adopted which deeply disturbs oversensitive consciences, especially those of new converts. This is the problem of the 'weaker brother' of whom Paul writes in connection with idol-meats. Since idols were nothing, Paul himself had liberty of conscience to eat these meats. But for the sake of 'weaker' Christians with a less well-educated conscience, who would be offended to see him eat, he refrained, at least in specific situations in which such offence might be caused. The principle still applies today. Scripture takes conscience seriously and tells us not to violate it. It needs to be educated in order to become 'strong,' but while it remains 'weak' it must be respected. A strong conscience will give us freedom; but love limits liberty.

(g)   The church's influence on culture

We deplore the pessimism which leads some Christians to disapprove of active cultural engagement in the world, and the defeatism which persuades others that they could do no good there anyway and should therefore wait in inactivity for Christ to put things right when he comes. Many historical examples could be given, drawn from different ages and countries, of the powerful influence which — under God — the church has exerted on a prevailing culture, purging, claiming, and beautifying it for Christ. Though all such attempts have had defects, they do not prove the enterprise mistaken.

We prefer, however, to base the church's cultural responsibility on Scripture rather than on history. We have reminded ourselves that our fellow men and women are made in God's image, and that we are commanded to honour, love, and serve them in every sphere of life. To this argument from God's creation we add another from his kingdom which broke into the world through Jesus Christ. All authority belongs to Christ. He is Lord of both universe and church. And he has sent us into the world to be its salt and light. As his new community, he expects us to permeate society.

Thus we are to challenge what is evil and affirm what is good; to welcome and seek to promote all that is wholesome and enriching in art, science, technology, agriculture, industry, education, community development and social welfare; to denounce injustice and support the powerless and the oppressed; to spread the good news of Jesus Christ, which is the most liberating and humanizing force in the world; and actively to engage in good works of love. Although, in social and cultural activity as in evangelism, we must leave the results to God, we are confident that he will bless our endeavours and use them to develop in our community a new consciousness of what is 'true, noble, right, pure, lovely, and honourable' (Phil. 4:8, TEV). Of course, the church cannot impose Christian standards on an unwilling society, but it can commend them by both argument and example. All this will bring glory to God and greater opportunities of humanness to our fellow human beings whom he made and loves. As the Lausanne Covenant put it, 'churches must seek to transform and enrich culture, all for the glory of God' (para. 10).

Nevertheless, naive optimism is as foolish as dark pessimism. In place of both, we seek a sober Christian realism. On the one hand, Jesus Christ reigns. On the other, he has not yet destroyed the forces of evil; they still rampage. So in every culture Christians find themselves in a situation of conflict and often of suffering. We are called to fight against the 'cosmic powers of this dark age' (Eph. 6:12, TEV). So we need each other. We must put on all God's armour, and especially the mighty weapon of believing prayer. We also remember the warnings of Christ and his apostles that before the end there will be an unprecedented outbreak of wickedness and violence. Some events and developments in our contemporary world indicate that the spirit of the coming Antichrist is already at work not only in the non-Christian world, but both in our own partially Christianized societies and even in the churches themselves. 'We therefore reject as a proud, self-confident dream the notion that man can ever build a utopia on earth' (Lausanne Covenant, para. 15), and as a groundless fantasy that society is going to evolve into perfection.

Instead, while energetically labouring on earth, we look forward with joyful anticipation to the return of Christ, and to the new heavens and new earth in which righteousness will dwell. For then not only will culture be transformed, as the nations bring their glory into the New Jerusalem (Rev. 21:24–26), but the whole creation will be liberated from its present bondage of futility, decay and pain, so as to share the glorious freedom of God's children (Rom. 8:18–25, TEV). Then at last every knee will bow to Christ and every tongue openly proclaim that he is Lord, to the glory of God the Father (Phil. 2:9–11).

Questions for Discussion

1. Is your local church 'free' to develop its own selfhood? If not, what forces are hindering it? See Section 8 a-d.
2. Section 8 d has some hard things to say about 'power-structures.' Do you agree? If so, can you do anything about it?
3. 'Provincialism' (8 e) and 'syncretism' (8 f) are both mistakes of a church which is trying to express its identity in local cultural forms. Is your church making either mistake? How can they be avoided without repudiating indigenous culture?
4. Should the church in your country be doing more to 'transform and enrich' its national culture? If so, in what way?

9. Culture, Christian Ethics and Lifestyle

Having considered in Section 7 some of the cultural factors in Christian conversion, we come finally to the relations between culture and Christian ethical behaviour. For the new life Christ gives his people is bound to issue in a new lifestyle.

(a) Christ-centredness and Christ-likeness

One of the themes running right through our consultation has been the supreme lordship of Jesus Christ. He is Lord of the universe and the church; he is Lord of the individual believer also. We find ourselves gripped by the love of Christ. It hems us in and leaves us no escape. Because we enjoy newness of life through his death for us, we have no alternative (and desire none) but to live for him who died for us and rose again (2 Cor. 5:14,15). Our first loyalty is to him, to seek to please him, to live a life worthy of him, and to obey him. This necessitates the renunciation of all lesser loyalties. So we are forbidden to conform ourselves to this world's standards, that is, to any prevailing culture which fails to honour God, and are commanded instead to be transformed in our conduct by renewed minds which perceive the will of God.

God's will was perfectly obeyed by Jesus. Therefore, 'the most outstanding thing about a Christian should not be his culture, but his Christlikeness.' As the mid-second century *Letter to Diognetus* put it: 'Christians are not distinguished from the rest of mankind by country or by speech or by customs . . . they follow the customs of the land in clothing and food and other matters of daily life, yet the condition of citizenship which they exhibit is wonderful . . . In a word, what the soul is in the body, that Christians are in the world.'

(b) Moral standards and cultural practices

Culture is never static. It varies both from place to place and from time to time. And throughout the long history of the church in different countries, Christianity has, in some measure, destroyed culture, preserved it, and in the end created a new culture in place of the old. So everywhere Christians need to think seriously about just how their new life in Christ should relate to contemporary culture.

In our consultation's preliminary papers two rather similar models were set before us. One suggested that there are several categories of customs which need to be distinguished. The first includes those practices which the convert will be expected to renounce immediately as being wholly incompatible with the Christian Gospel (e.g., idolatry, the possession of slaves, witchcraft and sorcery, head hunting, blood feuds, ritual prostitution, and all personal discriminations based on race, colour, class or caste). A second category might comprise institutionalized customs which could be tolerated for a while but would be expected to disappear gradually (e.g., systems of caste, slavery, and polygamy). A third category might relate to marriage traditions, especially questions of consanguinity, on which the churches are divided, while into a fourth category would be put the so-called *adiaphora* or 'matters indifferent,' which relate only to customs and not to morals, and therefore may be preserved without any compromise (e.g., eating and bathing customs, forms of public greeting to the opposite sex, hair and dress styles, etc.).

The second model we have considered distinguishes between 'direct' and 'indirect' encounters between Christ and culture, which correspond approximately to the first and second categories of the other model. Applied to 19th century Fiji in the case-study presented to us, it was assumed that there would be 'direct encounter' with such inhuman practices as cannibalism, widow-strangling, infanticide, and patricide, and that converts would be expected to abandon these customs upon conversion. 'Indirect' encounter would take place, however, either when the moral issue was not so clear-cut (e.g., some marriage customs, initiation rites, festivals and musical celebrations involving song, dance and instruments) or when it becomes apparent only after the convert has begun to work out his or her new faith in the applied Christian life. Some of these practices will not need to be discarded, but rather to be purged of unclean elements and invested with Christian meaning. Old customs can be given new symbolism, old dances can celebrate new blessings, and old crafts can serve new purposes. To borrow an expression from the Old Testament, swords can be hammered into ploughs and spears into pruning-knives.

The Lausanne Covenant said: 'The Gospel does not presuppose the superiority of any culture to another, but evaluates all cultures according to its own criteria of truth and righteousness, and insists on moral absolutes in every culture' (para. 10). We wish to endorse this, and to emphasize that even in this present age of relativity moral absolutes remain. Indeed, churches which study the Scriptures should not find it difficult to discern what belongs to the first or 'direct encounter' category. Scriptural principles under the guidance of the Holy Spirit will also guide them regarding the category of 'indirect encounter.' An additional test proposed is to ask whether a practice enhances or diminishes human life.

It will be seen that our studies have focused mainly on situations where younger churches have to take up a moral stance against certain evils. But we have been reminded that the church needs to confront evil in western culture too. In the 20th century West, often more sophisticated but no less horrible examples of the evils which were opposed in 19th century Fiji exist. Parallel to cannibalism is social injustice which 'eats' the poor; to widow-strangling, the oppression of women; to infanticide, abortion; to patricide, a criminal neglect of senior citizens; to tribal wars, World Wars I and II; and to ritual prostitution, sexual promiscuity. In considering this parallelism, it is necessary to remember both the added guilt adhering to the nominally Christian nations, and also the courageous Christian protest against such evils, and the immense (though incomplete) successes which have been won in mitigating these evils. Evil takes many forms, but it is universal, and wherever it appears Christians must confront and repudiate it.

(c)   The process of cultural change

It is not enough for converts to make a personal renunciation of the evils in their culture; the whole church needs to work for their elimination. Hence, the importance of asking how cultures change under the influence of the Gospel. Of course, the evil and the demonic are deeply entrenched in most cultures, and yet Scripture calls for national repentance and reform, and history records numerous cases of cultural change for the better. In fact, in some cases culture is not as resistant to necessary change as it may appear. Great care is needed, however, when seeking to initiate it.

First, 'people change as and when they want to.' This seems to be axiomatic. Further, they want to change only when they perceive the positive benefits which change will bring them. These will need to be carefully argued and patiently demonstrated, whether Christians are advocating in a developing country the benefits of literacy or the value of clean water, or in a western country the importance of stable marriage and family life.

Secondly, cross-cultural witnesses in the Third World need to have great respect for the in-built mechanisms of social change in general, and for the 'correct procedures of innovation' in each particular culture.

Thirdly, it is important to remember that virtually all customs perform important functions within the culture, and that even socially undesirable practices may perform 'constructive' functions. That being so, a custom should never be abolished without first discerning its function and then substituting another custom which performs the same function. For example, it may be right to wish to see abolished some of the initiatory rites associated with the circumcision of adolescents and some of the forms of sex education which accompany it. This is not to deny that there is much of value in the processes of initiation; great care must be taken to see that adequate substitutes are provided for the rites and forms of initiation which the Christian conscience would desire to see abolished.

Fourthly, it is essential to recognize that some cultural practices have a theological undergirding. When this is so, the culture will change only when the theology changes. Thus, if widows are killed in order that their husbands may not enter the next world unattended, or if older people are killed before senility overtakes them, in order that in the next world they may be strong enough to fight and hunt, then such killings, because founded on a false eschatology, will be abandoned only when a better alternative, the Christian hope, is accepted in its place.

Questions for Discussion

1. Can 'Christ-likeness' be recognized in every culture? What are its ingredients?
2. In your own culture, what would you expect a new convert to renounce immediately?
3. Take some 'institutionalized custom' in your country which Christians hope will 'disappear gradually' (e.g., polygamy, the caste system, easy

divorce, or some form of oppression). What active steps should Christians be taking to work for change?

Conclusion

Our Consultation has left us in no doubt of the pervasive importance of culture. The writing and the reading of the Bible, the presentation of the Gospel, conversion, church and conduct — all these are influenced by culture. It is essential, therefore, that all churches contextualize the Gospel in order to share it effectively in their own culture. For this task of evangelization, we all know our urgent need of the ministry of the Holy Spirit. He is the Spirit of truth who can teach each church how to relate to the culture which envelops it. He is also the Spirit of love, and love is 'the language — which is understood in every culture of man.' So may God fill us with his Spirit! Then, speaking the truth in love, we shall grow up into Christ who is the head of the body, to the everlasting glory of God (Eph. 4:15).

NOTE: Unattributed quotations in this report have been drawn from various papers presented at this Consultation.

APPENDIX A

The Consultation Program and Papers

January 7	**Culture and Revelation** (cultural factors in the Bible)	
	Old Testament:	S. Ananda Kumar
	New Testament:	I. Howard Marshall
	Towards a Theology of Culture:	Bruce J. Nicholls
January 8	**Culture and Hermeneutics** (understanding the Bible today)	
	A Theological Perspective:	C. René Padilla
	An Anthropological Perspective:	Charles R. Taber
January 9	**Culture and Evangelization** (the content and communication of the gospel)	
	A Theological Perspective:	James I. Packer
	An Anthropological Perspective:	Jacob A. Loewen
January 10	**Culture and Conversion** (the implications of culture in the conversion experience)	
	The East African Setting:	Donald R. Jacobs
	Theological Dimensions from a Korean Perspective:	Harvie M. Conn
	A Personal Case-study:	Orlando E. Costas

January 11   **Culture and Churches** (Christian churches and their immersion
              in culture)
              A Dynamic Equivalence Model: Charles H. Kraft
              A Socio-Historical Critique: Alfred C. Krass
              A Case-study from Indonesia: I. Wayan Mastra

January 12   **Culture and Ethics** (the contextualization of the Gospel in
              Christian behavior)
              The Christian Lifestyle: Gottfried Osei-Mensah
              A Case-study from Oceania: Alan R. Tippett

Background Papers
              Religion and Culture,
                a Historical Survey: Stephen C. Neill

              Conversion and Convertibility,
              with special reference to
              Muslims: Kenneth Cragg

APPENDIX B

In Attendance

PARTICIPANTS (Signatories of the Lausanne Covenant and/or committed to its
framework and understanding of mission)

Dr. Saphir Athyal, Principal (President) of Union Biblical Seminary, Yavatmal, India

Dr. Kwame Bediako, Lecturer in Biblical Studies and Theology, Christian Service
        College, Kumasi, Ghana

Prof. Dr. Peter P. J. Beyerhaus, Professor of Missiology and Ecumenics, Tübingen
        University, West Germany

Prof. Robinson Cavalcanti, Professor of Political Science at Recife Federal and Rural
        Universities of Pernambuco, Brazil

Dr. Chongnahm Cho, President and Professor, Seoul Theological Seminary, Bucheon
        City, Korea

Dr. Harvie M. Conn, Associate Professor of Missions and Apologetics, Westminster
        Theological Seminary, Chestnut Hill, Philadelphia, Pennsylvania

Rev. Dr. Orlando E. Costas, Director, Latin American Evangelical Center for Pastoral
        Studies (CELEP), San Jose, Costa Rica

Mr. Edward R. Dayton, Director, MARC, Monrovia, California

Cand. theol. Tormod Engelsviken, Teacher of Theology, Fjellhaug School of Missions,
        Oslo, Norway

Dr. John A. Gration, Associate Professor of Missions, Wheaton Graduate School,
        Wheaton, Illinois

Dr. Donald R. Jacobs, Director, Mennonite Christian Leadership Foundation

Dr. F. S. Khair–Ullah, Director, Creative Writing Project of M.I.K. Pakistan

Dr. Charles H. Kraft, Professor of Anthropology and African Studies, School of World Mission, Fuller Theological Seminary, Pasadena, California

Rev. Dr. S. Ananda Kumar, Professor of Biblical Studies, Karnataka Theological College, Karnataka State, South India

Dr. Jacob A. Loewen, Translations Consultant for East Central Africa with the United Bible Societies

Dr. I. Howard Marshall, Reader in New Testament Exegesis, University of Aberdeen, Scotland

Dr. I. Wayan Mastra, Chairman of the 'Gereja Kristen Protestan di Bali,' Indonesia

Mr. Bruce J. Nicholls, Executive Secretary, Theological Commission, World Evangelical Fellowship

Rev. Gottfried Osei-Mensah, Executive Secretary, Lausanne Committee for World Evangelization

Rev. Dr. James I. Packer, Associate Principal, Trinity College, Bristol, England

Dr. C. René Padilla, Director of Ediciones Certeza, International Fellowship of Evangelical Students

Dr. William E. Pannell, Assistant Professor of Evangelism, Fuller Theological Seminary, Pasadena, California

Rev. Pedro Savage (Consultation Coordinator), Coordinator, Latin American Theological Fraternity, staff member of Partnership in Mission and of Latin American IFES

Rev. John Stott (Consultation Chairman), Rector Emeritus, All Souls' Church, Langham Place, London

Dr. Charles R. Taber, Director, Institute of World Studies/Church Growth, Milligan College, Tennessee

Rev. Tite Tienou, Director of Bible School Bobo Dioulasso, Upper Volta, and Executive Secretary of A.E.A.M. Theological Commission

Dr. Alan R. Tippett, Hon. Research Fellow, St. Mark's Library, Canberra, A.C.T., Australia

Rev. Canon James Wong, Anglican Pastor and Coordinator of Asian Leadership Conference on Evangelism, Singapore

CONSULTANTS (in general sympathy with the Lausanne Covenant)

Bishop Kenneth Cragg, Reader in Religious Studies, University of Sussex, and Assistant Bishop of Chichester, England

Rev. Alfred C. Krass, Co-Editor of *The Other Side* magazine

Canon Prof. John Mbiti, Director, the Ecumenical Institute, Bossey, Switzerland

Bishop Stephen C. Neill, Resident Scholar, Wycliffe Hall, Oxford, England

VISITOR (Contributing to a consultation committed to the Lausanne Covenant)

Rev. Louis J. Luzbetak, President, Divine Word College, Epworth, Iowa

POSTSCRIPT

The seventeen papers of the Willowbank Consultation, with slight alterations to their order and their text, were edited by John Stott and Robert Coote, and published by Hodder and Stoughton in 1981 under the title *Down to Earth*, sub-titled 'Studies in Christianity and Culture'.

After a brief Foreword which opens up the topic of 'Gospel and Culture', and a historical introduction, 'Religion and Culture', by Bishop Stephen Neill, the book is divided into three parts.

Part I is headed 'Culture and the Bible'. Its five chapters handle the place of culture both in the writing of Scripture (Old and New Testaments) and in the reading of it (theological and anthropological perspectives on hermeneutics).

Part II is entitled 'Culture, Evangelism and Conversion'. Its six chapters handle the place of culture in both the preaching and the receiving of the Gospel, that is, in evangelism and conversion. Again, theological and anthropological perspectives are developed, first on the content and communication of the Gospel, and then on the experience of conversion. Case studies are included from East Africa, Korea and the Muslim world.

Part III is called 'Culture, Churches and Ethics'. Its five chapters consider the post-conversion place of culture, that is, in the development of both the church and the Christian lifestyle. Case studies on contextualization are contributed from Indonesia (Bali) and Oceania (Fiji).

The book ends with the full text of the Willowbank Report.

4

— 1978 —

The Glen Eyrie Report on Muslim Evangelization

♦♦♦♦♦

The North American Conference on Muslim
Evangelization, Glen Eyrie, Colorado Springs,
15–21 October 1978

EXPLANATORY PREFACE

The North American Conference on Muslim evangelization, jointly sponsored by the North American LCWE and World Vision International, was held at Glen Eyrie, Colorado Springs, from 15 to 21 October 1978.

The Glen Eyrie Report grew out of this historic conference. It was initially drafted by Dr. Arthur Glasser, Dean of the School of World Mission, Fuller Theological Seminary, who was assisted by Dr. Robert Douglas of Pepperdine University, and Rev. Don McCurry, the Conference Director. The major part of the report was read at the conference, and suggestions made from the participants were incorporated into it. Following the conference, the completed report was circulated among the Steering Committee and further modified. The document before you is not an official conference statement, but is a highly valuable and informative report on the conference.

—The Glen Eyrie Report—

CONTENTS

INTRODUCTION: THE BACKGROUND

During mid-October 1978, a week-long consultation was convened at Glen Eyrie, Colorado Springs, to explore the responsibilities of North American Christians towards the Muslim world. This was part of a continuum that began with the *International Congress on World Evangelization* at Lausanne in 1974. At that time many were deeply stirred by what God was doing in their midst, but were moved to penitence by their flawed and limited commitment to the missionary task. At Lausanne they entered into a solemn covenant with God and with each other to pray, to plan and to work together for the evangelization of the world. Their concern was: 'Let the Earth Hear His Voice', and their focus was on 'unreached people.' Of particular interest to many of the participants was the large bloc of unreached Muslims.

Two subsequent conferences heightened this concern to reach the unreached. *The Pasadena Consultation* (1977) celebrated the diversity of peoples and cultures making up the human race. Its participants made a particular effort to relate this reality to the worldwide missionary task. They were in deep agreement that Scripture supports the Christian witness that seeks to preserve cultural diversity, for this will 'honor God, respect man, enrich life and promote evangelization' (Par. 4).

Later, *The Willowbank Consultation* (1978) was convened to explore in depth the interrelation of the Gospel of Jesus Christ and culture. Upon this sequence the *North American Conference on Muslim Evangelization* was built to focus on reaching these unreached Muslim peoples and to explore the wide range of implications of the Gospel in their Islamic cultures.

The days at Glen Eyrie were very full, and session followed session in relentless sequence. When a pattern began to emerge which seemed to indicate the overruling providence of God in our midst, we began to prepare this report. It is neither an official statement nor a declaration, much less a covenant; so none of us has signed it. But we send it out as reflecting the mood of the participants and indicating the highlights of what took place in our midst. We commend it to our fellow Christians throughout the world for study, and as a reminder that the Lord will truly meet with his people when they concern themselves with the unfinished task of evangelizing the Muslim world.

1. PRE-CONFERENCE PREPARATION: THE FERMENT

Those invited to participate were drawn from a wide range of church traditions, missionary experience, specialized training and evangelical commitment. All were concerned with Muslim evangelization. They represented a variety of roles and disciplines: mission executives, field missionaries, mission professors, Islamicists, anthropologists, theologians and media experts. In addition, the conveners invited a sizeable number of men and women from churches in the Middle East, Asia and Africa. They too represented different roles and disciplines: pastors, theologians, Islamicists and active laymen.

During the six months prior to the conference, forty foundation papers were prepared by selected authors — men and women — to alert the participants to the complexity of issues related to the task before them.

Ten papers were conceptual, in that they explored its major underlying postulates.

'*The Gospel and Culture,*' Paul G. Hiebert
'*The Cross-Cultural Communication of the Gospel to Muslims,*' Donald N. Larson
'*The Incarnational Witness to the Muslim Heart,*' Bashir Abdol Massih
'*The Muslim Convert and His Culture,*' Harvie M. Conn
'*Dynamic Equivalence Churches in Muslim Society,*' Charles H. Kraft
'*Power Encounter in Conversion from Islam,*' Arthur F. Glasser
'*Contextualization: Indigenization and / or Transformation,*' Charles R. Taber
'*New Theological Approaches in Muslim Evangelism,*' Bruce J. Nicholls
'*An "Engel Scale" for Muslim Work?*' David A. Fraser
'*Resistance/Receptivity Analysis of Muslim Peoples,*' Don M. McCurry

Sixteen papers described key 'givens' in the Christian encounter with Islam today.

'*Islamic Theology: Limits and Bridges,*' Kenneth Cragg
'*Popular Islam: The Hunger of the Heart,*' Bill Musk
'*The Comparative Status of Christianity and Islam in the West,*' R. Max Kershaw
'*The Comparative Status of Christianity and Islam in Sub-Sahara Africa,*' Gerald O. Swank
'*The Comparative Status of Christianity and Islam in North Africa,*' Gregory M. Livingston
'*The Comparative Status of Christianity and Islam in the Middle East,*' Norman A. Horner

119

'The Comparative Status of Christianity and Islam in Turkey,' Mehmet Iskender

'The Comparative Status of Christianity and Islam in Iran,' David G. Cashin

'The Comparative Status of Christianity and Islam in the Sub-Continent,' Richard Bailey

'The Comparative Status of Christianity and Islam in Southeast Asia,' Frank Cooley, Peter Gowing, Alex Smith, Warren Meyers

'The Comparative Status of Christianity and Islam in Russia and China,' J. Robert Overbrook

'The Current Status of Christian Literature for Muslims,' Raymond H. Joyce

'The Current Status of Bible Translations in Muslim Languages,' William D. Reyburn

'The Current Status of Radio Broadcasting to Muslim Peoples,' Fred D. 'Bud' Acord

'An Overview of Missions to Muslims,' George M. Peters

'A Selective Bibliography for Christian Muslim Workers,' Warren W. Webster

The final fourteen papers defined concrete responses deemed essential to effective missionary service among Muslims.

'The Call to Spiritual Renewal,' J. Edwin Orr

'The Development of New Tools to Aid Muslim Evangelization,' Donald R. Rickards

'Levels, Styles and Locations of Training Programs,' Vivienne Stacey

'Building the Network of Research Centers,' Roland E. Miller

'The Value and Methodology of Planning Strategies,' Edward R. Dayton

'Tentmaking Ministries in Muslim Countries', J. Christy Wilson, Jr.

'The Need for a North American Nerve Center,' Ralph D. Winter

'Dialogue: Relevancy to Evangelism,' Daniel Brewster

'North American Ties to Third World Missions to Muslims,' Waldron Scott

'The Need for a New Journal on Missions to Muslims,' C. George Fry

'Food and Health as Partners of Muslim Evangelism,' Robert C. Pickett and Rufino L. Macagba, Jr.

'The Role of Local Churches in God's Redemptive Plan for the Muslim World,' Frank S. Khair-Ullah

'The Christian Approach to the Muslim woman and Family,' Valerie Hoffman

'To Reach the Unreached,' the report to the Lausanne Committee for World Evangelization of its Strategy Working Group.

Uppermost in these foundation papers was the overriding concern that Jesus Christ be known, loved and served in the midst of each of the more than 3,500 separate peoples making up this massive religious community.

The conferees not only studied these papers beforehand; they were required to draft written responses to the ten conceptual papers. This generation of intellectual ferment and expansive dreaming was deemed essential to the success of the conference. All were greatly stimulated by this process, particularly the authors who were inevitably informed, enriched and balanced by the friendly counsel of those whose expertise differed from their own. In fact, this intense pre-conference interaction heightened the expectation with which all gathered at Glen Eyrie to study the Scriptures and to involve themselves in corporate reflection, discussion, planning and prayer.

2. CONTRITION AND REPENTANCE: THE ESSENTIAL

At the opening session of the conference, this mood of expectancy was overshadowed by a painful reality. The keynote address raised the question: 'Why is not the Muslim world better evangelized?' The probing went deeper. Related questions were asked: 'Why is it that barely two percent of North American Protestant missionaries are involved in this work? Why their limited understanding of Islam and Islamic culture? Why their long persistence in using inappropriate and ineffective methods to communicate the Gospel to Muslims?'

These questions were joined by others in the days that followed. Indeed, as the week progressed we became inwardly convinced that we first had to take the measure of what these questions implied. We came under the compulsion of a sense of sorrow, and experienced a renewed hunger for the forgiving grace and mighty working of God in our lives. The more we listened to one another, particularly to those God was manifestly using to reach Muslims for Christ, the more we felt we should give expression in this report to our sense of contrition.

a. The Need for Love

In so many ways we North Americans have failed. And our personal failures are a reflection of the larger tragedy of the Christian Church. Over the centuries Christians in both the West and the East have all too readily cherished and cultivated an antipathy towards Muslims, and have expressed it by largely neglecting their obligation under God to share Jesus Christ with them.

We stand appalled that relatively few Muslims have entered into life through responding to the Gospel. And we grieve that at this late hour in the history of the church there exist so few vital and outgoing congregations of Muslim believers in Jesus among this largely accessible people. And yet, it is our fault. We Christians have loved so little, and have put forth such little effort to regard Muslims as people like ourselves. They too bear the image and likeness of God. They, too, deserve the love and respect God would have his people accord all men. Although we know that their inmost needs — like ours — can be satisfied only by Christ, we somehow draw back from sharing him with them. They deserve a Christian presence in their midst that is neither tentative nor timid — the sort that is imbued with vigorous faith and counts on 'the God who only does wondrous things.' But this demands more of us than we have been willing to give. And our North American mission agencies continue to conduct the sort of culturally insensitive, unplanned missionary work in their midst that falls far short of the ideal of Christian presence in Muslim society.

b. The Need for Respect

And we North American Christians also tend to be critical of Islamic culture. In our pride and ethnocentrism we have forgotten that our own culture is terribly flawed. True, it reflects the creativity of a pluralistic society, but it also expresses our fallenness. Since Christ judges all cultures and is seeking through the Gospel to infuse and transform them with his presence, he would have us discern and appreciate the redeemable in Islamic culture.

An aspect of our concern should be the cultivation of a new awareness of the nature of the Islamic faith. It touches every aspect of the lives of Muslims. They are determined that God's rule shall range publicly over every detail of the life of their nations.

In sharpest contrast, of course, Jesus Christ offers men a *truly* holistic Gospel. Indeed, his is the Gospel of the kingdom. It embraces the totality of human existence. We North American Christians are only beginning to discover that all too often we have preached a westernized, truncated message that does not do full justice to the biblical revelation.

We are challenged when we stand before the world of Islam. But as evangelicals, we refuse to confine our mission to the development of better Christian-Muslim relations or to involvement in social service on their behalf. Jesus Christ has defined our agenda, and because we love him we are constrained to embrace as well the mandate he has given the church to evangelize the Muslim world.

3. THE LISTENING PROCESS: MUTUAL INTERDEPENDENCE

Early in the week we began to take the measure of the Muslim world: its extent, size, people diversity and many variations of religious faith and practice. Simultaneously, we began to implement the planning process which the conveners deemed essential to the spiritual productivity of the conference. Indeed, their structuring of the day-to-day sequence was in response to the encouragement received from Christians worldwide. One group had drafted a statement with the buoyant exhortation: 'Commit yourselves to work together in the unity of the Holy Spirit and in the bond of peace. Anticipate and plan for a great turning to Christ by millions of Muslims.'

a. A New Approach

All felt that we had to make a decisive break with the past. We were reminded of an earlier conference in Cairo in 1906 convened by that great American missionary statesman, Samuel M. Zwemer. It brought together more than 60 representatives of almost 30 missions and churches, and marked 'the beginning of a new era in the Christian mission to Muslims.' This was followed by a similar conference he convened in Lucknow in 1911. And yet, such enormous changes have taken place in the Muslim world since, that all of us felt a new forward step was called for. The North American church tolerates too limited a knowledge of Islam and Muslim peoples. Its mission involvement in the Muslim world is marginal at best. Moreover, it is dominated by a methodology that demands critical revision. New approaches are needed in North American missionary training programs. On and on. An entirely new pattern of interaction was needed between western missionaries and their brothers and sisters in the Muslim world. Actually, it was precisely for this reason that so many Muslim converts and national church leaders from the Middle East, Africa and Asia had been invited to participate in every workshop and in every discussion and planning session. North Americans were encouraged to be 'swift to hear' and discouraged from initiating any planning on their own.

These key evangelical men and women from the Middle East, Asia and Africa are themselves deeply and fruitfully involved in the task of Muslim evangelization. Hence, every effort was made to listen to their non-North American perspectives. They were given very specific assignments by the western participants: 'Help us in learning how to work together. Be patient with those of us who are slow learners. Pray for those of us who appear insensitive to your concerns. And above all, do help us to see God's world through your uniquely different eyes.' Needless to say, they exceeded themselves in meeting the high demands of this task.

The witness of these consultants was wonderfully reinforced by a series of short addresses given by western missionaries — men and women — likewise fruitful in their evangelistic work among Muslims. The note uniformly struck by each was that in the course of their service, however, they had to break with the 'older' patterns in which they had been trained. They had to rethink before God what he would have them do. This impulse to review their ministry and alter it significantly came in every instance from their non-western friends. This confirmed to all of us the essentiality of such collaboration. It exposed the folly of North Americans thinking they can go it alone. It underscored the exciting possibilities for new perspectives on mission to Muslims arising from the deliberate creation of patterns of mutual interdependence between eastern and western Christians. The implications are far-reaching.

One missionary in Lebanon had to receive from an Arab scholar insight into how he might escape the sterile apologetic pattern of the past and recast his entire evangelistic approach, via the Quran, as well as the Bible. A woman missionary in Pakistan, after struggling unsuccessfully for some years to interject her 'western' Jesus into Muslim culture, was brought lovingly inside that culture with the help of Muslim friends, and in time discovered an 'eastern' Jesus that was more than able to meet their needs. A team of two women deliberately turned from a barren, traditional approach to adopt step by step the unexpected thesis that 'women are the key.' This resulted in the Gospel being deeply and widely planted in a previously unevangelized rural community in Pakistan. A highly trained missionary in India had to be pointedly counselled by a national church leader so that he might recast his approach from friendly manipulation to the sort of friendship evangelism that makes one love Muslims for what they are, and not for what we want them to become.

Several other reports were given in similar vein. All spoke of non-western input. All described the sense of release and gratitude that came through this helpful counsel. All bore witness that a sovereign God is working significantly in Muslim hearts today. Our faith was challenged by the evidence, whether in Iran or Tunisia, in Israel or Egypt, in Syria and Bangladesh and Indonesia. As we listened, we almost came to the conclusion that given half a chance, and provided the evangelist's approach is more relational than cognitive, there is the possibility that any Muslim will come to love Jesus.

b.   The Cost

But there is a price to be paid. All who spoke shared in one way or another the fact that this listening to non-western friends and responding, this re-thinking and changing one's methodology and planning, involved them in spiritual crisis. All knew pain and brokenness. Their testimonies endorsed what the early Franciscans gave to those who would serve Christ among Muslims. 'Go out' they said:

> '. . . not as the Latins were wont to do — with weapons — but with words; not with force — but reason; not with hatred — but love, the kind of love that should exist between Christians and non-Christians, the same love with which the apostles approached the Gentiles, the love that God himself had for those who did not serve him' (Abbot Peter of Cluny).

What did this mean to us? No easy triumphalism on our part, although we were convinced of the final triumph of God in history, when every knee shall bow to Jesus Christ. And no 'gimmick' methodology either, for we must face the Cross and enter into the trauma of conflict with 'the powers', while seeking to witness simply and lovingly to Jesus Christ. Only thereby shall we be used of God to turn Muslims 'from darkness to light and from the power of Satan to God' (Acts 26:18). If one would be God's instrument to plant the church in a Muslim society, he has no alternative but to follow the methodology of the Apostle Paul who wrote:

'It is now my happiness to suffer for you. This is my way of helping to complete, in my poor human flesh, the full tale of Christ's afflictions still to be endured, for the sake of his body which is the church' (Col. 1:24, NEB).

c. The Keys

The more we listened to the testimonies of field missionaries and of non-western consultants, the more aware we became of the heavy demands God would make on all who would serve him among Muslims. The keys to effective mission were defined and underscored again and again:

- *The cruciality of transparency before others.*
- *The centrality of love in all our dealings.*
- *The cultivation of a sensitive regard for truthfulness, about oneself and about the stark demands of the Gospel.*
- *The inevitability that tears of compassion will flow.*
- *The demanding but encouraging possibilities of prayer and fasting.*
- *The need for courage, patience and persistence.*
- *The ability to absorb scorn and suffering.*
- *The essentiality of unwavering faith and joyful praise: our God is the God of the impossible.*

To conclude this section: effective Muslim evangelism can be accomplished only through humble respect for Islamic cultures, and by seeking to master the use of these keys, and through deliberately adopting a pattern of intercommunication and conscious interdependence between national

Christians and western missionaries. And this pattern must be sustained by the interdependence of the structures to which they belong. Gone is the day when western missionaries can regard themselves as sufficient for the task. It was at Glen Eyrie that we resolved, as never before, to make the most of the opportunities given to us by God — to develop a loving sense of responsibility to the whole household of faith, particularly to all Christians and churches in the Muslim world. From henceforth, we are determined to regard ourselves willingly accountable to one another, that together God might work through us to the achieving of his redemptive purpose for the Muslim world.

4. THE PLANNING PROCESS: UTILIZING ALL RESOURCES

A great concern of those who participated in the Lausanne Congress (1974) was that there be an end to the 'sinful individualism and needless duplication' that all too often have marred the missionary service of evangelicals. They pledged themselves 'to seek a deeper unity in truth, worship, holiness and mission' and urged 'the development of regional and functional cooperation for the furtherance of the church's mission, for strategic planning, for mutual encouragement, and for the sharing of resources and experience' (Para 7). However, the participants did not go much further in their deliberations than to note that 'the development of strategies for world evangelization calls for imaginative pioneering methods.' In fact, there was a certain drawing back from anything more specific because of the fear that 'those activistic, pragmatic Americans' would somehow organize the Holy Spirit right out of the task of world evangelization!

Not a few of the addresses contained expressions of this concern. The desire was to submit to the lordship of Jesus Christ and focus attention on his sovereignty. To follow him and to serve as he directs is the highest virtue. No small effort was put forth to support from Scripture this thesis that God alone has the initiative! And no plenary address was more heartily received than the one which included the following:

> 'Effective mission does not spring from human blueprints . . . I don't believe the early Christians had much of a strategy . . . the Gospel spread out in an apparently haphazard way as men obeyed the leading of the Spirit, and went through the doors he opened' (Report: pp. 166, 174).

The participants at Glen Eyrie shared this concern. God must be God! His missionary servants must labor under his direction, and solely for his glory. They must resist the arrogance that boasts of having within themselves all that is needed to evangelize the Muslim world. No human being, no matter how able, dare affirm that he or she knows what to do and how to do it!

a. Biblical Foundations for Planning

And yet, when the conveners sought direction from the Lord touching the inner structure of the conference, they felt that Lausanne 1974 gave them the mandate not only to pray, but to expect God's guidance and surprises. It also gave them the obligation to think strategically about the evangelization of the Muslim world. They were convinced that such an obligation was also

128

biblically enjoined. Does not Scripture speak specifically? 'We should make plans . . . counting on God to direct us . . . [and] the final outcome is in God's hands' (Prov. 16:9,1, LB).

However, in order to bring the subject of planning into New Testament focus, it was decided that each day should begin with an exploration into relevant aspects of the strategies and patterns of the witness and service of the apostolic church. This resulted in the selection of the following themes and texts:

> The long-range plan of the apostle Paul to establish a missionary base at Rome from which to evangelize Spain (Rom. 1:1–17; 15: 1–29).
> The day-to-day movements of his missionary team in establishing a foothold in unevangelized Europe (Acts 16:1–34).
> The apostolic conviction of the essentiality of cultural adaptation if one is to be effective in his cross-cultural witness to Jesus Christ (John 4:1–42; 1 Cor. 9:16–23).
> The inescapable necessity of accepting suffering and self-denial if one is to be fruitful in his cross-cultural missionary service (Phil. 3:1–21).
> The Jerusalem church pattern for resolving 'new convert' problems arising from cultural differences (Acts 15:1–29).
> The possibilities for courageous and victorious witness in the face of civil and religious opposition (Acts 4:1–35).

But then followed a measure of agony. Large sections of three days were taken with the assignment to develop a method for strategic planning and then with the task of applying that method to a series of specific situations. This found many of us involved in a process that was largely unfamiliar. Some tended to dismiss the planning as an American aberration, only to fall vulnerable to the rebuke: 'What a shame — yes, how stupid! to decide before knowing the facts!' (Prov. 18:13, LB). But in the end the great majority felt the instructional experience had been most helpful. 'It is pleasant to see plans develop . . .' (Prov. 13:19a, LB).

These good feelings developed when we became particularly involved in examining critically actual missionary situations in the Muslim world. It was then that we sensed in new ways the manner in which even the planning process was a vital exercise in partnership with God. We were agreed that from henceforth we should incorporate this larger experience of being 'God's fellow workers' into our future ministry among Muslims (I Cor. 3:9–15).

b. A Productive Planning Sequence

As to the 'planning sequence' that we finally adopted and which we commend to the wider church, the following seemed essential:

> State the philosophy, policies, assumptions and purpose of the mission: 'Why has God brought our mission or parachurch agency into existence?'
> Describe the actual field situation — the specific people to whom God has called us: 'What are the dominant felt needs of the people we are to evangelize?'

Define the mission's role in terms of its potential and its limitations: 'What aspects of the need of this people does God want us to meet?'

Set measurable goals — a work plan — for the mission to carry out, which express its faith in the working of God: 'What is to be the schedule and sequence of our work?'

Detail the specific obstacles that in all probability will stand in the way of the goals being reached: 'What problems should we anticipate and prepare for?'

Specify the means and methods that conceivably might be blessed of God in reaching this people: 'How are we to go about our assignments?'

Appraise the resources already available (people, funds, facilities, etc.) and determine the additional resources that will be needed to complete the task: 'What do we have and what shall we need?'

Anticipate that from time to time there will be evaluation of the work, and adjustment and modification of the plans, as we remain in dynamic interaction with God: 'What have we accomplished with the resources which God has given us?'

Needless to say, involvement in this process convinced us in a most telling fashion that there is no normative approach to Muslim evangelization. Every situation is unique and must be examined on its own. It is only when we ask these basic questions, however, that we become utterly convinced of the essentiality of the planning process. Only thereby can we avoid the 'sinful individualism and needless duplication' which Lausanne 1974 deplored.

But we also learned something else of tremendous significance. Every small group and workshop in our conference was so structured that each contained the sort of participant mix that inevitably brought enrichment and balance to our insights, but also brought tension. How could it be otherwise with theologians working alongside anthropologists, communicators trying to understand Islamicists, field missionaries interacting with national church leaders, and mission executives seeking to work harmoniously with mission professors? All were competent, and the perspectives of one and all were valid. And the insight of each participant informed the rest. Here was interdisciplinary dialogue at its best. Suffice it to say that in these planning exercises the 'listening process' came fully into its own. But it was not easy for this diversity to come to productive agreement. The process took time and prayer, and the loving acceptance of one another. But when agreement was achieved, all knew that a planning process had been uncovered and experienced which must indeed precede all future evangelical activity on behalf of the Muslim world. 'Plans go wrong with too few counselors; [but] many counselors bring success' (Prov. 15:22, LB).

5. THE INESCAPABLE REALITY: CAESAR AND THE POWERS

Good planning is essential if we are to make use of the resources God has given us. On this we are agreed. But we also are aware of the spiritual struggle involved in carrying out even the best of God-given plans. No one was deceived at this point, for the participants in the conference were anything but novices in the service of God. Indeed, all those actively engaged in making Jesus Christ known, loved and obeyed throughout the Muslim world know that they are engaged in constant spiritual warfare with the principalities and powers of evil. And there is always Caesar, who is never the friend of Jesus Christ.

It was inevitable that whenever the subject of conflict and suffering was broached, there were those who quickly reminded us — and did so correctly — that for much of this Christians had only themselves to blame. Not all missionaries have been wise and holy, noble and loving. Some have tended to misrepresent and belittle the moral and religious stature of Muhammad and the Quran. All too many have been uncritically defensive of Christian missions in the Muslim world during the long years of western political dominance. As a result, they have been largely indifferent to the task of reducing the mistrust and misunderstanding which accentuated past tensions and rivalries. And they have given the impression that they lack concern for the deterioration of Christian values in the Christian world, while openly encouraging the process of secularization in the Muslim world.

It was humbling for us to be confronted by this evidence of cultural imperialism, coupled with aggressive and insensitive proselytism. We were agreed that much within the modern missionary movement needs rectification. And yet, we were also reminded that this was not the whole story.

Religious Freedom

We had to consider the plight of those Christians scattered throughout the Muslim world who are limited in the exercise of their religious freedom. Many have either fled or withdrawn into ghetto communities, because they found it impossible to act as responsible citizens toward their nation. They have been denied the right to erect or acquire buildings for public worship, religious education and social activity. And these restrictions are contrary to Islamic law. Actually, however, this discrimination is but a part of a larger contemporary problem — Muslims and Christians are both being denied their human rights in various parts of the world. Both know insecurity. Both are

131

under heavy and varied pressures to conform. Both need freedom to protect their human dignity, to exercise their particular religion and to propagate their faith. Whereas we would contend for 'the full right to convince and be convinced', and would deplore all that stands in the way of this freedom, we are obliged to confess that we have all too often been unaware of the obligation to support our Muslim neighbors in their efforts to obtain their human rights.

This does not mean that we have forgotten the somber reality of the Law of Apostasy (*irtidad*), and the particular problems and perils it poses for those who submit to the lordship of Jesus Christ in Muslim lands. Even at this late hour in the long history of Muslim-Christian relations, reports are not infrequent of harsh discrimination, community hostility, violence against persons and buildings, and the suffering of the oppressed. We pray that Muslim leaders will sense anew their God-given obligation to promote justice and freedom. We pray that the conduct of Muslim states will increasingly approximate to *The Universal Declaration of Human Rights* by which they agreed to respect

'. . . human rights and fundamental freedoms, including freedom of thought, conscience, religion or belief, for all without distinction as to race, sex, language or religion.'

Finally, there was deepest agreement that when the issue is Jesus Christ, and when persecution has broken out because of loving attempts to name his Name, no redress should be sought. In one workshop the question was asked: 'How should the converts stand up to potential serious persecution, which could expel them from their land and livelihood?' All sorts of suggestions came to the fore, but the conversation was abruptly terminated when a convert from Islam said, in effect, what the apostle Paul advised long ago: 'Let no one be moved by these afflictions, for you yourselves know that this is to be our lot.' It is 'through many tribulations that we enter the kingdom of God' (1 Thess. 3:3; Acts 14:22).

6. THE UNFINISHED AGENDA: LOOKING AHEAD

It was inevitable that, as the conference progressed, workshops and discussion groups increasingly faced the future. When they did so, many issues surfaced that called for exploration, and old questions arose that demanded new answers. In the process all of us became aware of the wide variety of tasks which will have to be undertaken if the church seriously desires to evangelize the Muslim world. Fortunately, the conveners had anticipated this ferment and had planned the sequence of sessions to encourage this transition to practical matters.

More than a whole day was devoted to uncovering and defining the details of this 'unfinished agenda.' And the more we became involved, the more we came to appreciate the significance of the planning process we had sought to master earlier in the week. How essential it became to all our final deliberations!

This work began when the decision was taken to divide the participants along the lines of their specialties. This meant that each group of participants met on its own — overseas consultants along with North Americans — whether theologians, missionaries, anthropologists, communication experts, mission professors, Islamicists or mission executives.

Each specialty group was commissioned to ask itself: 'What specific contribution can and should we make to further Muslim evangelization?' On the first time around, more than thirty major and relevant tasks were defined as needing urgent attention. And the momentum kept increasing.

The growing ground swell of suggestions demanded that task forces be formed to suggest the first steps in translating them into specific plans. The process then reached the stage where objectives were defined and goals set. Discussions swirled around such tangibles as means, methods, resources and timetables. In the end a lengthy plenary session heard the reports and provided the occasion for yet more input. In many ways, this final gathering was the most stimulating and fruitful session of the whole conference. All that followed was largely taken up with inspiration, worship and summarization. All were agreed that the Lord had graciously welded us into a dynamic, creative oneness. When report after report was received, there seemed to be an almost apostolic dimension to our determination to lay all these matters before the whole church and invite the participation of all like-minded Christians all over the world. 'It seemed good to the Holy Spirit and to us' (Acts 15:28).

This brief report cannot detail the extensive output of the six task forces. What follows is but a summary of high points to encourage this participation. Indeed, an ever-widening circle of concerned Christians will be needed in the days ahead if the church is to carry to completion the evangelization of the Muslim world.

a. Human Rights

Recognizing that both Muslim and non-Muslim governments, both Muslim and Christian religious organizations, have violated human freedom by various forms of coercion, especially depriving people of the freedom to change or not to change their religion, we see the desirability of establishing an international Christian-Muslim office on human rights, to receive complaints, investigate them, and make recommendations for redress to the concerned parties.

b. Resource and Research Center

Recognizing the need for developing vital and continuous inter-communication among all those involved in Muslim evangelization, we purpose to establish a central resource and research center in the United States,* to be followed as need arises by regional centers in all major segments of the Muslim world. This center shall be organized and directed by an experienced missionary scholar, supported by researchers from a variety of church traditions, trained in anthropology and Islamics. It shall also recruit consultants who can visit and serve the churches. It shall gather a wide range of pertinent information on the location, character and size of all Muslim people groups, along with their psychographic and demographic characteristics. Its archival structure shall include a resource library containing all types of media communication.

Recognizing the need for an expanded body of information about unreached Muslim peoples, we purpose that this center shall establish a research consortium for the coordination of pertinent data. The director shall authorize that linkage be established with all major research agencies worldwide, in order to develop working relationships with missions serving among Muslims, and to gather relevant information from those educational and research institutions currently doing mission-related research. The center shall also publish a monthly newsletter to channel data on available services to churches and missions throughout the Muslim world.

This research center shall encourage all theological and missionary training schools in North America to strengthen their course offerings in Islamics and to prepare suitable syllabuses and textbooks for foundation courses on mission to Muslims.

c. Evangelism

Recognizing that the major untapped force for evangelism among Muslims is the Christian community scattered throughout the Muslim world, we shall

---

*This purpose was fulfilled in the establishment in Pasadena of the Samuel Zwemer Institute, which was later re-named The Zwemer Institute of Muslim Studies.

seek to concentrate our attention on all existing churches, training and motivating both pastors and people to a new awareness of Islam. We shall seek with them to develop and refine new and more appropriate evangelistic methods for introducing the Gospel to Muslims. Particular attention will be given to the use of relevant Quranic themes in the initial stages of evangelistic encounter.

d.   Communication Patterns

Recognizing the importance of communicating Christian truth in ways consonant with communication patterns already in use in Muslim societies, we propose that the research center shall stimulate the development of extensive research activities within strategic segments of the Muslim world, with a view to developing appropriate methods and materials, along with teaching guides.

1.   *For Non-Literate People*: to enable the poet, singer or chanter to communicate the Gospel and Bible stories in such a fashion that the way will be prepared for the teaching of reading.

2.   *For Women and Children*: to study their varied roles at different levels in Muslim societies, respecting the code of modesty and sexual segregation where this prevails; to provide for more meaningful home-oriented women's activities; to recognize the authority of men who are heads of households through seeking to witness to entire families; to work through those women who are recognized as religious or community leaders; and to present more winsomely the Christian alternative to the demonic influences which particularly assail women in Muslim societies.

e.   Church Planting — Converts in Congregations

Recognizing that the evangelization of the Muslim world largely depends on the spiritual vitality and outgoing love of national churches in its midst, we purpose to pray that God will increasingly bring renewal to these privileged Christians. We anticipate that under his blessing those involved in evangelizing Muslims will be able to engage in more than seed-sowing. We believe that discipling and church planting will also take place.

This anticipated growth will possibly heighten the difficulty converts encounter in seeking a church home which receives them warmly and completely. We purpose through deliberately contrived study programs to make every effort to change the attitudes of Christians towards Muslim converts. Only those churches interested in winning Muslims to Christ will be interested in what happens to them after conversion.

However, where there is resistance or reluctance on the part of national Christians to involve themselves in this task, we shall seek to develop separate

Muslim convert churches. These latter congregations shall be encouraged to develop culturally appropriate forms of worship which arise out of the natural expression of earlier worship patterns, which will be true to biblical teaching, and yet will neither deliberately flaunt our Christian liberty nor carelessly involve the believers in syncretistic belief or conduct.

f.   Theological Research: A study group

Recognizing the need for extensive theological reflection on the contextualizing of the Gospel and the church in Islamic culture, we purpose that the center shall stimulate the forming of a theological study group, which will undertake a systematic exploration of the many theological issues raised at this conference which bear on the task of evangelizing Muslims.

Because Islam and Christianity hold certain tenets in common, but differ markedly in others, we purpose that the study group shall seek to identify and explore the theological issues which are related to effective communication of the Gospel to Muslims. This group will be authorized to produce a comparative study of significant Christian-Islamic theological vocabulary, and follow this with a manual of the actual bridges and blocks in Christian witness to Islam. The bridges would include such concepts as God, Creation, Prophets, Sacrifice, the Word of God, the Judgment, Satan, Heaven and Hell, the Virgin Birth, Healing Ministry, and the Second Coming of Christ, the felt needs of men and women and the Lord's Prayer. The blocks would include such controversial issues as man's need of Redemption, the essentiality of the Cross, the Substitutionary Atonement, the Trinity, the Incarnation, religious terminology, the meaning of history and its relation to politics, the integrity of the Bible, Islamic family and social pressures, and the reasons behind the all too frequent failure of the church to express true Christian community. Since these studies will be greatly enriched if accompanied by an exploration into the reasons behind the variations in Muslim response to the Christian message, we encourage the center to undertake this research assignment. Particular attention shall be given to their relation to those significant points of contact with popular Islam at the primary level of experience.

This group shall conduct a feasibility study to ascertain the type of publication needed to share its findings among Christians worldwide.

g.   Muslims in North America

Recognizing the growing presence of Muslims throughout Canada and the United States, we propose that the center shall seek to create an in-depth demographic profile of their distribution, and make a comprehensive study of what Christian work is being done among them. All this shall be undertaken with a view to planning strategies for their evangelization. Not only do we pray that convert churches shall emerge in Muslim communities; our concern is also that American churches shall be so informed that they will increasingly take this responsibility on themselves in a meaningful and effective fashion, incorporating into their congregations those converts who desire to worship with them.

(*Note*: Many other practical suggestions were made during the closing hours of the conference. All were carefully recorded and are being referred to the continuation committee for attention. They range from missionary and lay leadership training to matters pertaining to the task of evangelism among black Muslims, immigrants, and international students.)

CONCLUSION: HOPE IN GOD

At Glen Eyrie we sensed anew our individual and collective responsibility to devote heart, soul, conscience and resources to the task of making Jesus Christ known to the many diverse peoples of the Muslim world. Before we parted, we gathered at his table to worship and to receive grace for the many demands he will place upon us in the days ahead. We reaffirmed that he is both the light of the world and the hope of the world. He is Jesus Christ, the Lord over all, the one who makes all things new. It is he who encourages us to move forward with hope.

We hope in the forgiveness of God who is the best of forgivers. We know that he has put away our past failures through his suffering love in Jesus Christ. And it is in Christ, the one who has borne our infirmities, that we presume to make our new start.

We also have hope for the forgiveness of our Muslim friends and neighbors, that they will indeed not count our failures against us, but will give us their friendship and love.

And for the future we place all our hope in the Spirit and power of God. It is his salvation that he desires to communicate through us, and therefore it is he who will enable us: to witness powerfully and understandingly; to serve with compassion; to live neighborly and in every way to share with Muslims the boundless grace of God.

We ask him to help us to be the true servants of his love throughout the Muslim world.

We cannot but supplement the dominant concern of Lausanne 1974 with the thrust of Glen Eyrie 1978:

'Let the earth hear his voice'
and
'May Muslims feel his touch.'

POSTSCRIPT

The Gospel and Islam, edited by Don M. McCurry, is a massive 638-page compendium which contains the papers and research of the North American Conference on Muslim Evangelization. It begins with two keynote addresses. The first, by Don McCurry and entitled 'A Time for New Beginnings', emphasizes the need for a greater respect for Islamic cultures and a more culturally sensitive approach to Muslims. The second was given by Stan Mooneyham. Basing himself on the Parable of the Sower, he spoke about 'the quality of the soil' (degrees of Muslim responsiveness), 'the attitude of the sower' (deficiencies in missionary understanding, communication and love) and 'the prospects for the harvest' (grounds for optimism). The text of these two addresses is followed by the Conference Report drawn up by Arthur Glasser.

The rest of the compendium consists of the forty foundation papers, together with a summary of participants' responses to each and of the author's rejoinders to these. In this way the reader is enabled to follow the progress of the debate. The forty papers are grouped under three headings which might be called principles, facts and methods. The first ten papers explore the basic principles of Christian witness to Muslims — incarnational, and cross-cultural. The next sixteen supply facts and figures of the comparative status of Christianity and Islam in different countries and regions, and the current status of Christian resources. The final fourteen papers describe priorities and methods in Muslim evangelization.

The Gospel and Islam was published by MARC in 1979; an abridged edition also appeared in 1984.

5

— 1980 —

An Evangelical Commitment to Simple Lifestyle

♦♦♦♦♦

The International Consultation on Simple Lifestyle,
High Leigh, nr. Hoddesdon, Hertfordshire, England,
17–21 March 1980

EXPLANATORY PREFACE

'An Evangelical Commitment to Simple Lifestyle' was written and endorsed by the International Consultation on Simple Lifestyle, held at Hoddesdon, England, from March 17 to 21, 1980. The Consultation was sponsored by the Lausanne Committee for World Evangelization's Theology and Education Working Group and the World Evangelical Fellowship's Theological Commission's Unit on Ethics and Society.

—An Evangelical Commitment to Simple Lifestyle—

CONTENTS

INTRODUCTION

'Life' and 'lifestyle' obviously belong together and cannot be separated. All Christians claim to have received a new life from Jesus Christ. What lifestyle, then, is appropriate for them? If the life is new, the lifestyle should be new also. But what are to be its characteristics? In particular, how is it to be distinguished from the lifestyle of those who make no Christian profession? And how should it reflect the challenges of the contemporary world — its alienation both from God and from the earth's resources which he created for the enjoyment of all?

It was such questions as these which led the participants in the Lausanne Congress on World Evangelization (1974) to include in paragraph 9 of their Covenant these sentences:

'*All us us are shocked by the poverty of millions and disturbed by the injustices which cause it. Those of us who live in affluent circumstances accept our duty to develop a simple lifestyle in order to contribute more generously to both relief and evangelism.*'

These expressions have been much debated, and it became clear that their implications needed to be carefully examined.

So the Theology and Education Group of the Lausanne Committee for World Evangelization and the Unit on Ethics and Society of the World Evangelical Fellowship's Theological Commission agreed to co-sponsor a two-year process of study, culminating in an international gathering. Local groups met in 15 countries. Regional conferences were arranged in India, Ireland and the United States. Then from March 17 to 21, 1980, at High Leigh Conference Centre (about 17 miles north of London, England) an International Consultation on Simple Lifestyle was convened. It brought together 85 evangelical leaders from 27 countries.

Our purpose was to study simple living in relation to evangelism, relief and justice, since all three are mentioned in the Lausanne Covenant's sentences on simple lifestyle. Our perspective was, on the one hand, the teaching of the Bible; and, on the other, the suffering world — that is, the billions of men, women and children who, though made in his image and the objects of his love, are either unevangelized or oppressed or both, being destitute of the Gospel of salvation and of the basic necessities of human life.

During the four days of the consultation we lived, worshiped and prayed together; we studied the Scriptures together; we listened to background papers (to be published in a book) and heard some moving testimonies; we struggled to relate the theological and economic issues to one another; we debated these in both plenary sessions and small groups; we laughed and cried and repented and made resolutions. Although at the beginning we sensed some tension between representatives of the First and Third Worlds, yet by the end the Holy Spirit of unity had brought us into a new solidarity of mutual respect and love.

Above all, we tried to expose ourselves with honesty to the challenges of both the Word of God and the world of need, in order to discern God's will and seek his grace to do it. In this process our minds were stretched, our consciences pricked, our hearts stirred and our wills strengthened.

'An Evangelical Commitment to Simple Lifestyle' (whose original text was drafted out of the papers and the discussion) was carefully studied during three exacting hours of plenary debate, and numerous alterations were agreed upon. The revised text was re-submitted at a final plenary session and, with a few further and minor amendments, was approved. None of the participants was asked to subscribe to it by personal signature, but it carries the substantial endorsement of the Consultation. As individuals, too, we all made our own private commitment, in response to its call.

We recognize that others have been discussing this topic for several years, and we are ashamed that we have lagged behind them. We have no wish, therefore, to claim too much for our Consultation or commitment. Nor have we any grounds for boasting. Yet for us the week was historic and transforming. So we send this statement on its way for the study of individuals, groups and churches, with the earnest hope and prayer that large numbers of Christians will be moved, as we have been, to resolve, commitment and action.

John Stott
Chairman
Theology and
Education Working Group
Lausanne Committee for
World Evangelization

Ronald J. Sider
Convenor
Unit on Ethics and Society
Theological Commission of the
World Evangelical Fellowship

October, 1980

Quotations are from the New International Version.

Preamble

For four days we have been together, 80 Christians from 27 countries, to consider the resolve expressed in the Lausanne Covenant (1974) to 'develop a simple lifestyle'. We have tried to listen to the voice of God, through the pages of the Bible, through the cries of the hungry poor, and through each other. And we believe that God has spoken to us.

We thank God for his great salvation through Jesus Christ, for his revelation in Scripture which is a light for our path, and for the Holy Spirit's power to make us witnesses and servants in the world.

We are disturbed by the injustice of the world, concerned for its victims, and moved to repentance for our complicity in it. We have also been stirred to fresh resolves, which we have expressed in this Commitment.

1. Creation

We worship God as the Creator of all things, and we celebrate the goodness of his creation. In his generosity he has given us everything to enjoy, and we receive it from his hands with humble thanksgiving (1 Tim. 4:4; 6:17). God's creation is marked by rich abundance and diversity, and he intends its resources to be husbanded and shared for the benefit of all.

We therefore denounce environmental destruction, wastefulness and hoarding. We deplore the misery of the poor who suffer as a result of these evils. We also disagree with the drabness of the ascetic. For all these deny the Creator's goodness and reflect the tragedy of the fall. We recognize our own involvement in them, and we repent.

2. Stewardship

When God made man, male and female, in his own image, he gave them dominion over the earth (Gen. 1:26–28). He made them stewards of its resources, and they became responsible to him as Creator, to the earth which they were to develop, and to their fellow human beings with whom they were to share its riches. So fundamental are these truths that authentic human fulfilment depends on a right relationship to God, neighbor, and the earth with all its resources. People's humanity is diminished if they have no just share in those resources.

By unfaithful stewardship, in which we fail to conserve the earth's finite resources, to develop them fully, or to distribute them justly, we both disobey God and alienate people from his purpose for them. We are determined, therefore, to honor God as the owner of all things, to remember that we are stewards and not proprietors of any land or property that we may have, to use them in the service of others, and to seek justice with the poor who are exploited and powerless to defend themselves.

We look forward to 'the restoration of all things' at Christ's return (Acts 3:21). At that time our full humanness will be restored; so we must promote human dignity today.

3. Poverty and Wealth

We affirm that involuntary poverty is an offence against the goodness of God. It is related in the Bible to powerlessness, for the poor cannot protect themselves. God's call to rulers is to use their power to defend the poor, not to exploit them. The church must stand with God and the poor against injustice, suffer with them, and call on rulers to fulfil their God-appointed role.

We have struggled to open our minds and hearts to the uncomfortable words of Jesus about wealth. 'Beware of covetousness', he said, and 'a person's life does not consist in the abundance of his possessions' (Luke 12:15). We have listened to his warnings about the dangers of riches. For wealth brings worry, vanity and false security, the oppression of the weak and indifference to the sufferings of the needy. So it is hard for a rich person to enter the kingdom of heaven (Matt. 19:23), and the greedy will be excluded from it. The kingdom is a free gift offered to all, but it is especially good news for the poor because they benefit most from the changes it brings.

We believe that Jesus still calls some people (perhaps even us) to follow him in a lifestyle of total, voluntary poverty. He calls all his followers to an inner freedom from the seduction of riches (for it is impossible to serve God and money) and to sacrificial generosity ('to be rich in good works, to be generous and ready to share' — 1 Tim 6:18). Indeed, the motivation and model for Christian generosity are nothing less than the example of Jesus Christ himself, who, though rich, became poor that through his poverty we might become rich (2 Cor. 8:9). It was a costly, purposeful self-sacrifice; we mean to seek his grace to follow him. We resolve to get to know poor and oppressed people, to learn issues of injustice from them, to seek to relieve their suffering, and to include them regularly in our prayers.

4. The New Community

We rejoice that the church is the new community of the new age, whose members enjoy a new life and a new lifestyle. The earliest Christian church, constituted in Jerusalem on the Day of Pentecost, was characterized by a quality of fellowship unknown before. Those Spirit-filled believers loved one another to such an extent that they sold and shared their possessions. Although their selling and giving were voluntary, and some private property was retained (Acts 5:4), it was made subservient to the needs of the community. 'None of them said that anything he had was his own' (Acts 4: 32). That is, they were free from the selfish assertion of proprietary rights. And as a result of their transformed economic relationships, 'there was not a needy person among them' (Acts 4:34).

This principle of generous and sacrificial sharing, expressed in holding ourselves and our goods available for people in need, is an indispensable characteristic of every Spirit-filled church. So those of us who are affluent, in any part of the world, are determined to do more to relieve the needs of less privileged believers. Otherwise, we shall be like those rich Christians in Corinth who ate and drank too much while their poor brothers and sisters were left hungry, and we shall deserve the stinging rebuke Paul gave them for despising God's church and desecrating Christ's body (1 Cor. 11:20–24). Instead, we determine to resemble them at a later stage when Paul urged them out of their abundance to give to the impoverished Christians of Judea 'that there may be equality' (2 Cor. 8:10–15). It was a beautiful demonstration of caring love and of Gentile-Jewish solidarity in Christ.

In this same spirit, we must seek ways to transact the church's corporate business together with minimum expenditure on travel, food and accommodation. We call on churches and para-church agencies in their planning to be acutely aware of the need for integrity in corporate lifestyle and witness.

Christ calls us to be the world's salt and light, in order to hinder its social decay and illumine its darkness. But our light must shine and our salt must retain its saltness. It is when the new community is most obviously distinct from the world — in its values, standards and lifestyle — that it presents the world with a radically attractive alternative and so exercises its greatest influence for Christ. We commit ourselves to pray and work for the renewal of our churches.

5. Personal Lifestyle

Jesus our Lord summons us to holiness, humility, simplicity and contentment. He also promises us his rest. We confess, however, that we have often allowed unholy desires to disturb our inner tranquillity. So without the constant renewal of Christ's peace in our hearts, our emphasis on simple living will be one-sided.

Our Christian obedience demands a simple lifestyle, irrespective of the needs of others. Nevertheless, the fact that 800 million people are destitute and that about 10,000 die of starvation every day make any other lifestyle indefensible.

While some of us have been called to live among the poor, and others to open our homes to the needy, all of us are determined to develop a simpler lifestyle. We intend to re-examine our income and expenditure, in order to manage on less and give away more. We lay down no rules or regulations, for either ourselves or others. Yet we resolve to renounce waste and oppose extravagance in personal living, clothing and housing, travel and church building. We also accept the distinction between necessities and luxuries, creative hobbies and empty status symbols, modesty and vanity, occasional celebrations and normal routine, between the service of God and slavery to fashion. Where to draw the line requires conscientious thought and decision by us, together with members of our families. Those of us who belong to the west need the help of our Third World brothers and sisters in evaluating our standards of spending. Those of us who live in the Third World acknowledge that we too are exposed to the temptation to covetousness. So we need each other's understanding, encouragement and prayers.

6. International Development

We echo the words of the Lausanne Covenant: 'We are shocked by the poverty of millions, and disturbed by the injustices which cause it'. One quarter of the world's population enjoys unparalleled prosperity, while another quarter endures grinding poverty. This gross disparity is an intolerable injustice; we refuse to acquiesce in it. The call for a New International Economic Order expresses the justified frustration of the Third World.

We have come to understand more clearly the connection between resources, income and consumption: people often starve because they cannot afford to buy food, because they have no income, because they have no opportunity to produce, and because they have no access to power. We therefore applaud the growing emphasis of Christian agencies on development rather than aid. For the transfer of personnel and appropriate technology can enable people to make good use of their own resources, while at the same time respecting their dignity. We resolve to contribute more generously to human development projects. Where people's lives are at stake, there should never be a shortage of funds.

But the action of governments is essential. Those of us who live in the affluent nations are ashamed that our governments have mostly failed to meet their targets for official development assistance, to maintain emergency food stocks or to liberalize their trade policy.

We have come to believe that in many cases multi-national corporations reduce local initiative in the countries where they work, and tend to oppose any fundamental change in government. We are convinced that they should become more subject to controls and more accountable.

7. Justice and Politics

We are also convinced that the present situation of social injustice is so abhorrent to God that a large measure of change is necessary. Not that we believe in an earthly utopia. But neither are we pessimists. Change can come, although not through commitment to simple lifestyle or human development projects alone.

Poverty and excessive wealth, militarism and the arms industry, and the unjust distribution of capital, land and resources are issues of power and powerlessness. Without a shift of power through structural change these problems cannot be solved.

The Christian church, along with the rest of society, is inevitably involved in politics, which is 'the art of living in community'. Servants of Christ must express his lordship in their political, social and economic commitments and their love for their neighbors by taking part in the political process. How, then, can we contribute to change?

First, we will pray for peace and justice, as God commands. Secondly, we will seek to educate Christian people in the moral and political issues involved, and so clarify their vision and raise their expectations. Thirdly, we will take action. Some Christians are called to special tasks in government, economics or development. All Christians must participate in the active struggle to create a just and responsible society. In some situations obedience to God demands resistance to an unjust established order. Fourthly, we must be ready to suffer. As followers of Jesus, the Suffering Servant, we know that service always involves suffering.

While personal commitment to change our lifestyle without political action to change systems of injustice lacks effectiveness, political action without personal commitment lacks integrity.

8. Evangelism

We are deeply concerned for the vast millions of unevangelized people in the world. Nothing that has been said about lifestyle or justice diminishes the urgency of developing evangelistic strategies appropriate to different cultural environments. We must not cease to proclaim Christ as Savior and Lord throughout the world. The church is not yet taking seriously its commission to be his witnesses 'to the ends of the earth' (Acts 1:8).

So the call to a responsible lifestyle must not be divorced from the call to responsible witness. For the credibility of our message is seriously diminished whenever we contradict it by our lives. It is impossible with integrity to proclaim Christ's salvation if he has evidently not saved us from greed, or his lordship if we are not good stewards of our possessions, or his love if we close our hearts against the needy. When Christians care for each other and for the deprived, Jesus Christ becomes more visibly attractive.

In contrast to this, the affluent lifestyle of some western evangelists when they visit the Third World is understandably offensive to many.

We believe that simple living by Christians generally would release considerable resources, finance and personnel for evangelism as well as for development. So by our commitment to a simple lifestyle we recommit ourselves wholeheartedly to world evangelization.

9. The Lord's Return

The Old Testament prophets both denounced the idolatries and injustices of God's people and warned of his coming judgment. Similar denunciations and warnings are found in the New Testament. The Lord Jesus is coming back soon to judge, to save and to reign. His judgment will fall upon the greedy (who are idolaters) and upon all oppressors. For on that day the King will sit upon his throne and separate the saved from the lost. Those who have ministered to him by ministering to one of the least of his needy brothers and sisters will be saved, for the reality of saving faith is exhibited in serving love. But those who are persistently indifferent to the plight of the needy, and so to Christ in them, will be irretrievably lost (Matt. 25: 31–46). All of us need to hear again this solemn warning of Jesus, and resolve afresh to serve him in the deprived. We therefore call on our fellow Christians everywhere to do the same.

Our Resolve

So then, having been freed by the sacrifice of our Lord Jesus Christ, in obedience to his call, in heartfelt compassion for the poor, in concern for evangelism, development and justice, and in solemn anticipation of the day of judgment, we humbly commit ourselves to develop a just and simple lifestyle, to support one another in it, and to encourage others to join us in this commitment.

We know that we shall need time to work out its implications and that the task will not be easy. May Almighty God give us his grace to be faithful! Amen.

APPENDIX A

In Attendance

Those attending the consultation were divided into three categories, 'participants,' 'consultants,' and 'visitors.' The 'participants' were those who were either signatories of the Lausanne Covenant or persons fully committed to its framework and understanding of mission. 'Consultants' were persons invited because they had some special contribution to make to the meeting. They were in general sympathy with the Lausanne Covenant. The one or two 'visitors' were persons who, having read the Covenant, were willing to take part constructively in a consultation which was committed to it.

In listing them below, however, we have placed them in alphabetical order and have not felt it necessary to indicate to which category each belonged.

Tokunboh Adeyemo, Nigeria/Kenya
John F. Alexander, U.S.A.
Pedro Arana, Peru
Ramez Atallah, Egypt/Canada
Jorge Atiencia, Colombia
Kwame Bediako, Ghana
Ulrich Betz, West Germany
Wayne Bragg, U.S.A.

Robinson Cavalcanti, Brazil
Donald Cameron, Australia
John Capon, England
Mark Cerbone, U.S.A.
Harvie Conn, U.S.A.
Donald Dayton, U.S.A.
Robert DeMoss, U.S.A.
Oeistein de Presno, Norway

Linda Doll, U.S.A.
Ron Elsdon, Ireland
Leif Engedal, Norway
Rob von Essen, Holland
Richard Foster, U.S.A.
John Gladwin, England
Jorgen Glenthoj, Denmark
J. van der Graff, Holland
Paul Hampsch, U.S.A.
Donald Hay, England
Horst-Klaus Hofmann, West Germany
Robert Hughes, U.S.A.
Simon Ibrahim, Nigeria
Neuza Itioka, Brazil
Arthur Johnston, U.S.A.
L. de Jong, Holland
Pippa Julings, England
Sione Kami, New Guinea
Israel Katoke, Tanzania
Graham Kerr, U.S.A.
Andrew Kirk, England
Alan Kreider, U.S.A./England
Daniel Lam, Hong Kong/England
Fritz Lampartner, West Germany
Gregorio Landero, Colombia
Daryl LaRusso, U.S.A.
Barnabas Lee, Korea
Magnus Malm, Sweden
Vishal Mangalwadi, India
Ted Martin, Jr., U.S.A.
Tad Maruyama, Japan
Charles Massey, U.S.A.
Bruce McConchie, Australia
Peter Meadows, England

Karl-Heinz Michel, West Germany
Alex and John Mitchell, England
Nobumasa Mitsuhashi, Japan
George Monsma, Jr., U.S.A.
B. Howard Mudditt, England
Jeremy Mudditt, England
Alan Nichols, Australia
Lennart Nordin, Sweden
Gottfried Osei-Mensah, Ghana/Kenya
René Padilla, Argentina
Clark Pinnock, Canada
Tacito Pinto, Brazil/Italy
M. G. Reuben, India
D. John Richard, India
Bong Rin Ro, Taiwan
Colleen Samuel, India
Vinay Samuel, India
Waldron Scott, U.S.A.
Ronald Sider, U.S.A.
Kevin Smith, Australia
John Stott, England
Gordon Strachan, Scotland
Morris Stuart, England/Australia
Chris Sugden, England/India
Dick Van Halsema, U.S.A.
J. A. Emerson Vermaat, Holland
Jim Wardwell, U.S.A.
David Watson, England
Dolphus Weary, U.S.A.
Waldo Werning, U.S.A.
Derek Williams, England
David Wong, Singapore
Florence Yeboah, Ghana
Rolf Zwick, West Germany

APPENDIX B

The Papers and their Writers

Day 1   (1)   *Living More Simply for Evangelism and Justice* — Ronald J. Sider

      (2)   *Simple Lifestyle and Evangelism* — David Watson

Day 2   (3)   *A Just and Responsible Lifestyle: An Old Testament Perspective* — Vinay K. Samuel & Christopher Sugden

      (4)   *New Testament Perspectives on Simple Lifestyle* — C. René Padilla

Day 3   (5) *The International Socio-Economic-Political Order and Our Lifestyles* — Donald A. Hay

Day 4   (6) *Simple Lifestyle from the Perspective of Church History* — Tadatake Maruyama

       (7) *The Church as a New Community which Fosters a Simple Lifestyle* — Gottfried Osei-Mensah

The Planning Committee

Co-ordinator
Ronald J. Sider

Ramez Atallah
Saphir Athyal
David J. Bosch
Frederick Catherwood
P. T. Chandapilla
Harvie Conn
Leighton Ford
Donald E. Hoke
Israel Katoke

Assistant Co-ordinator
Mark Cerbone

Andrew Kirk
Festo Kivengere
Frederick Catherwood
Samuel Moffett
George Monsma, Jr.
René Padilla
Russ Reid
John Stott

APPENDIX C

Bibliography

For all the papers and testimonies from the Consultation itself, see Ronald J. Sider, ed., *Lifestyle in the Eighties: An Evangelical Commitment to Simple Lifestyle* (London: Paternoster, 1982.)

Barnet, Richard, *The Lean Years: Politics in the Age of Scarcity.* New York: Simon and Schuster, 1980.

Brandt, Willy, *et al., North-South: A Program For Survival.* London: Pan Books, 1980.

Eller, Vernard, *The Simple Life: The Christian Stance Toward Possessions.* Grand Rapids: Eerdmans, 1973.

Elsdon, Ronald, *Bent World.* Downers Grove: Intervarsity, 1981.

Foster, Richard, *The Freedom of Simplicity*, New York: Harper, 1981.

Johnston, Arthur, *The Battle for World Evangelism.* Wheaton: Tyndale House, 1978.

Mooneyham, W. Stanley, *What Do You Say to a Hungry World?* Waco, Texas: Word Books, 1975.

Nelson, Jack, *Hunger for Justice: The Politics of Food and Faith*. Mary-Knoll, NY: Orbis Books, 1980.

Ramientos, Neve, *Christian Social Concern: The Mission of the Church in Asia*. (Asian Perspective No. #18; Asia Theol. Ass., P.O. Box #73 — Ila Shihlin, Taipei, Taiwan.)

Schumacher, E. F., *Small is Beautiful: Economics as if People Mattered*. New York: Harper, 1973.

Scott, Waldron, *Bring Forth Justice*. Grand Rapids: Eerdmans, 1980.

Sider, Ronald J., *Cry Justice: The Bible on Hunger and Poverty*. New York: Paulist Press, 1980.

Sider, Ronald J., ed. *Living More Simply: Biblical principles and Practical Models*. Downers Grove: Intervarsity, 1980.

Sider, Ronald J., *Rich Christians in an Age of Hunger: A Biblical Study*. Downers Grove: Intervarsity, 1977.

Stott, John,. *Christian Counter-Culture: The Message of the Sermon on the Mount*. Downers Grove: Intervarsity Press, 1978.

Taylor, John V., *Enough is Enough*. London: SCM Press, 1975.

White, John, *The Golden Cow: Materialism in the Twentieth Century Church*. Downers Grove: Intervarsity, 1979.

Ziesler, J. A., *Christian Asceticism*. Grand Rapids: Eerdmans, 1973.

POSTSCRIPT

A 'Commentary and Exposition' of *An Evangelical Commitment to Simple Lifestyle* was written, at the request of John Stott and Ronald Sider, by Alan Nichols, who at that time was Executive Director of the Mission of St. James and St. John, an Anglican family welfare agency in Melbourne, Australia. His exposition was published as LOP 20 and is still available.

Lifestyle in the Eighties: 'an evangelical commitment to Simple Lifestyle', edited by Ronald Sider, was published by Paternoster Press in 1982. It is divided into four sections:-

Section I gives the full text of the Commitment.

Section II contains the seven 'Background Papers', which develop the concept of a simple lifestyle in relation to evangelism and justice, Old and New Testaments, economics and church history, and the life of God's new community.

Section III consists of 'Testimonies' by seven Christian leaders from different parts of the world, who had personally struggled to develop a simple lifestyle.

In Section IV there are fifteen Bible studies which had been prepared by Harvie Conn. Each begins with a cluster of texts, and is followed by a brief comment and some challenging questions.

6

— 1980 —

The Thailand Statement

◆◆◆◆◆

The Consultation on World Evangelization,
Pattaya, Thailand, 16–27 June 1980

EXPLANATORY PREFACE

LCWE's 'Consultation on World Evangelization' (COWE), under the title 'How Shall They Hear?', was held in Pattaya, Thailand, from 16th to 27th June 1980. The chairman was Leighton Ford and the director David Howard. Over 800 people attended from a wide diversity of cultural backgrounds.

For five of its ten days COWE divided into seventeen 'mini-consultations', each of which concentrated on Christian witness to a particular people or group. Each mini-consultation's report was published as a Lausanne Occasional Paper (LOPs 5–19 and 22–23). A list of these is given on page 163.

—The Thailand Statement—

CONTENTS

INTRODUCTION

We have gathered at Pattaya, Thailand, for the Consultation on World Evangelization, over 800 Christians from a wide diversity of backgrounds, nations and cultures.

We have spent 10 days together in a fellowship of study, praise and prayer. We have celebrated God's great love for us and for all humanity. We have considered before him and under his Word the command of our Lord Jesus Christ to proclaim the Gospel to all people on earth. We have become freshly burdened by the vast numbers who have never heard the good news of Christ and are lost without him. We have been made ashamed of our lack of vision and zeal, and of our failure to live out the Gospel in its fulness, for these things have lessened our obedience and compromised our witness. We have noted that there are hard places where opposition is strong and evangelism is difficult. At the same time, we have rejoiced to hear how God is at work in his world, and how he is making many peoples receptive to his Word.

Our consultation has been held in the ancient Kingdom of Thailand, and we are grateful for the welcome which we have received from the hospitable Thai people. In particular, we have enjoyed fellowship with Thai church leaders, and have sought to share the concern of their hearts that, after more than 150 years of Protestant missions, considerably less than 1% of their country's 46 million people confess Jesus Christ as Saviour and Lord.

Close by, on the country's eastern border, are hundreds of thousands of refugees from neighbouring countries. They symbolize both the political ferment of the world and the tragic suffering of millions of human beings. We denounce the injustice of which they are victims, and have struggled to understand and feel their plight. We thank God for those Christians who have been among the first to go to their aid. We thank him also that growing numbers of them, uprooted from their ancestral homes and cultural inheritance, are finding in Jesus Christ a new security and a new life. We have made a solemn resolution to involve ourselves more actively in the relief and rehabilitation of refugees throughout the world.

1. The Mandate for World Evangelization

We believe that there is only one living and true God, the Creator of the universe and the Father of our Lord Jesus Christ; that he has made all men, women and children in his own likeness; that he loves all those whom he has made, although they have rebelled against him and are under his judgment;

and that he longs for their salvation. He sent his Son Jesus Christ to die for sinners and, having raised him from the dead, has given him universal authority, that every knee should bow to him and every tongue confess him Lord. This exalted Jesus now sends us, on whom he has had mercy, into the world as his witnesses and servants.

As his witnesses he has commanded us to proclaim his good news in the power of the Holy Spirit to every person of every culture and nation, and to summon them to repent, to believe and to follow him. This mandate is urgent, for there is no other Saviour but Jesus Christ. It is also binding on all Christian people. As the Lausanne Covenant declares, the evangelistic task 'requires the whole church to take the whole gospel to the whole world' (para. 6).

We are also the servants of Jesus Christ who is himself both 'the servant' and 'the Lord.' He calls us, therefore, not only to obey him as Lord in every area of our lives, but also to serve as he served. We confess that we have not sufficiently followed his example of love in identifying with the poor and hungry, the deprived and the oppressed. Yet all God's people 'should share his concern for justice and reconciliation throughout human society and for the liberation of men from every kind of oppression' (Lausanne Covenant, para. 5).

Although evangelism and social action are not identical, we gladly reaffirm our commitment to both, and we endorse the Lausanne Covenant in its entirety. It remains the basis of our common activity, and nothing it contains is beyond our concern, so long as it is clearly related to world evangelization.

2. The Primacy of Evangelization

The Lausanne Covenant declares that 'in the church's mission of sacrificial service evangelism is primary' (para. 6). This is not to deny that evangelism and social action are integrally related, but rather to acknowledge that of all the tragic needs of human beings none is greater than their alienation from their Creator and the terrible reality of eternal death for those who refuse to repent and believe. If therefore we do not commit ourselves with urgency to the task of evangelization, we are guilty of an inexcusable lack of human compassion.

Some two-thirds of the world's four and a half billion people have had no proper opportunity to receive Christ. We have considered the value of thinking of them not only as individuals but also as 'people groups' who perceive themselves as having an affinity with one another. Many are within easy reach of Christians. Large numbers of these are already Christian in name, yet still need to be evangelized because they have not understood the Gospel or have not responded to it. The great majority of people in the world, however, have no Christian neighbours to share Christ with them. They can therefore be reached only by cross-cultural messengers of the Gospel. We confidently expect that these will increasingly come from all countries, as the Christian mission becomes universalized, and we will work to keep this challenge before the churches.

3. Some Vital Aspects of Evangelization

At Lausanne our theme was 'Let the earth hear his voice'; in Thailand it has been 'How shall they hear?' So we have searched the Scriptures daily in order to learn more about the God who speaks, the message he has spoken, and the people to whom and through whom he speaks.

We have reaffirmed our confidence in the truth and power of God's Word, and our desire to let his voice penetrate our cultural defences. We have recognized the local church as the principal agency for evangelism, whose total membership must therefore be mobilized and trained. We have heard the call to be sensitive to other people's cultural patterns and not to try to impose on them our own. We have also acknowledged the indispensable necessity of the work of the Holy Spirit, and of prayer to the sovereign Lord for boldness to speak for him.

For five of our ten days together we have divided into 17 mini-consultations, all of which have concentrated on how to reach particular peoples for Christ. These mini-consultations have built upon a lengthy study programme in which hundreds of groups throughout the world have been involved. Our purpose has been to consider important issues of theology and methodology, in relation to our approach to different peoples, in order to develop realistic strategies for evangelism.

Many of the reports have called for a change in our personal attitudes. The following four have been particularly emphasized:

The first is *love*. Group after group has asserted that 'we cannot evangelize if we do not love.' We have had to repent of prejudice, disrespect and even hostility towards the very people we want to reach for Christ. We have also resolved to love others as God in Christ has loved us, and to identify with them in their situation as he identified himself with us in ours.

Secondly, *humility*. Our study has led us to confess that other people's resistance to the Gospel has sometimes been our fault. Imperialism, slavery, religious persecution in the name of Christ, racial pride and prejudice (whether anti-black or anti-white, anti-Jewish or anti-Arab, or any other kind), sexual oppression, cultural insensitivity, and indifference to the plight of the needy and the powerless — these are some of the evils which have marred the church's testimony and put stumbling blocks in other people's road to faith. We resolve in future to spread the Gospel with greater humility.

Thirdly, *integrity*. Several groups have written about the character and conduct of the message-bearer. Our witness loses credibility when we contradict it by our life or lifestyle. Our light will shine only when others can see our good works (Matt. 5:16). In a word, if we are to speak of Jesus with integrity, we have to resemble him.

The fourth emphasis has to do with *power*. We know that we are engaged in a spiritual battle with demonic forces. Evangelism often involves a power encounter, and in conversion Jesus Christ demonstrates that he is stronger than the strongest principalities and powers of evil by liberating their victims. Strategy and organization are not enough; we need to pray earnestly for the power of the Holy Spirit. God has not given us a spirit of fear, but of boldness.

4. Cooperation in World Evangelization

We have been deeply concerned during our consultation to strengthen evangelical cooperation in global evangelization, for no single agency could accomplish this enormous task alone.

We joyfully affirm the unity of the body of Christ and acknowledge that we are bound together with one another and with all true believers. While a true unity in Christ is not necessarily incompatible with organizational diversity, we must nevertheless strive for a visible expression of our oneness. This witnesses to Christ's reconciling power and demonstrates our common commitment to serve him. In contrast, competitive programs and needless duplication of effort both waste resources and call into question our profession to be one in Christ. So we pledge ourselves again, in the words of the Lausanne Covenant, 'to seek a deeper unity in truth, worship, holiness and mission' (para. 7).

It is imperative that we work together to fulfil the task of world evangelization. Cooperation must never be sought at the expense of basic biblical teaching, whether doctrinal or ethical. At the same time, disagreement on non-essentials among those equally concerned to submit to Scripture should not prevent cooperation in evangelism. Again, cooperation must never inhibit the exercise of the diverse gifts and ministries which the Holy Spirit gives to the people of God. Nor should the diversity of gifts and ministries be made an excuse for non-cooperation.

Yet obstacles to cooperation remain, which involve genuine problems and complex issues. Some of these reflect either the social, political, geographical and cultural circumstances or the ecclesiastical traditions from which we come. Others reflect tensions between different forms of ministry (e.g., between traditional church structures and those which are not directly accountable to churches) or between different evangelistic strategies and methodologies. These and other tensions are real and must be frankly faced. They do not release us, however, from our responsibility to explore with creativity different levels of cooperation in evangelism. We are determined to work more closely together. The Scripture urges us to 'stand firm in one spirit, with one mind striving side by side for the faith of the gospel' (Phil. 1:27).

We believe that God has given a special role to the Lausanne Committee for World Evangelization to act as a catalyst for world evangelization. We desire therefore to give it a further mandate to stimulate evangelism throughout the world, on the basis of the Lausanne Covenant, and in growing cooperation with others of like mind.

5. Our Commitment to Christ

In the light of his clear command to go and make disciples of all nations, his universal authority and his love for all humanity, we solemnly make the following commitment to Christ, which we shall seek his grace to fulfill:

1. We pledge ourselves to *live* under the lordship of Christ, and to be concerned for his will and his glory, not our own.
2. We pledge ourselves to *work* for the evangelization of the world, and to bear witness by word and deed to Christ and his salvation.
3. We pledge ourselves to *serve* the needy and the oppressed, and in the name of Christ to seek for them relief and justice.
4. We pledge ourselves to *love* all those we are called to serve, even as Christ loved us, and to identify with them in their needs.
5. We pledge ourselves to *pray* for the church and for the world, that Christ will renew his church in order to reach his world.
6. We pledge ourselves to *study* God's Word, to seek Christ in it, and to relate it to ourselves and our contemporaries.
7. We pledge ourselves to *give* with the generosity of Christ, that we may share with others what he has given to us.
8. We pledge ourselves to *go* wherever Christ may send us, and never to settle down so comfortably that we cannot contemplate a move.
9. We pledge ourselves to *labour* to mobilize Christ's people, so that the whole church may take the whole gospel to the whole world.
10. We pledge ourselves to *cooperate* with all who share with us the true Gospel of Christ, in order to reach the unreached peoples of the world.
11. We pledge ourselves to *seek* the power of the Spirit of Christ, that he may fill us and flow through us.
12. We pledge ourselves to *wait* with eagerness for Christ's return, and to be busy in his service until he comes.

We believe that God, who has uniquely exalted his Son Jesus Christ, has led us to make these pledges to him. With hope and prayer we invite all Christ's followers to join us in our commitment, so that we may work together for the evangelization of the world.

POSTSCRIPT

(A)   A List of the 17 Mini-Consultation Reports

The Consultation on World Evangelization (COWE), held at Pattaya in Thailand in June 1980, divided for five of its ten days into seventeen 'mini-consultations'. These focused on how to reach particular peoples for Christ. Each produced a report, which was published as a 'Lausanne Occasional Paper' (LOP).

The major part of each report went through a draft and a revised draft, which involved all members of the mini-consultation concerned. It was also submitted to a wider 'sub-plenary' group for comment. But the responsibility for the final text rests with each mini-consultation and its chairman.

LOP 5   Christian Witness to Refugees
LOP 6   Christian Witness to Chinese People
LOP 7   Christian Witness to the Jewish People
LOP 8   Christian Witness to Secularized People
LOP 9   Christian Witness to Large Cities
LOP 10   Christian Witness to Nominal Christians among Roman Catholics
LOP 11   Christian Witness to New Religious Movements
LOP 12   Christian Witness to Marxists
LOP 13   Christian Witness to Muslims
LOP 14   Christian Witness to Hindus
LOP 15   Christian Witness to Buddhists
LOP 16   Christian Witness to Traditional Religionists of Asia and Oceania
LOP 17   Christian Witness to Traditional Religionists of Latin America and
         the Caribbean
LOP 18   Christian Witness to People of African Traditional Religions
LOP 19   Christian Witness to Nominal Christians among the Orthodox
LOP 22   Christian Witness to the Urban Poor
LOP 23   Christian Witness to Nominal Christians among Protestants

N.B. A compendium, which binds together the 17 mini-consultation reports and is entitled *How Shall They Hear?*, was published by LCWE after the consultation, with a brief foreword by Saphir Athyal, the program chairman. It contains no other material.

(B)   Lausanne Occasional Paper 24

Entitled *Co-operating in World Evangelization*, 'a handbook on Church/ Para-church relationships', this LOP emerged from the discussions during Pattaya 1980 of the International Commission on Evangelical Co-operation.

Keith Price chaired the commission and edited the report. After a theological preamble on biblical incentives and limits to cooperation, and an introduction on the need for open dialogue between church leaders and leaders of para-church agencies, the report concentrates on five major hindrances to cooperation. These are (1) dogmatism about non-essentials, (2) the threat of conflicting authorities, (3) strained relationships, (4) rivalry between ministries, and (5) suspicion about finances.

Two appendices relate to the validity of para-church agencies and the nature of the church. The report concludes with the prayer 'that God will make us neither wall-builders nor empire-builders, but bridge-builders in his great kingdom' (p.82).

(C)   The Plenary Papers

Two main series of addresses were given at COWE, morning and evening, as follows:

Mornings

How shall they hear?	Gottfried Osei–Mensah
The God who speaks:	Gottfried Osei–Mensah
The Word he has spoken:	Saphir Athyal
The Word he has spoken:	Chow Lien Hwa
The People to whom he speaks:	Tom Houston
The People through whom he speaks:	Emilio Antonio Nuñez

Evenings

Opening address:	Leighton Ford
The Place of the Bible in world evangelization:	John Stott
The Place of Communication in world evangelization:	Vigo Sogaard
The Place of the Holy Spirit in world evangelization:	Luis Palau
The Place of the Local Church in world evangelization:	Gordon MacDonald
The Place of Prayer in world evangelization:	John Reid
The Place of Resources in world evangelization:	Chua Wee Hian and Stanley Mooneyham
The Place of Biblical Unity in world evangelization:	John Richard
Closing address:	Billy Graham

7

— 1982 —

The Grand Rapids Report on Evangelism and Social Responsibility: An Evangelical Commitment

⧫⧫⧫⧫⧫

The International Consultation on the Relationship between Evangelism and Social Responsibility, Grand Rapids, Michigan, 19–25 June 1982

EXPLANATORY PREFACE

This Report, *Evangelism and Social Responsibility*, was written during the international Consultation on the Relationship between Evangelism and Social Responsibility, held at Grand Rapids, Michigan, June 19–25, 1982. It was drafted by members of the consultation, the drafting committee being under the chairmanship of the Rev. John Stott, who was also responsible for the final editing. The consultation was sponsored by the Lausanne Committee for World Evangelization and the World Evangelical Fellowship. Its co-chairmen were Gottfried Osei-Mensah and Bong Rin Ro, and its co-ordinator Dick Van Halsema. In arranging for the publication of this report and encouraging the study of it, neither the Lausanne Committee for World Evangelization nor the World Evangelical Fellowship necessarily endorses every opinion expressed in it.

—Evangelism and Social Responsibility—
An Evangelical Commitment

CONTENTS

Evangelicals and evangelism have always been bracketed. So much so that the adjectives 'evangelical' and 'evangelistic' have often been identified in the popular mind. It is not at all surprising, therefore, that whenever evangelicals have become concerned about social issues, some eyebrows have been raised, and questions have been asked whether the cause of the Gospel is not about to be betrayed.

The history of the ecumenical movement has unfortunately strengthened evangelical suspicions of social involvement. Modern ecumenism was born in the missionary enthusiasm — even euphoria — of the 1910 World Missionary Conference in Edinburgh. John Mott, its chairman, described as a 'longstanding reproach' to the church the fact that there were still millions of people who had never heard of Christ. The church must develop a strategic plan, he urged, 'for the evangelization of the whole of this multitude'. From this high point of commitment to world evangelism, however, there seems to have been a steady decline. The convening by evangelicals of the two Congresses on World Evangelization at Berlin in 1966 and at Lausanne in 1974 must unfortunately be understood, at least in part, as a loss of confidence in the World Council of Churches. But then leaders of the World Council have also been justly critical of many of us evangelicals for our lack of social concern.

This polarization became particularly visible in 1980 when the conference *Your Kingdom Come* (sponsored by the WCC's Commission on World Mission and Evangelism) was held in Melbourne in May, and the following month the consultation *How Shall They Hear?* (sponsored by the Lausanne Committee) took place at Pattaya, Thailand. Neither group had intended that these meetings should be juxtaposed in this way, although perhaps it served to highlight the continuing tension. A number of evangelicals attended both conferences and found reasons for hope in both. For a perusal of the documents makes it plain that there was much common ground between them. Nevertheless, the emphasis was different. At Melbourne the necessity of proclamation was clearly recognized, but the cries of the poor, the hungry and the oppressed predominated. At Pattaya also the cries of the needy were heard (one mini-consultation focused on refugees, and another on the urban poor), but the call to proclaim the Gospel to the unevangelized predominated.

This, then, was the historical run-up to the Consultation on the Relationship between Evangelism and Social Responsibility held at Grand Rapids in June 1982. The planning group took great pains to ensure a balanced representation among participants between geographical regions, denominational backgrounds and evangelical viewpoints. It also defined clearly the goals of the consultation. It expressed its resolve to study 'Scripture, history, theology and the contemporary church, and the interaction among them', and its hope and prayer for God's blessing in the following ways:

'1. that we shall come to understand each other better and to appreciate each other's points of view more fully.
2. that we shall reach a greater unity of mind on the relationship between evangelism and social responsibility, not by a superficial semantic consensus but by a real theological agreement according to Scripture.
3. that we shall commit ourselves, and encourage other believers to commit themselves, to a yet more active fulfilment of our evangelistic and social responsibilities.'

In spite of these declared goals, I confess that I arrived in Grand Rapids with a considerable degree of apprehension. The papers and responses, circulated in advance, had not only been critical of each other's positions but even in some cases sharply so. How then could we possibly expect to reach accord? Yet underneath our natural fears there was a confidence that God could unite us, if we humbled ourselves under the authority of his Word. And so it proved. For me it was another and dramatic demonstration of the value of international conferences. When we remain apart from one another, and our only contact with one another is the lobbing of hand grenades across a demilitarized zone, our attitudes inevitably harden and our mental images of each other become stereotyped. But when we meet face to face (or, as our American friends vividly express it, 'eyeball to eyeball'), and listen not only to each other's arguments but to the cherished convictions which lie behind the arguments, then we develop towards one another a new understanding, respect and love. This is not to say that we agree about everything (as our report makes plain), but that our agreements are far greater than our residual differences.

The group entrusted with the task of drafting the report consisted of Gottfried Osei-Mensah from Africa and Bong Rin Ro from Asia (co-chairmen of the consultation), David Wells (USA), Samuel Olson (Latin America) and myself (Europe). Early drafts were approved by the group, and then submitted to plenary sessions throughout the Friday and the Saturday morning of the consultation. The revised draft, incorporating a large number of requested amendments, was re-submitted to participants by mail. A very few minor adjustments have subsequently been made to the text.

As we look back on our Grand Rapids experience, we are profoundly grateful to God for the common mind and heart which he gave us. We commend our Report to the study of individual Christians and of local churches. And we pray that our verbal commitment to the evangelistic and social responsibilities which God has laid upon us will express itself in increasingly practical and dedicated action.

John R. W. Stott
Chairman, Drafting Committee

INTRODUCTION

(a) The Context of the Consultation

Jesus Christ calls all his followers to witness to him in word and deed, that is, to share his good news with others and to serve them according to their needs.

In the Lausanne Covenant, which was adopted at the end of the International Congress on World Evangelization in 1974, paragraph 4 is entitled 'The Nature of Evangelism' and paragraph 5 'Christian Social Responsibility'. But the Covenant leaves these two duties side by side without spelling out their relationship to each other, except to say in paragraph 6 that 'in the church's mission of sacrificial service, evangelism is primary'.

As the years have passed, it has become increasingly necessary to complete Lausanne's unfinished business and to define more clearly what is included in 'social responsibility', whose responsibility it is, and how it relates to evangelism. For many fear that the more we evangelicals are committed to the one, the less we shall be committed to the other; that if we commit ourselves to both, one is bound to suffer; and in particular that a preoccupation with social responsibility will be sure to blunt our evangelistic zeal.

So, in the conviction that evangelical Christians, who seek to live under the lordship of Christ and the authority of Scripture, and who pray to be guided by the Holy Spirit, should not be divided on an issue of such importance, it was decided to call an international consultation to study the matter. Jointly sponsored by the Lausanne Committee for World Evangelization and the World Evangelical Fellowship, the consultation would focus on Scripture, church history, modern theologies and the contemporary church, in order to help participants understand each other better, reach a greater unity of mind, and commit themselves to a yet more active fulfilment of their evangelistic and social responsibilities.

We have not been disappointed. Fifty evangelical leaders from 27 different countries have spent a week together at Grand Rapids, Michigan. Each day began with Bible study and prayer. Eight papers, and the responses to them, have been presented to us. The issues raised by them we have discussed in both small groups and plenary sessions, and we have been encouraged by case studies from several different cultures. Throughout the week, through patient listening to one another, we have grown in mutual understanding and respect. Although our agreement is not total, it is substantial, and we have been given grace to face our disagreements with charity.

This statement is a summary of the consensus which has emerged, but it makes no attempt to conceal our differences. Although participants have not

171

been asked to endorse it individually, they thoroughly scrutinized its first draft and amended it. We now publish it with the desire to share with others the fruits of our discussion and in the hope that they will be stimulated, as we have been, to more conscientious evangelism and social responsibility.

(b)   Scripture and Culture

The stated goals of the consultation indicated that we would focus first and foremost on Holy Scripture. We have been determined, therefore, to let our minds be formed not by any human ideology but by the Word of God.

We have found it a struggle, however. For all of us are to some extent conditioned by the cultural environment in which we live, by our ideological settings and theological traditions, and this tends to determine what we are able to 'see' in Scripture. It is not that God's Word is unclear in itself, nor that its meaning is captive to any culture. The problem lies rather within our minds as we read. The assumptions we bring with us, which are often insufficiently examined and corrected in the light of God's Word, distort our understanding of it. 'Now we see in a mirror dimly' (1 Cor. 13:12).

How else can we explain some of the painful anomalies that soon came to light in our discussion? To give a few examples: we heard of some Christians in a Confucian culture who, because of its assumption of the ultimate harmony of all things, have surrendered their belief in the uniqueness of Christ as Saviour. Under the pressure of religious pluralism, others have fallen into universalism. In some parts of the United States there are churches which still close their doors to blacks, and remain oblivious to the indignities to which discrimination has brought them, while at the same time proclaiming the love of God. In South Africa, social policy and legislation are built on the theory of the inviolable diversity of the races. Many churches, whose members are sincere Christian people, nevertheless share this view of racial irreconcilability, while continuing to preach the good news of reconciliation. In Europe and North America, secularism — which is a child of the Enlightenment — has even invaded the lives of Christians and effectively banished the reality of God from much of what they do.

It is easy to censure fellow believers in distant parts, however, and to occupy ourselves with removing splinters from their eyes while failing to perceive the logs in our own. It has become apparent during our consultation that those of us who live in affluence do not feel the pain and humiliation of poverty as readily as do those who live among the poor. To the former, social responsibility may remain a topic for academic debate; to the latter, it is a self-evident Christian obligation. Yet moral blind spots are not peculiar to white or black, affluent or poor, north or south. They are a symptom of that fall in which we have all participated. It is our sin, as it comes to expression in our various cultural assumptions and tries to find justification in them, which often blinds our eyes to what God wants us to see in his Word. An acknowledgement of this tragic fact at the beginning of our consultation challenged us to listen all the more attentively to one another and to God's Word.

1   A CALL TO WORSHIP AND THANKSGIVING

God created and redeemed our world in order to reveal his infinite majesty and his eternal love. Therefore, the primary sin is to refuse to honour him as God or to give him thanks (Rom. 1:21), while the supreme duty of his redeemed people is to worship him in humble praise and obedience. 'We love, because he first loved us' (1 John 4:19).

From this adoring and loving encounter with God, there immediately flows a desire to share his love with our fellow human beings, both by telling them how God in Christ has loved them and by serving them in deeds of mercy and justice.

Only if they are rooted in a vertical relationship to God in worship can the church's two ministries of *kerygma* (proclamation) and *diakonia* (service) be held in proper balance and tension. Only in this way, too, can evangelism and social responsibility be kept from degenerating into merely human activity and even propaganda. The mission of any church can fall into this trap.

It is therefore urgent to heed the pre-eminent call to worship and thanksgiving.

2   A CALL TO WORLD EVANGELIZATION

(a)   Contemporary Need

When we met at Lausanne in 1974, we calculated that more than 2,700 million people were still unevangelized. Now, eight years later, we believe that the number has risen to three billion, and that this comprises many thousands of people groups. We cannot think of them as statistics, however. They are human beings like ourselves. Yet, though created by God like God and for God, they are now living without God. The tragedy of this is painful, and the task of overcoming it is enormous. It calls for concerted prayer and evangelism on an unprecedented scale.

(b)   A Definition

But what is evangelism? This is the definition given in the Lausanne Covenant (para. 4):

> To evangelize is to spread the good news that Jesus Christ died for our sins and was raised from the dead according to the Scriptures, and that as the reigning Lord he now offers the forgiveness of sins and the liberating gift of the Spirit to all who repent and believe. Our Christian presence in the world is indispensable to evangelism, and so is that kind of dialogue whose purpose is to listen sensitively in order to understand. But evangelism itself is the proclamation of the historical, biblical Christ as Savior and Lord, with a view to persuading people to come to him personally and so be reconciled to God. In issuing the gospel invitation we have no liberty to conceal the cost of discipleship. Jesus still calls all who would follow him to deny themselves, take up their cross, and identify themselves with his new community. The results of evangelism include obedience to Christ, incorporation into his church and responsible service in the world.

We heartily endorse this statement, and we wish to emphasize that reconciliation to God lies at the very heart of the good news. Our only criticism is that the statement sounds somewhat impersonal, since neither the evangelist nor the evangelized is characterized in it as a person of flesh and blood. Yet that is what they both are, and evangelism involves a personal encounter between them. The most essential qualities of gospel messengers are loyalty to the biblical Gospel and personal authenticity. They must embody the good news they proclaim. Few things repel people more than hypocrisy, and few things attract them more than integrity.

As for the persons who hear the Gospel, we acknowledge the need to approach them with great sensitivity. Many will already have been convicted of their sin and guilt, and it will be possible at once to share with them the good news of forgiveness. Others will be oppressed by a different sense of alienation. So we shall have to begin where they are, with their 'felt needs', and then lead them to where they have to come, that is, to Christ as Saviour from their deepest need — their sinful separation from God.

(c) Motivation for Evangelism

There are many incentives to evangelism. To begin with, there is simple obedience to the Great Commission, and to the Lord of the Great Commission, to whom all authority has been given (Matt. 28:18–20). Then there is the terrible knowledge we have that human beings without Christ are lost or 'perishing' (e.g., John 3:16; I Cor. 1:18), and our earnest desire in love to reach them with the Gospel before it is too late. Another powerful motive is zeal or 'jealousy' for the glory of Christ, whom God has super-exalted in order that every knee should bow to him and every tongue confess him Lord (Phil. 2:9–11).

Yet we believe that the most basic of all motives lies in the very nature of God himself, and in his saving work by which he revealed himself. We do not exaggerate when we affirm that the living God is a missionary God. He created all humankind, is 'the God of the spirits of all flesh', and when calling Abraham promised through his posterity to bless 'all the families of the earth'.

Next, Jesus Christ during his public ministry sent his disciples to 'the lost sheep of the house of Israel', and subsequently he commissioned them to go and make disciples of all the nations. Between these two missions lay his death and resurrection. He died on the cross for the sins of the world, and was raised and exalted to be Lord. The church's universal mission derives from Christ's universal authority.

Thirdly, the Holy Spirit is a missionary Spirit, and Pentecost was a missionary event. He gave his people power for witness, as Jesus promised, and thrust them out to the ends of the earth, as Jesus foretold (Acts 1:8).

This Trinitarian basis for mission is primary. It is the missionary heart of God himself, Father, Son and Holy Spirit. If he yearns in his love for his lost world, we his people must share his yearning. Commitment to world mission is unavoidable, and indifference to it inexcusable.

3 A CALL TO SOCIAL RESPONSIBILITY

(a) Contemporary Need

We are appalled to know that about 800 million people, or one-fifth of the human race, are destitute, lacking the basic necessities for survival, and that thousands of them die of starvation every day. Many more millions are without adequate shelter and clothing, without clean water and health care, without opportunities for education and employment, and are condemned to eke out a miserable existence without the possibility of self-improvement for themselves or their families. They can only be described as 'oppressed' by the gross economic inequality from which they suffer and the diverse economic systems which cause and perpetuate it.

The oppression of others is political. They are denied fundamental human rights by totalitarian regimes of the extreme left or right, while if they protest they are imprisoned without trial, tortured, and killed. Yet others suffer discrimination on account of their race or sex. And all of us are oppressed by global problems which seem to defy solution — conditions of over-population and famine, the exploitation of non-renewable resources of energy, the spoliation of the environment, community violence, war, and the ever-present threat of a nuclear holocaust.

All these are rooted in the profound sinfulness of humankind, and they demand from the people of God a radical response of compassion. Only the Gospel can change human hearts, and no influence makes people more human than the Gospel does. Yet we cannot stop with verbal proclamation. In addition to worldwide evangelization, the people of God should become deeply involved in relief, aid, development and the quest for justice and peace.

(b) A Definition

Here is the paragraph on 'Christian Social Responsibility' in the Lausanne Covenant (para 5):

> We affirm that God is both the Creator and the Judge of all men. We therefore should share his concern for justice and reconciliation throughout human society and for the liberation of men from every kind of oppression. Because mankind is made in the image of God, every person, regardless of race, religion, color, culture, class, sex or age, has an intrinsic dignity because of which he should be respected and served, not exploited. Here too we express penitence both for our neglect and for having sometimes regarded evangelism and social concern as mutually

177

exclusive. Although reconciliation with man is not reconciliation with God, nor is social action evangelism, nor is political liberation salvation, nevertheless we affirm that evangelism and socio-political involvement are both part of our Christian duty. For both are necessary expressions of our doctrines of God and man, our love for our neighbour and our obedience to Jesus Christ. The message of salvation implies also a message of judgment upon every form of alienation, oppression and discrimination, and we should not be afraid to denounce evil and injustice wherever they exist. When people receive Christ they are born again into his kingdom and must seek not only to exhibit but also to spread its righteousness in the midst of an unrighteous world. The salvation we claim should be transforming us in the totality of our personal and social responsibilities. Faith without works is dead.

(c) Motivation for Social Responsibility

Again, as in evangelism so in social responsibility, we discern the fundamental basis for our actions in the character of God himself. He is the God of justice, who in every human community hates evil and loves righteousness. He is also the God of mercy. In the first Bible study of our consultation we read of him that, though he made the universe, he nevertheless humbles himself to care for the needy, 'executes justice for the oppressed', and 'gives food to the hungry'. In addition, 'the Lord sets the prisoners free; the Lord opens the eyes of the blind. The Lord lifts up those who are bowed down; the Lord loves the righteous. The Lord watches over the sojourners, he upholds the widow and the fatherless; but the way of the wicked he brings to ruin' (Psalm 146:5–9). We recognize that we have neither the authority nor the power to do every-thing God does. Nevertheless, since this text shows us the kind of God he is, and since these concerns of his were further expressed in the demands of his law and prophets, it is indisputable what kind of people we should be, seeking justice, freedom and dignity for all, especially the powerless who cannot seek it for themselves.

It is no surprise that Jesus reflected this lovingkindness of God his Father. He had compassion on the hungry, the sick, the bereaved, the outcast. He had compassion on the crowds because they were harassed and helpless, like sheep without a shepherd. And always his compassion issued in appropriate action.

Moreover, the first fruit of the Holy Spirit is love (Gal. 5:22). It is therefore he who gives his people a tender social conscience, and impels them to immerse themselves in humanitarian relief, development, and the search for justice.

Thus we find that there is a Trinitarian basis for our social duties, just as there is for our evangelistic outreach. We who claim to belong to God and who worship him as Father, Son and Holy Spirit, must express our worship in these activities. *Orare est laborare* — to work is to pray.

4 THE RELATIONSHIP BETWEEN EVANGELISM AND SOCIAL RESPONSIBILITY

(a) Historical Background

It appears to us that evangelism and social concern have been intimately related to one another throughout the history of the church, although the relationship has been expressed in a variety of ways. Christian people have often engaged in both activities quite unselfconsciously, without feeling any need to define what they were doing or why. So the problem of their relationship, which led to the convening of this consultation, is comparatively new, and for historical reasons is of particular importance to evangelical Christians.

The Great Awakening in North America, the Pietistic Movement in Germany, and the Evangelical Revival under the Wesleys in Britain, which all took place in the early part of the 18th century, proved a great stimulus to philanthropy as well as evangelism. The next generation of British evangelicals founded missionary societies and gave conspicuous service in public life, notably Wilberforce in the abolition of the slave trade and of slavery itself, and Shaftesbury in the improvement of conditions in the factories.

But at the end of the 19th century and the beginning of the 20th, the so-called 'social gospel' was developed by theological liberals. Some of them confused the kingdom of God with Christian civilization in general, and with social democracy in particular, and they went on to imagine that by their social programmes they could build God's kingdom on earth. It seems to have been in over-reaction to this grave distortion of the Gospel that many evangelicals became suspicious of social involvement. And now that evangelicals are recovering a social conscience and rediscovering our evangelical social heritage, it is understandable that some of our brothers and sisters are looking askance at us and suspecting us of relapsing into the old heresy of the social gospel. But the responsible social action which the biblical Gospel lays upon us, and the liberal 'social gospel' which was a perversion of the true Gospel, are two quite different things. As we said in the Lausanne Covenant, 'we . . . reject as a proud self-confident dream the notion that man can ever build a utopia on earth' (para. 15).

Another cause of the divorce of evangelism and social responsibility is the dichotomy which has often developed in our thinking. We tend to set over against one another in an unhealthy way soul and body, the individual and society, redemption and creation, grace and nature,

179

heaven and earth, justification and justice, faith and works. The Bible certainly distinguishes between these, but it also relates them to each other, and it instructs us to hold each pair in a dynamic and creative tension. It is as wrong to disengage them, as in 'dualism', as it is to confuse them, as in 'monism'. It was for this reason that the Lausanne Covenant, speaking of evangelism and socio-political involvement, affirmed that they 'are both part of our Christian duty' (para 5).

(b)   Particular Situations and Gifts

In wanting to affirm that evangelism and social responsibility belong to each other, we are not meaning that neither can ever exist in independence of the other. The Good Samaritan, for example, if we may characterize him as a Christian, could not have been blamed for tending the wounds of the brigands' victim and failing to preach to him. Nor is Philip to be blamed for preaching the Gospel to the Ethiopian eunuch in his chariot and failing to enquire into his social needs. There are still occasions when it is legitimate to concentrate on one or other of these two Christian duties. It is not wrong to hold an evangelistic crusade without an accompanying programme of social service. Nor is it wrong to feed the hungry in a time of famine without first preaching to them, for, to quote an African proverb, 'an empty belly has no ears'. It was similar in the days of Moses. He brought the Israelites in Egypt the good news of their liberation, 'but they did not listen to him, because of their broken spirit and their cruel bondage' (Ex. 6:9).

There is another justification for sometimes separating evangelism and social action, in addition to the existential demands of a particular situation: namely, the distribution of spiritual gifts. The church is a charismatic community, the body of Christ, whose members are endowed by the Holy Spirit with different gifts for different forms of ministry. Some are gifted to be 'evangelists' (Eph. 4:11), while others are called to 'service' (Rom. 12:7; I Pet. 4:11) or to 'acts of mercy' (Rom. 12:8). Whatever our gifts may be, we are neither to depreciate them nor to boast of them (I Cor. 12:14–26), but rather to use them for the common good.

The best example of the outworking of this principle occurs in Acts 6 where the apostles, who had been called to 'prayer and the ministry of the word', were in danger of becoming preoccupied with 'serving tables', that is, with caring for the material needs of the church's widows. So seven men were appointed to perform this social service, although Stephen and Philip also did some preaching (Acts 6:8–15; 8:5–13). This left the apostles free to concentrate on the pastoral ministry for which they had been commissioned, although they also retained a social concern (e.g., Gal. 2:10). Still today, Christ calls some to pastoral, others to social, others to evangelistic ministries; in fact, there is a wide diversity of spiritual gifts, callings and ministries within the body of Christ.

(c) Three Kinds of Relationship

Having seen that both particular situations and specialist callings can legitimately separate our evangelistic and social responsibilities, we are now ready to consider how in general they relate to one another. What has emerged from our discussion is that there is no one relationship in which they are joined, but that there are at least three equally valid relationships.

First, social activity is a *consequence* of evangelism. That is, evangelism is the means by which God brings people to new birth, and their new life manifests itself in the service of others. Paul wrote that 'faith works through love' (Gal. 5:6), James that 'I will show you my faith by my works' (James 2:18), and John that God's love within us will overflow in serving our needy brothers and sisters (I John 3:16–18). As Robert E. Speer wrote about the Gospel in 1900: 'Wherever it goes, it plants in the hearts of men forces that produce new lives; it plants in communities of men forces that create new social combinations.' We have heard of evangelists in our own day who, during their missions or crusades, actively encourage Christians (including new converts) to become involved in programs to meet specific local, human needs. This effectively highlights the serving dimension of Christian conversion and commitment.

We can go further than this, however. Social responsibility is more than the consequence of evangelism; it is also one of its principal aims. For Christ gave himself for us not only 'to redeem us from all iniquity' but also 'to purify for himself a people of his own who are zealous for good deeds' (Tit. 2:14). Similarly, through the Gospel we are 'created in Christ Jesus for good works which God prepared beforehand, that we should walk in them' (Eph. 2:10). Good works cannot save, but they are an indispensable evidence of salvation (James 2:14–26).

In saying this, we are not claiming that compassionate service is an automatic consequence of evangelism or of conversion, however. Social responsibility, like evangelism, should therefore be included in the teaching ministry of the church. For we have to confess the inconsistencies in our own lives and the dismal record of evangelical failure, often as a result of the cultural blind spots to which we have already referred. This has grave consequences. When we do not allow the Word of God to transform us in all areas of our personal and social life, we seem to validate the Marxist criticism of religion.

Secondly, social activity can be a *bridge* to evangelism. It can break down prejudice and suspicion, open closed doors, and gain a hearing for the Gospel. Jesus himself sometimes performed works of mercy before proclaiming the good news of the kingdom. In more recent times, we were reminded, the construction of dams by the Basel missionaries in Northern Ghana opened a way for the Gospel, and much missionary medical, agricultural, nutritional and educational work has had a similar effect. To add a contemporary western example, a recent crusade in an American city was preceded and accompanied by a 'Love in Action' program, with the evangelist's encouragement. Several 'social uplift' groups co-operated and were able to extend their ministries to the inner city poor. As a result, we were told, a number of people came under the sound of the Gospel who would not otherwise have come to the crusade.

Further, by seeking to serve people, it is possible to move from their 'felt needs' to their deeper need concerning their relationship with God. Whereas, as another participant put it, 'if we turn a blind eye to the suffering, the social oppression, the alienation and loneliness of people, let us not be surprised if they turn a deaf ear to our message of eternal salvation.' We are aware of the danger of making 'rice Christians', that is, of securing converts only because of the physical benefits we offer. But we have to take this risk, so long as we retain our own integrity and serve people out of genuine love and not with an ulterior motive. Then our actions will be 'not bribes but bridges — bridges of love to the world.'

Thirdly, social activity not only follows evangelism as its consequence and aim, and precedes it as its bridge, but also accompanies it as its *partner*. They are like the two blades of a pair of scissors or the two wings of a bird. This partnership is clearly seen in the public ministry of Jesus, who not only preached the Gospel but fed the hungry and healed the sick. In his ministry, *kerygma* (proclamation) and *diakonia* (service) went hand in hand. His words explained his works, and his works dramatized his words. Both were expressions of his compassion for people, and both should be of ours. Both also issue from the lordship of Jesus, for he sends us out into the world both to preach and to serve. If we proclaim the good news of God's love, we must manifest his love in caring for the needy. Indeed, so close is this link between proclaiming and serving, that they actually overlap.

This is not to say that they should be identified with each other, for evangelism is not social responsibility, nor is social responsibility evangelism. Yet, each involves the other.

To proclaim Jesus as Lord and Saviour (evangelism) has social implications, since it summons people to repent of social as well as personal sins, and to live a new life of righteousness and peace in the new society which challenges the old.

To give food to the hungry (social responsibility) has evangelistic implications, since good works of love, if done in the name of Christ, are a demonstration and commendation of the Gospel.

It has been said, therefore, that evangelism, even when it does not have a primarily social intention, nevertheless has a social dimension, while social responsibility, even when it does not have a primarily evangelistic intention, nevertheless has an evangelistic dimension.

Thus, evangelism and social responsibility, while distinct from one another, are integrally related in our proclamation of and obedience to the Gospel. The partnership is, in reality, a marriage.

(d) The Question of Primacy

This brings us to the question whether the partnership between evangelism and social responsibility is equal or unequal, that is, whether they are of identical importance or whether one takes precedence over the other. The Lausanne Covenant affirms that 'in the church's mission of sacrificial service evangelism is primary' (para. 6). Although some of us have felt uncomfortable about this phrase, lest by it we should be breaking the partnership, yet we are able to endorse and explain it in two ways, in addition to the particular situations and callings already mentioned.

First, evangelism has a certain priority. We are not referring to an invariable *temporal* priority, because in some situations a social ministry will take precedence, but to a *logical* one. The very fact of Christian social responsibility presupposes socially responsible Christians, and it can only be by evangelism and discipling that they have become such. If social activity is a consequence and aim of evangelism (as we have asserted), then evangelism must precede it. In addition, social progress is being hindered in some countries by the prevailing religious culture; only evangelism can change this.

Secondly, evangelism relates to people's eternal destiny, and in bringing them good news of salvation, Christians are doing what nobody else can do. Seldom if ever should we have to choose between satisfying physical hunger and spiritual hunger, or between healing bodies and saving souls, since an authentic love for our neighbour will lead us to serve him or her as a whole person. Nevertheless, if we must choose, then we have to say that the supreme and ultimate need of all humankind is the saving grace of Jesus Christ, and that therefore a person's eternal, spiritual salvation is of greater importance than his or her temporal and material well-being (cf. II Cor. 4:16–18). As the Thailand Statement expressed it, 'Of all the tragic needs of human beings none is greater than their alienation from their Creator and the terrible reality of eternal death for those who refuse to repent and believe.' Yet this fact must not make us indifferent to the degradations of human poverty and oppression. The choice, we believe, is largely conceptual. In practice, as in the public ministry of Jesus, the two are inseparable, at least in open societies. Rather than competing with each other, they mutually support and strengthen each other in an upward spiral of increased concern for both.

(e) Some Examples

The three relationships between evangelism and social responsibility need not occur in isolation from each other. Instead, they often blend together in such a way that it is difficult to distinguish them. This was made clear to us as we listened to a number of case studies.

The 'Precious Jewels Development' project in Cebu City, Philippines, is a many-pronged effort by Christians to serve their neighbours, improving their means of local livelihood, offering education and child care, developing a nutritional programme, and giving emergency relief. In one respect, it is simply an expression of love, the natural consequence of the knowledge of Christ which the Gospel has brought. In another, it has been a bridge to evangelism. Non-Christians 'opened themselves' to Christians. Their reserve was melted, and they became ready to hear the Gospel. Thus, social service, evangelism's consequence and bridge, also became its partner. God himself was loving them, one of them said, through the preaching of the Gospel and the meeting of their practical needs.

Another project in the Philippines ('Project Gamtabeng') has come to the aid of a hill tribe whose very existence was threatened by urbanization and industrialization. Medical, agricultural and educational development have gone hand in hand with evangelism and church planting. A convert summed up the project's aims by saying 'Through Project Gamtabeng, I became an heir to my Father's heaven and earth.'

We also heard about some nomadic Maasai people of Northern Kenya who had come to Christ. Amidst dancing and singing, they were being welcomed into the church by the Anglican bishop. As they celebrated, however, he noticed that half of them were either blind or nearly so. 'This convinced me,' he said, 'that we cannot evangelize the spiritually blind and leave them in their physical blindness.' Immediately, therefore, a health care program was developed.

Next, we were told of an Indian couple, both doctors, who have laboured for more than 20 years in Jamkhed, Maharashtra. They trained despised outcaste widows in the elements of pre- and post-natal care, proved their credentials as healers by establishing a small operating theatre, and taught out of the gospels how Jesus gave dignity to women. As a result, child mortality has been reduced almost to zero, social justice has increased and fear has diminished, and many people in seventeen villages, which for 50 years had not responded to the good news, are now turning to Jesus.

In addition, we learned about the Voice of Calvary ministries in Mississippi, where for 22 years the Gospel has been shared, and the physical, spiritual, economic, social and material needs of people have been met. Evangelism, community development and racial reconciliation through the church have gone hand in hand. The reason for this holistic ministry is that its pioneer came face to face with the cycle of poverty in which the people were trapped. They were so pre-occupied with the struggle to survive, that they could not attend to spiritual realities. It would have been almost impossible to offer Jesus Christ to them and ignore their other needs. So the Gospel of love is verbalized and actualized simultaneously.

5   THE GOOD NEWS OF THE KINGDOM

Having suggested three ways in which evangelism and social responsibility are related to one another, we come to an even more basic way in which they are united, namely by the Gospel. For the Gospel is the root, of which both evangelism and social responsibility are the fruits. As good news of God's love in Christ, the Gospel demands both to be preached and to be lived. Once we have come to know it, we are obliged to share it with others and to 'adorn' it by good deeds (Tit. 2:10).

So what is the good news? No simple answer can be given, since a variety of models is developed in the New Testament. At this Consultation, however, we have concentrated on two comprehensive models. We have thought of the Gospel both as 'good news of salvation' (Eph. 1:13) and as 'good news of the kingdom of God' (Matt. 4:23; Mark 1: 14,15; Luke 4:43).

(a)   Salvation

We are all agreed that salvation is a broad term, in the sense that it embraces the totality of God's redemptive purpose.

It begins with *new life*. Through the substitutionary death and historical resurrection of Jesus, the individual believer is 'ransomed, healed, restored, forgiven'. Saved from guilt and the judgment of God, he or she is adopted into God's family as his child.

Salvation continues with the *new community*. For salvation in the Bible is never a purely individualistic concept. As in the Old Testament, so in the New, God is calling out a people for himself and binding it to himself by a solemn covenant. The members of this new society, reconciled through Christ to God and one another, are being drawn from all races and cultures. Indeed, this single new humanity — which Christ has created and in which no barriers are tolerated — is an essential part of the good news (Eph. 2:11–22).

Thirdly, salvation includes the *new world* which God will one day make. We are looking forward not only to the redemption and resurrection of our bodies, but to the renovation of the entire created order, which will be liberated from decay, pain and death (Rom. 8:18–25). Of this cosmic renewal the resurrection of Christ was the beginning and the pledge.

Having agreed on these three dimensions of salvation (personal, social and cosmic), we went on to pose a further question: is salvation experienced only by those who consciously confess Christ as Lord and Saviour? Or is it right in addition to refer to the emergence of justice and peace in the wider

185

community as 'salvation', and to attribute to the grace of Christ every beneficial social transformation? Some of us do not find salvation-language inappropriate for such situations, even when Christ is not acknowledged in them. Most of us, however, consider that it is more prudent and biblical to reserve the vocabulary of salvation for the experience of reconciliation with God through Christ and its direct consequences. None of us would dream of following those who have portrayed Hitler's Germany or Mao's China or Castro's Cuba as having experienced 'salvation', though all of us are united in wishing to honour Christ as universal Lord.

(b) The Kingdom of God

It is well known that Jesus came preaching the kingdom of God. According to the Synoptic Gospels, the kingdom was the major theme of his sermons and parables. Although 'the kingdom of God' is largely replaced by 'eternal life' in John's Gospel and by the lordship of Christ in Paul's letters, so that we recognize the diversity of salvation models and wish to avoid committing ourselves exclusively to any one of them, nevertheless the kingdom is a richly suggestive concept, with significant applications to the modern world. Hence our decision to focus on it.

The kingdom of God is the rule of God, and the whole Bible declares that God is King. As the Creator, he is both king of nature (sustaining what he has made) and king of history (ordering the life of nations). 'The Lord reigns' is a frequent shout of joy in the Old Testament, expressing Israel's confidence in the providential rule of God over the world. Over themselves Israel knew that Yahweh reigned in a special way. For even after the people had demanded a king like other nations, Israel did not cease to be a theocracy. Yet her kings were only a poor approximation to Yahweh's ideal of kingship. So he began to promise through his prophets that one day he would send his own king, anointed with his Spirit, to reign in righteousness and peace over all peoples and for ever.

'The time has come,' Jesus announced as he began his public ministry, 'the kingdom of God is near. Repent and believe the good news' (Mark 1:15). Thus Jesus brought the kingdom with him. 'Eschatology invaded history.' 'The person of Jesus and the presence of God's kingdom are inseparably connected.' Only those enter it who humble themselves like a little child and are born again.

The kingdom of God is both a present reality and a future expectation. As a present reality, now that Jesus' physical presence has been withdrawn from the earth, his Holy Spirit establishes it in the lives of his people. For the King must never be thought of apart from his subjects, the messianic community, over which he rules. Moreover, his rule takes the form of both total blessing (salvation, in fact) and total demand (obedience and service).

Christians have often debated the relationship between the church and the kingdom. We must not identify them, but neither must we separate them. The church is the community in which God's kingly rule is revealed, which therefore witnesses to the divine rule, and is the first fruits of the redeemed humanity (James 1:18). It lives by new values and standards, and its relationships have been transformed by love. Yet it continues to fail. For it lives in an uneasy tension between the 'already' and the 'not yet', between the present reality and the future expectation of the kingdom.

(c) The Signs of the Kingdom

Evangelism is the proclamation of this kingdom in the fulness of its blessings and promise, which are also called 'salvation'. Moreover, Jesus did more than preach the kingdom; he demonstrated its reality with 'signs of the kingdom', public evidence that the kingdom he was talking about had come. We believe that signs should validate our evangelism, too, and we have spent time discussing what they should be.

Since 'the reason the Son of God appeared was to destroy the devil's work' (I John 3:8), he inevitably came into collision with the prince of darkness. The signs of the kingdom were evidences that the devil was retreating before the advance of the King. As Jesus put it, once the strong man has been overpowered by the stronger one, his possessions can be taken from him (Matt. 12:29; Luke 11:22).

The signs reflect this. We list them in approximately the order in which they appeared, although this is not necessarily an order of importance.

The *first* sign of the kingdom was (and still is) Jesus himself in the midst of his people (Lk. 17:21; Matt. 18:20), whose presence brings joy, peace, and a sense of celebration (John 15:11; 16:33; Mk. 2:18–20).

The *second* is the preaching of the Gospel. There was no Gospel of the kingdom to proclaim until Christ arrived. Now that he has come, however, the good news of the kingdom must be preached to all, especially to the poor (Lk. 4:18,19; 7:22). The preaching of the kingdom points people to the kingdom itself.

The *third* sign of the kingdom was exorcism. We refuse to demythologize the teaching of Jesus and his apostles about demons. Although the 'principalities and powers' may have a reference to demonic ideologies and structures, we believe that they certainly are evil, personal intelligences under the command of the devil. Demon possession is a real and terrible condition. Deliverance is possible only in a power encounter in which the name of Jesus is invoked and prevails.

The *fourth* sign of the kingdom was the healing and the nature miracles — making the blind see, the deaf hear, the lame walk, the sick whole, raising the dead (Lk. 7:22), stilling the storm, and multiplying loaves and fishes. We all agree that these were not only signs pointing to the reality of the kingdom's arrival, but also anticipations of the final kingdom from which all disease, hunger, disorder and death will be for ever banished. We also agree that God is still free and powerful, and performs miracles today, especially in frontier situations where the kingdom is advancing into enemy-held territory. Some of us think we should expect miracles as commonly as in the ministry of Jesus and his apostles (e.g., John 14:12), while others draw attention to the texts which describe these miracles as authenticating their unique ministry (e.g., Heb. 2:3,4; II Cor. 12:12).

A *fifth* sign of the kingdom is the miracle of conversion and the new birth. Whenever people 'turn to God from idols, to serve the living and true God' (I Thess. 1:9,10), a power encounter has taken place in which the spell of idols, whether traditional or modern, and of the spirits, has been broken. God's power for salvation is displayed in the Gospel (Rom. 1:16), and converts who have been rescued from darkness to light and from the power of Satan to God (Acts 26:18) are said to have 'tasted . . . the powers of the age to come' (Heb. 6:5).

A *sixth* sign of the kingdom is the people of the kingdom, in whom is manifested that cluster of Christlike qualities which Paul called 'the fruit of the Spirit'. For the gift of the Spirit is the supreme blessing of the kingdom of God. Where he rules, love, joy, peace and righteousness rule with him (Gal. 5:22,23; Rom. 14:17). Moreover, love issues in good works. Thus, if the Gospel is good news of the kingdom, good works are the signs of the kingdom. Good news and good works, evangelism and social responsibility, are once again *seen* to be indissolubly united.

The *seventh* sign of the kingdom, we suggest, is suffering. It was necessary for the King to suffer in order to enter into his glory. Indeed, he suffered for us, leaving us an example that we should follow in his steps (I Pet. 2:21). To suffer for the sake of righteousness or for our testimony to Jesus, and to bear such suffering courageously, is a clear sign to all beholders that we have received God's salvation or kingdom (Phil. 1:28,29; cf. II Thess. 1:5).

(d)   The Extent of the Kingdom

If these are the signs of the kingdom, manifesting its present reality and pointing forward to its final consummation, how extensive is the kingdom they signify?

In one sense, as we have seen, God's rule extends only over those who acknowledge it, who have bowed their knee to Jesus and confessed his lordship (Phil. 2:9–11). These God 'has delivered . . . from the dominion of darkness and transferred to the kingdom of his beloved Son' (Col. 1:13). Apart from them, the whole world is 'in the power of the evil one', its 'ruler' and 'god' (I John 5: 19; John 12:31; II Cor. 4:4), for 'we do not yet see everything in subjection to' Jesus (Heb. 2:8; cf. Ps. 110:1; Acts 2:35).

Yet in another sense, the risen Lord claimed that 'all authority in heaven and on earth' had been given to him (Matt. 28:18). For already God has 'put

all things under his feet and has made him head over all things for the church'
(Eph. 1:22). His titles are 'King of kings and Lord of lords' and 'the ruler of
princes on earth' (Rev. 1:5; 19:16).

How can these two perspectives be fused? How can Christ claim universal
authority if the whole world still lies in Satan's power? The answer is that over
his redeemed people Jesus is King *de facto*, while it is only *de jure* that he is
presently King over the world, his right being still challenged by the usurper.
Perhaps, therefore, we should reserve the expression 'the kingdom of God'
for the acknowledged rule of Christ, since this is the new thing he inaugurated
at his coming, while referring to the more general 'sovereignty' of God over
all things.

It is important to maintain the tension between what Christ rules *de facto*
and *de jure*. For if we assume that all authority has in fact been given to him,
we shall not take seriously the evil powers which have not yet capitulated. If,
on the other hand, our horizon is bounded by the community in which the
King is consciously confessed, we may be tempted to dismiss the rest of the
world as beyond redemption. From these extremes of naive optimism and
dark pessimism we return to the radical realism of the Bible, which recognizes
both the defeat of evil and its refusal to concede defeat. This double conviction
will persuade us to work hard in evangelism and in the quest for justice, while
at the same time putting our whole trust and confidence in God.

During the interim period between the two comings of Christ, between his
victory over evil and evil's final capitulation and destruction, what should be
the relations between the kingdom community and the world?

First, the new community should constitute a challenge to the old. Its
values and ideals, its moral standards and relationships, its sacrificial lifestyle,
its love, joy and peace — these are the signs of the kingdom, as we have seen,
and present the world with a radically alternative society. All our words of
love and deeds of love must express our wholehearted submission to the Lord
of love himself.

Secondly, as the world lives alongside the kingdom community, some of
the values of the kingdom spill over into society as a whole, so that its
industry, commerce, legislation and institutions become to some degree
imbued with kingdom values. So-called 'kingdomized' or 'Christianized'
society is not the kingdom of God, but it owes a debt to the kingdom which
often is unrecognized.

The 'overspill' model has its limitations, however, because it pictures the
two communities as independent of one another, like two vessels standing
side by side, the contents of one spilling over into the other. The salt, light
and yeast metaphors which Jesus employed are more dynamic, since each
implies the penetration of the old community by the new. The light shines
into the darkness, the salt soaks into the meat, the yeast causes fermentation
in the dough. So Jesus intends his followers neither to withdraw from the
world in order to preserve their holiness, nor to lose their holiness by
conforming to the world, but simultaneously to permeate the world and to

retain their kingdom distinctives. Only so can they share the good news with credibility. Only so can they be effective agents for cultural, social and political change. Indeed, as 'the Lord blessed the Egyptian's house for Joseph's sake' (Gen. 39:5), so we believe he blesses the world through the ministry of, and for the sake of, his redeemed people.

Meanwhile, we do not forget that God is directly at work in his world, apart from the agency of his people. In his common grace he continues without intermission to sustain the earth and its creatures, to grant life and health, to give sunshine and rain, to maintain the cycle of the seasons, to cause the ground to be fruitful, to preserve society from disintegration, and to give to all humankind (who bear his image and have his law written in their hearts — Rom. 2:14,15) a certain appreciation of justice, freedom, beauty, dignity and peace.

While we gladly recognize these works of God in the world, both directly and through his people, they are not what Jesus meant by his kingdom. It is, therefore, our urgent responsibility to summon all people in Christ's name to turn and humble themselves like little children, as we have sought to humble ourselves, in order to enter the kingdom and receive its priceless blessing, the salvation of God (Matt. 18:3).

6 HISTORY AND ESCHATOLOGY

We devoted a whole day of our consultation to 'history and eschatology', that is, to the relationship between *on the one hand* what we do now in the historical process and what God is doing since the last days when the kingdom was inaugurated, and *on the other* what God is going to do on the last day when he ushers in the fulness of the kingdom.

(a) False Dreams

We saw our study as being all the more important because we human beings are inveterate dreamers. We cannot live only for today; we must have some hope for tomorrow which will sustain us in our pilgrimage. Consequently, like the pseudo-prophets of the Old Testament, we have a constant tendency to fabricate false dreams, visions which come out of our own minds, and not from the Lord (cf. Jer. 23:25–32).

We have been conscious of the special need to distinguish the social responsibility to which we as Christians are called, its reasons and its content, from that which modern ideologies have generated. Both dogmatic and messianic Marxisms, for example, proclaim a bogus millennium which recognizes neither the Creator of the world, nor his Christ. Yet they anticipate that by changing social structures, frequently by violent means, they will by human effort alone bring about a fully just and perfect society. A program for change such as this, because it denies the stubborn reality of evil and ignores our deepest human needs, is bound to end in failure, even in disaster.

We also reject the messianic western dream which aims at erecting a counterfeit materialistic kingdom. We recognize, of course, the divine command to subdue the earth and harness its resources for the good of all. But selfish secular materialism pursues its own economic growth irrespective of the need to conserve the environment and to serve the development of the poorer nations. It is characterized by self-absorbed individualism and insensitive affluence, which are incompatible with Christian — let alone truly human — values, and which unwittingly foster increasing inequality between the rich and the poor.

Again, we cannot join those who call for a new political world order, based on a new world religion concocted from a synthesis of all religions, as the only means of escaping from the threats of global calamity. We, too, recognize with sober realism the terrible potential for destruction in human life. But we are convinced that only the power of God manifest in the forgiveness and

191

recreative power of Christ can restore to us that order, meaning, freedom, dignity and responsibility which the world so desperately needs.

It was, therefore, with relief that we turned from all ideological substitutes to the authentic Christian hope, to the vision of the triumphant return of Jesus, and of the kingdom he will consummate, which God has revealed to us in his Word. Our concern was to relate this hope to history, and to our concrete duties within history. In particular, we asked ourselves whether there is any connection between our eschatological outlook and the attitude we adopt towards evangelism and social responsibility. We are conscious that more biblical study and historical research are needed before we will be ready to handle this question with greater confidence. For the present, we feel able to contribute only tentatively to the debate.

(b)   Differing Millenarian Views

To begin with, we thought about the millennium and about its influence on Christian behaviour at different periods of church history. We tried to discern whether there is any correlation between the three traditional varieties of millennialism and the vigour with which social responsibility and evangelism have been pursued in the history of the church. Without doubt, our understanding of the millennium affects the way in which we view the world. The degree of hope which we sustain seems to be proportionate to the degree to which we see the kingdom of God as an already present reality or as a largely future expectation.

Since all three views of the millennium were represented at our consultation, and since we desired to give one another liberty on this matter and not to convert one another to our own position, we moved on from our millenarian differences to seek a common eschatological motivation for evangelism and social responsibility. Of course, Christians are given in the New Testament many other reasons and motives for good living and good works, which we did not consider. The following eschatological incentives were put forward.

(c)   Judgment to Come

The first was judgment. A great deal of teaching by Jesus and his apostles linked present responsibility with future judgment. Jesus told us to be alert, sober and busy in his service, because we do not know when our Lord will come. But we do know that when he comes he will call us to account (e.g., Mark 13:33–36; Luke 12:35–40; Matt. 25:14–30).

The conscientious dedication of the apostle Paul to evangelism seems to have been related directly to his sense of accountability. 'Knowing the fear of the Lord,' he wrote, 'we persuade men.' 'Men-persuading' is a clear reference to his evangelistic methods, as we know from the Acts, and 'the fear of the Lord' to appearing before Christ's judgment seat, of which he has written in the previous verse (II Cor. 5:10,11).

The same motivation can sustain us in our works of philanthropy, as is evident from the sheep and the goats passage which we studied together one morning. In this solemn description of the day of judgment, the 'sheep' or the 'righteous', who are 'blessed' and welcomed into the kingdom, are those who have ministered to Christ in the hungry and thirsty, the naked and sick, the strangers and the prisoners. The 'goats', on the other hand, who are 'cursed' and dismissed to eternal punishment, are those who have failed to minister to Christ in the needy. Whether Christ's 'brethren' are his followers in general, as other passages seem to indicate (e.g., Matt. 12:46–50; Heb. 2:10–18), or in particular his messengers, as may be suggested by the 'cup of cold water' passage (Matt. 10:9–15, 40–42), or may include the rest of needy humankind with whom Christ humbly identifies himself, the principal message is the same. As the rest of the New Testament teaches, the dead will be judged 'by what they have done' (e.g., Rev. 20:13), and our deeds will include either the loving service of those in need or a scandalous indifference to their plight. These will be an acid test whether we are true believers, or unbelievers.

Neither of these two passages of Scripture can possibly mean that we can gain entry to heaven by our good works. To interpret them in this way would be to turn the Gospel upside down. What they are emphasizing is that though we are justified by grace alone through faith alone, we shall be judged by those good works of love through which our secret faith is made public.

(d)   The Eschatological Vision

We are united in rejecting utopic visions, which are dreams of human accomplishment. The eschatological vision is totally different, however, because it is a revelation of what God himself is going to do in the end. This vision can give both direction and inspiration to our present duty. We do not, of course, presume to imagine that we can do now what God will do then. Nor will every part of our life on earth have a counterpart in the final state (e.g., there will be no marriage after the Resurrection — Mk. 12:25).

Nevertheless, the glimpses God has given us of the end disclose the kind of community life which is pleasing to him. Twice Peter tells us 'what sort of persons' we ought to be in this life on account of what is going to happen at the end. He likens the coming destruction of the present evil order to the flood, except that it will be by fire instead of water, and urges us in consequence to 'lives of holiness and godliness'. Then he passes from the destruction of the old order to the creation of the new. He argues that because in the new heavens and the new earth 'righteousness dwells', therefore we must be zealous to be found by Christ 'without spot or blemish, and at peace'. In other words, because righteousness and peace will be characteristics of the eternal kingdom, we need to pursue them in the kingdom's present manifestation (II Pet. 3:1–14).

We believe that, in a similar way, the vision of the countless multitude before God's throne, redeemed from every nation (Rev.7:9), who will constitute the final fulfilment of God's promise to give Abraham a countless posterity (Gen. 12:1–3), should be a powerful incentive to us to obey the Great Commission, to go and make disciples of all nations, and to seek to make our churches a foretaste of the heterogeneous heavenly community.

If that aspect of the eschatological vision is a stimulus to evangelism, others should prove a stimulus to social responsibility. If in heaven they will 'hunger no more, neither thirst any more' (Rev. 7:16), should we not feed the hungry today? And if in the end 'they shall beat their swords into plough-shares, and their spears into pruning hooks, neither shall they learn war any more' (Micah 4:3; Is. 2:4), does that not mean that war is incompatible with the perfect will of God? Not that the state can now discard its responsibility to enforce justice and order (Rom. 13:1–4), any more than we can expect lambs and lions to lie down together now. But does not the promise of final peace tell us that, even if (as some Christians have always believed) war may be in some circumstances the lesser of two evils, we should all nevertheless seek to be peacemakers?

In these ways the eschatological vision can direct and motivate our Christian action, while at the same time we must never forget the fallenness of this world or the wickedness of the principalities and powers.

(e) Continuity

The words 'continuity' and 'discontinuity' have kept recurring throughout our consultation. That is to say, will the final kingdom enjoy some continuity with its present manifestation, or will the future be discontinuous with the present, so that nothing will survive the judgment except those who by God's sheer grace are the heirs of his kingdom?

We have not been able to reach complete agreement on this matter. Some of us, vividly aware of the evil of this present age and of the glory that is to be revealed, emphasize the destructive nature of God's judgment and the newness of his new creation. Others of us believe that, just as after the new birth we are not a different person but the same person remade, so the universe is going to experience a new birth (*palingenesia*, Matt. 19:28). That is, God is going to re-create it, and not create another universe *ex nihilo*. Indeed, Paul likens the pains of the created order to the birthpangs of the new (Rom. 8:18–25; cf. Mark 13:8).

We all believe this about our bodies, for the principle of continuity is evident in the resurrected body of Jesus. Although, as Paul expresses it, our new body will be as different from the old as a flower differs from its seed, nevertheless there will be a continuity between the two (I Cor. 15:35–46). And later he grounds his argument for sexual self-control and a right use of our bodies not only on what they are (members of Christ and temples of the Holy Spirit) but on what they are going to be: 'The body is not meant for immorality, but for the Lord, and the Lord for the body. And God raised the Lord and will also raise us up by his power' (I Cor. 6:12–20). On this double resurrection, of the Lord Jesus and of our bodies, the apostle bases his plea for purity.

We are on more uncertain ground, however, when we ask how many of our present works will be carried over into eternity. Certainly evangelism has eternal consequences, since converts receive God's free gift of eternal life. So does our teaching, if we build with 'gold, silver and precious stones' upon the foundation of Christ (I Cor. 3:10–15). But what about our social activity? We are told of those who 'die in the Lord' that 'their deeds follow them' (Rev. 14:13; cf. I Cor. 13:13). We also are told that the kings of the earth will 'bring their glory' into the New Jerusalem, and that they will 'bring into it the glory and the honour of the nations', while what will be excluded is everything 'unclean' (Rev. 21:24–27). This has seemed to many to teach that whatever is beautiful, true and good in human cultures, once purged of everything which defiles, will be consummated in the final kingdom. Those who have the assurance of this continuity find in it a strong incentive to social and cultural involvement.

(f) The Christian Hope

In whatever more precise ways we may formulate these motivations of judgment, vision and continuity, we are all agreed that our Christian hope focuses on the personal, visible and glorious return of our Lord Jesus Christ, on the resurrection from death, and on the perfected kingdom which his appearing will bring. Also, we are all agreed that we are to live our lives and do our works in the conscious expectation of his coming. This confidence will make us committed to world evangelization (Matt. 24:14), 'zealous for good deeds' (Tit. 2:13,14), faithful to one another in the fellowship (Heb. 10:25), and courageous in suffering (II Tim. 4:6–8; Rev. 2:25). With great firmness we therefore reject what has been called 'eschatological paralysis'. On the contrary, before the Lord comes, and in preparation for his coming, we are determined to get into the action. This is to 'live anticipatorily', to experience the power, enjoy the community and manifest the righteousness of the kingdom *now*, before it is consummated in glory.

7 GUIDELINES FOR ACTION

Much of our debate has been at a theological level, for we have felt the need to wrestle with the issues which relate to salvation and kingdom, history and eschatology. Nevertheless, all our theologizing has been with a view to determining what practical action we should take to forward the mission which God has given us. In particular, we have considered in what forms our evangelistic and social concerns should be expressed, what agencies should undertake the work, and how different political and cultural situations will affect it.

(a) Forms of Evangelism and Social Responsibility

We have all been familiar for years with different forms of evangelism (personal evangelism, local church evangelism, mass evangelism, cross-cultural evangelism, etc.). But we have been less clear about the different forms in which our social concern should be manifested. Throughout our consultation we have spoken of 'social responsibility', 'social ministries', 'social assistance', 'social service', 'social action', 'social justice', and (as in the Lausanne Covenant) 'socio-political involvement'. We believe that a failure to define these terms has contributed to the continuing suspicion which surrounds every Christian activity described as 'social'. It may be easiest to divide our Christian social responsibility into two kinds, which for simplicity's sake we will call 'social service' and 'social action', and which can be distinguished from each other in several ways:

Social service	Social action
Relieving human need	Removing the causes of human need
Philanthropic activity	Political and economic activity
Seeking to minister to individuals and families	Seeking to transform the structures of society
Works of mercy	The quest for justice

In making this necessary functional distinction, we recognize that in practice it is not as neat as it looks. On the one hand, social action of a political kind lacks integrity if it is not supported by a personal commitment to social service. On the other, some works of mercy have inescapably political implications — for example, teaching the oppressed to read

196

and write, visiting a banned person in South Africa, or sending food to Poland or North Vietnam.

1. Social Service and Evangelism

The first of these two kinds of social ministry is universally accepted as a Christian obligation; there is nothing controversial about it. Just as we are called to personal evangelism, so we are called to personal service. Jesus, we are told, both 'went about . . . preaching and bringing the good news', and 'went about doing good' (Luke 8:1; Acts 10:38).

All Christians should follow his example — although, to be sure, our way of sharing the good news may not be only by preaching. Both personal evangelism and personal service are expressions of compassion. Both are forms of witness to Jesus Christ. And both should be sensitive responses to human need. The evangelist seeks to discover the principal point of felt need — for example, a sense of guilt or shame or fear, moral failure, personal loneliness, a lack of self-worth or significance, domestic unhappiness, a hunger for transcendence, lack of education, social repression, or demonic activity. Similarly, a person's social needs may range from the physical (food, clothing, shelter or health care), through the psychological (anxiety, alienation, emotional unbalance) to the economic (poverty, illiteracy, unemployment). We will come to political needs later. Even in welfare states there are always areas of human need which government and voluntary agencies do not fully cover, and which Christians can take the initiative to meet.

'Development' could be put into a separate category, but it probably should be bracketed with philanthropic service, even though some community development projects embrace a whole village, town or district. It is very welcome that many welfare agencies have expanded their emphasis in recent years from aid to development, and many medical missions from curative medicine to community health. To help people learn to help themselves not only makes better sense economically, but it is also more conducive to human dignity. It is important, therefore, to ensure that self-help programs genuinely enable people to stand on their own feet and are not devious paternalistic ploys to reinforce dependence, even subservience.

If Christian people are to get involved in humanitarian work, whether in the form of helping a neighbour or of sharing in an aid or development project, considerable sacrifices in time, energy and money will be needed. Authentic personal evangelism is equally costly. We see Christ's call to service, both evangelistic and social, as an important challenge to our self-centred, self-loving 'me generation'.

2. Social Action and Evangelism

The other kind of social responsibility is the quest for justice. It looks beyond persons to structures, beyond the rehabilitation of prison inmates to the reform of the prison system, beyond improving factory conditions to securing a more participatory role for the workers, beyond caring for the poor to improving — and when necessary transforming — the economic system (whatever it may be) and the political system (again, whatever it may be), until it facilitates their liberation from poverty and oppression. Such social changes often necessitate political action (for politics is about power), and some evangelicals fear it because they imagine it will entail civil strife and even revolution. But this is not what we mean by 'socio-political involvement'. We are thinking rather of political processes which are consistent with biblical principles — such as the rights of the individual and of minorities, respect for civil authority, the welfare of the whole community, and justice for the oppressed.

The Bible lays great emphasis on both justice (or righteousness) and peace. For God is the author of both, and both are essential characteristics of his kingdom. We, therefore, who claim to be members of his kingdom, must not only seek justice for others but must 'do justice' ourselves (Mic. 6:8), in relation to our family, our fellow workers, and any servants or employees we may have. In the same way, it is not enough to 'seek peace and pursue it'; we must also ourselves, so far as it depends on us, 'live peaceably with all' (1 Pet. 3:11; Rom. 12:18). This applies to churches as well as individual Christians. If discrimination and disunity are tolerated in the church, how can we denounce them in the nation? Conversely, it is churches which visibly demonstrate the righteousness and peace of the kingdom which will make the greatest evangelistic and social impact on the world. The salt must retain its saltiness, Jesus said; otherwise, it is good for nothing (Matt. 5:13).

(b)   Agents of Evangelism and Social Responsibility

One of the points of tension emerging during the consultation has concerned the allocation of responsibilities. Granted that evangelism and social service/action are Christian responsibilities, who is responsible for what? What should be undertaken by individual Christians, what by groups, and in particular what is to be the role of the church as church?

1.   Evangelism and Social Service
We all agree that alongside personal evangelism there should be personal social service. Individual Christians should be involved in both, according to their opportunities, gifts and callings.

The parallel is similar in the local church. Just as each local church has an inescapable responsibility before God to bring the Gospel to all the people who reside and work in its neighbourhood, so the social needs of the neighbourhood should be a special concern of the local church.

There is also an important place for both church groups and para-church groups. We shall have more to say about the former when we come to our section on 'The Local Church in a Free Society'. Para-church organizations, both for evangelism and for social responsibility, have an indispensable part to play in Christian outreach, especially if they specialize in kinds of ministry which no church can manage on its own, and provided that they accept a measure of responsibility to the churches.

2.   Evangelism and Social Action

What about social action of a political kind, in distinction to social service of a philanthropic kind? Does social action belong to the mission of the church as church, or is it the prerogative of individual believers who make up the church, and of groups?

We have no doubt about individuals and groups. The church should encourage its members to become conscientious citizens, to take the initiative to found and operate social programs, to inform themselves about political issues, and to advocate or dissent according to their conscience.

Since individual action is usually limited in its effects, however, Christians should also be encouraged to form or join groups and movements which concern themselves with specific needs in society, undertake research into social issues, and organize appropriate action. We welcome the existence and activity of such groups, for they supplement the church's work in many important areas. Christians should also be encouraged to participate responsibly in the political party of their choice, their labour union(s) or business association(s), and similar movements. Whenever possible, they should form a Christian group within them, and/or start or join a Christian party, union or movement, in order to develop specifically Christian policies.

From the activity of individuals and groups, we come back to the church. Should the church get involved in politics, or keep out? Some argue that churches which engage in socio-political action, especially on controversial issues, lose members and missionaries, because the action stirs up controversy. Others counter that different factors like theological liberalism and loss of confidence in the Gospel are the real cause of dwindling numbers.

This issue is not only pragmatic, however; it is essentially theological. Behind the debate lie our differing ecclesiologies and, in particular, our differing understandings of the relationship between church and state, between the kingdom of God and what has been called the 'kingdom of Caesar'. At least three traditions on Christian political involvement, all deriving from the European Protestant Reformation, have been represented in our consultation. All agree that the kingdom of God is distinct from the political realm. One sees the kingdom as *opposed* to that realm, and pleads for a Christian community witness independent of political institutions. A second tradition sees the kingdom as *separate* from the political realm, though parallel to it, and urges that Christians participate in that realm, though as citizens (not as church members) guided by Christian moral principles. The third tradition sees the kingdom of God as penetrating and *transforming* the political realm; it argues that political involvement belongs to the witness not only of Christian individuals and groups but also of churches.

This discussion is far from being irrelevant to evangelism. People's hearts are often opened to the Gospel when they see that we genuinely care for them as persons rather than merely as souls. When they perceive that the Gospel is about the mercy and justice of God which were reconciled at Christ's cross, and see his mercy and justice still active in the situation today, they are likely to be the more ready to come to Christ.

(c)   The Local Church in a Free Society

In spite of our differing theological and cultural backgrounds, on account of which some of us assign social action (of a political kind) to individuals and groups rather than to churches, all of us agree that the church has definite evangelistic and social responsibilities. This applies especially to the local church, which should be committed to the total well-being of the community in which it is permanently situated. Some of these duties belong to all churches, others only to churches in a free or open society. We shall have more to say in the next section about the particular case of churches under repression.

1.   *Intercession*
'First of all,' wrote Paul to Timothy, 'I urge that supplications, prayers, intercessions, and thanksgivings be made for all men, for kings and all who are in high positions, that we may lead a quiet and peaceable life, godly and respectful in every way. This is good, and it is acceptable in the sight of God our Saviour, who desires all men to be saved and to come to the knowledge of the truth' (I Tim. 2:1–4). Thus does the apostle give priority to prayer among the church's public duties, in particular prayer for the civil authorities, and he goes on to link it to both peace and salvation.

We are convinced that the living God hears and answers the prayers of his people, that by prayer we can enter into the unseen spiritual conflict and bind Satan in the name of Christ, and that there is special power in corporate prayer when 'two of you (or more) agree on earth about anything you ask' (Matt. 18:19). Yet we are ashamed that our practice falls far short of our principle. Often the pastoral prayer in public worship is brief and perfunctory; the petitions are so unimaginative and stale as to border on 'vain repetitions'; and the people doze and dream instead of praying.

We resolve ourselves, and call upon our churches, to take much more seriously the period of intercession in public worship; to think in terms of 10 or 15 minutes rather than five; to invite lay people to share in leading, since they often have deep insight into the world's needs; and to focus our prayers both on the evangelization of the world (closed lands, resistant peoples, missionaries, national churches, etc.) and on the quest for peace and justice in the world (places of tension and conflict, deliverance from the nuclear horror, rulers and governments, the poor and needy, etc.). We long to see every Christian congregation bowing down in humble and expectant faith before our sovereign Lord.

2. Love

If evangelism and social responsibility are twins, their mother is love. For evangelism means words of love and social service/action means deeds of love, and both should be the natural overflow of a community of love. We do not think the local church can reach out to its neighbourhood with any degree of credibility unless and until it is filled with the love of God.

This love will manifest itself first in the *philadelphia* ('brotherly love') which binds Christian brothers and sisters together. Such a loving fellowship has great evangelistic power. For it is only when we love one another, as Christ has loved us, that everybody will know we are his disciples (John 13:34,35). Further, the invisible God who once made himself visible in Christ now makes himself visible in us, if we love one another: 'Nobody has ever seen God; but if we love one another, God abides in us and his love is perfected in us' (I John 4:12).

But the love of God cannot possibly be bottled up within the Christian community; it breaks out in compassion for the world. It yearns for the salvation of sinners, so that Christ's lost sheep may be gathered safely into his flock. It yearns also to alleviate the material needs of the poor, the hungry and the oppressed, so that if we close our hearts against the needy, we cannot claim that God's love abides in us (I John 3:17). Love for God and love for neighbour belong inextricably together, as Jesus taught (Mark 12:28–34; cf. I John 4:19–21).

We are convinced that the Christian impact on society (both evangelistic and social) depends even more on quality than on numbers, and that the distinctive quality of Christians is love.

3. Teaching

Every Christian congregation, of course, should be preaching and teaching the Gospel, year in year out, in season and out of season, with biblical faithfulness, contemporary relevance and urgent boldness. We believe the church languishes whenever the Word of God is neglected, and flourishes whenever it is honoured. We desire to call our churches back to biblical preaching for both evangelism and edification.

But we have to teach our people the law as well as the Gospel, that is, obedience as well as forgiveness, the moral demands of the kingdom as well as its gift of salvation. Indeed, it is the calling of preachers, like Paul in Ephesus, 'not to shrink from declaring' to the people 'anything that is profitable', indeed 'not to shrink from declaring to them the whole counsel of God' (Acts 20:20,27). This will include rebuking evil in all its ugly manifestations.

Thorough teaching of the Word of God is even more important in our day, in which many Christians are bewildered by contemporary problems. They read about them in the newspaper and hear about them on radio or television; shall such topics then be excluded from the pulpit? We are not now referring to issues which are controversial even among Christians (we will come to these in the next paragraph), but to fundamental modern challenges to the teaching of the Bible. People need help to resist the pressures of secular thought and to take a firm stand on the moral principles of Scripture. So we must help them to discern the moral issues in each question, to understand them and to hold them fast. In addition, they need to be made aware of how the socio-political and legislative processes work, and to have their confidence raised that they need not be the helpless victims either of an evil status quo or of revolutionary destruction, but can be active as society's salt and light in the fight to protect, re-establish or introduce Christian ethical values. This kind of consciousness-raising is particularly important for those church members who are community leaders, opinion formers and decision makers — for example, parents, teachers, journalists and politicians. In a democracy (in which government depends on the consent of the governed), legislation depends on public opinion. Our Christian responsibility is to get into the public debate about current issues, boldly affirm, practise and argue what the Bible teaches, and so seek to influence public opinion for Christ.

How, then, shall we handle controversial topics? Many voices during the consultation have urged us to be cautious. Modern problems of personal and social ethics (which are often inter-related) are legion: abortion, euthanasia, genetic engineering, homosexuality, racism, casteism and tribalism, sexism, human rights, environmental pollution, ideologies, polygamy, economic in-equality between and within nations, terrorism, war, nuclear disarmament, and many more. To some of these ethical questions the biblical answer is clear, and in most others a plain biblical principle is involved: here, then, the teaching of the church should be unequivocal and unanimous.

Yet, highly complex issues remain. So then, whenever the Word of God speaks clearly, the church must speak clearly also, as for example did the German Confessing Church in the Barmen Declaration of 1934, and the Norwegian Church while Norway was under German occupation in World War II. If such speech is condemned as political, we need to remember that silence would be political, too. We cannot avoid taking sides. But when the teaching of Scripture seems unclear, and human reason has to seek to develop a position out of biblical principles, then the church should make a pro-nouncement only after thorough study and consultation.

When the church cannot agree on an issue, then the issue cannot be dealt with in the name of the church; instead, Christian individuals and groups should handle it. The church should also be sensitive to anything (such as a divisive controversy) that would weaken its evangelistic outreach. But when the church concludes that biblical faith or righteousness requires it to take a public stand on some issue, then it must obey God's Word and trust him with the consequences.

We heard from the pastor of a black church in New England that their resolve to address themselves to social issues has greatly increased their evangelistic witness. Their procedure is one of thorough consultation, in order to ensure unity rather than division in the congregation. First, the pastor makes a presentation on some issue to his deacons, next the deacons take it to the church council, and then the church council refers it to the church members. At each successive stage, agreement is sought. The result has been that the church has had wider opportunities for witness, because it has become known as a socially concerned church, and so evangelism and social action have had a multiplying impact on one another.

All of us are agreed that a local church should not normally engage in partisan politics, either advocating a particular party or attempting to frame political programs. We also are agreed, however, that the local church has a prophetic ministry to proclaim the law of God and to teach justice, should seek to be the conscience of the community, and has a duty to help the congregation develop a Christian mind, so that the people may learn to think Christianly even about controversial questions.

4. Power

All of us agree that God gives power to his people — power for holiness, power for witness, and power for courageous action in the name of Christ. We all also agree that, in his sovereignty and his grace, God endows his people with a wide variety of spiritual gifts for service. Some of us lay particular emphasis on supernatural 'gifts of healing', 'the working of miracles' (I Cor. 12:9,10), and the casting out of demons, while others prefer to emphasize non-miraculous social gifts like contributing to the needs of others, giving aid, and doing 'acts of mercy' (Rom. 12:8). All spiritual gifts, whatever their nature, should be exercised with compassion under the anointing of the Holy Spirit and for the common good. They can meet social, physical and emotional as well as spiritual needs, contribute to the well-being of society as well as of the church, and, authenticating the Gospel, draw unbelievers to Christ.

5. Vocations

All Christians are called to both witness and service. Whenever the opportunity is given, we have a privileged duty to speak for Christ and to serve our neighbour. In addition to this general Christian calling, however, each of us has a special vocation. We have already written about the diversity of gifts, leading to a diversity of ministries, in the body of Christ.

The local church (especially its leadership) has a responsibility, therefore, to help its members (especially its young people) to recognize their gifts and so discover their vocation. Some churches set up a 'vocation group' for those of its members who are wanting to discern God's will for their lives, in order that they may pray together, seek advice and investigate a variety of possibilities.

On the one hand, the local church should continuously keep before its membership the possibility that God may be calling some of them to a full-time Christian ministry as cross-cultural missionaries, evangelists, pastors, teachers, or church workers of some other kind. And the local church should give its members opportunities to test their vocation in evangelistic missions, house-to-house visitation, youth outreach, Sunday school teaching, and in other ways.

On the other hand, full-time Christian ministry is not limited to these areas. Although it is a great and sacred calling to be a missionary or a pastor, we must not thereby imply that other callings are 'secular'. There is an urgent need to encourage more of our Christian young people to respond to God's call into the professions, into industry and commerce, into public office in the political arena, and into the mass media, in order that they may penetrate these strongholds of influence for Christ. And whatever our church members' vocations are, we need both to help train them to serve there as Christians and to support them in their service.

This brings us back to evangelism again. For in order to make an impact on our society for Christ, we need more Christians to permeate it as his salt and light; otherwise, our effectiveness will be very small. But in order to send more Christians into the world, we must win more people for Christ and disciple them. 'Our dire need,' one of our groups has written, 'is for an army of Josephs, Esthers, Daniels and Nehemiahs, who will have a determining voice in the affairs of our countries.'

6. *Groups*

Just as there are special vocations, so there should be specialist groups in every church. For it is certain that the local church as a unit cannot possibly engage in all the activities it is being urged to undertake. Therefore, it must delegate particular responsibilities to different groups.

To begin with, there should be evangelistic groups, all trained for evangelistic outreach, one perhaps maintaining regular door-to-door visitation in the district, another organizing and maintaining a Christian coffee-bar or infiltrating a non-Christian one, another serving as a music group or witness team, another arranging evangelistic home meetings or home Bible study and prayer meetings. As the church responds sensitively to the evangelistic needs which it perceives in its community, appropriate new groups can constantly be brought into being.

In addition, the church needs social service groups. One may organize literacy classes with an ethnic minority, another may visit senior citizens or hospital patients or prison inmates, another may initiate a development project in a local slum area, or found a co-operative with the poor, or a club with delinquent youth, while another may offer citizens' advice or legal aid to those who cannot afford to pay for it. Again, the possibilities are almost limitless.

Thirdly, the local church may decide to form one or more social action groups, if this is compatible with its understanding of the church's role in society. Such groups would doubtless devote a good deal of their time to study, in which they may seek the help of experts. They might take up a global problem, in order to educate themselves and (if given the opportunity) the church. Or they might address themselves to an ethical issue like abortion. If they reach a consensus and are able to carry the church with them, then no doubt their study would lead to action, whether in terms of political lobbying or non-violent protest or joining in some national demonstration. An alternative to church groups is the encouragement of church members to join non-church groups.

Whatever action a group takes, however, it would have to be clear itself and make clear to others whether it is operating on its own or has the backing of the church. All these groups — for evangelism, social service or social action — need to relate closely to the church, reporting back regularly and seeking advice and support. In this way the ministry of the church can be greatly diversified.

7. Resources

The evangelistic and social work of the church depends on money as well as people. How much of its income each local church decides to allocate to evangelism, and how much to social responsibility, will depend on its particular circumstances. This will have to be settled by prayerful consultation and not by a simple formula, and it will be related to what other churches, government and voluntary agencies are doing.

Each local church needs to remember, however, that it is a manifestation in its own community of the universal church of Christ. Therefore, it has an international as well as a local responsibility. The world-wide Christian community should seek to develop a true 'partnership . . . in giving and receiving' (Phil. 4:15). That is, gifts should flow in both directions, so that every giver is also a receiver, and every receiver a giver. For example, one church might send financial help to another, and in return receive a visit from an evangelist or Bible teacher of the other church. Such reciprocal Christian ministry can be extremely enriching, and should be fostered by mutual discussion of needs and resources.

The context for Christian thinking about resources should be the forecast that by the year A.D. 2000 the world's population is likely to exceed six billion people. This will dramatically increase the numbers of both unevangelized and needy people. Meanwhile, a comparatively small number of westerners who live around the North Atlantic, together with some wealthy minorities elsewhere, continue to consume a disproportionate percentage of Planet Earth's natural wealth.

If Christians are going to take seriously the double challenge to take the good news to all nations and to enable the poor to become self-reliant, a major redistribution of resources will be necessary. We are not now pronouncing on the controversial macro-question of how to redress the economic imbalance between rich and poor nations. Rather we are wanting wealthy local churches to remember that millions of poor people in the world are their Christian brothers and sisters. The Christian conscience cannot come to terms with the fact that they live and die in poverty, while so many of us enjoy an affluent lifestyle.

We are still committed to paragraph 9 of the Lausanne Covenant, which commented that we cannot attain our goals without sacrifice, and then went on: 'All of us are shocked by the poverty of millions and disturbed by the injustices which cause it. Those of us who live in affluent circumstances accept our duty to develop a simple lifestyle in order to contribute more generously to both relief and evangelism.' We are not naïve enough to imagine that the world's problems will be solved by such action. But we believe that a Christian lifestyle of contentment and simplicity fulfils the teaching of Scripture, expresses solidarity with the poor, and releases funds for evangelistic and social enterprises.

At present, only a tiny fraction of our total Christian resources is being applied to any kind of mission, evangelistic or social. How, then, can Christian people be motivated to give? The strongest argument for sacrificial giving is the one Paul used when appealing to the Christians of Corinth to be generous: 'For you know the grace of our Lord Jesus Christ, that though he was rich, yet for your sake he became poor, so that by his poverty you might become rich' (II Cor.8:9). Our Lord is generous; his people therefore must be generous, too. And the place to learn generosity is the local church.

(d) The Church under Repression

There are many settings in the world where today's church, like the early church, suffers from harassment or active persecution. We have thought particularly about churches repressed by Marxist, Muslim or extreme rightist regimes, and about minority churches repressed by state-related churches. In such situations, it has been suggested to us, the church has always faced three temptations — to *conform* (tailoring the Gospel to the prevailing ideology), to *fight* (losing its identity by resorting to worldly weapons), or to *withdraw* (denying its mission, betraying its calling, and losing its relevance). It also has been pointed out to us that there were three similar options in our Lord's day, represented by the Sadducees (the compromisers), the Zealots (the freedom fighters), and the Pharisees and Essenes (the escapists), and that these three groups formed an unholy alliance against Jesus, finding him a greater threat than each other.

Our brothers and sisters in repressive situations have recommended that, resisting these three temptations, the church should rather develop a critical involvement in society, while preserving its primary allegiance to Christ. Such a church will have little opportunity to preach openly or to exert a social influence, because it has been pushed to the margins of society and has no apparatus of power. The following guidelines for its evangelism and social responsibility have been proposed:

1. Consistency
Above all, the church must be true to its Lord, a Christ-centred community, and thus establish the credibility of its witness. There must be no dichotomy

between its profession and its practice. For being precedes acting, and seeing must accompany hearing.

2. Love

Churches under duress should remember the evangelizing power of a Christian community of love which, even when public worship and witness are forbidden, can bear its testimony by deeds of love. Each local church needs to be a model of just structures, harmonious relationships, and modest lifestyle. The people of God need also to remember that their 'enemies', who persecute them, are persons in whom is the image of God and for whom Christ died, and that a person is more important than the ideology which he or she holds. By the grace of God, they will be enabled to love their enemies, as Jesus taught.

3. Witness

Even under persecution, God opens spaces for his people to live and share the Gospel, especially in personal evangelism, and to demonstrate that the 'new man' of Marxist expectation can be created only by Jesus Christ. God will give opportunities also to serve human need. Even though centrally-planned economies in some countries have succeeded in abolishing extreme poverty, there still remain pockets of deep human need — the disillusioned, the elderly, the lonely, and the neglected minority groups. Christians will gladly love and serve them.

4. Solidarity

When the church has to act, especially in some kind of protest, who will take the initiative? It is too risky for pastors, and individuals are too weak. So members of the body of Christ must stand together, the local church for local issues, and the national church for national issues, knowing their legal rights and defending them (like the apostle Paul), and witnessing together to Christ.

5. Suffering

What if church and state appear to be on a collision course?

The general teaching of Scripture is plain. The institution of government has been established by God; and citizens are required to be subject to it — to obey the law, pay their taxes, fulfil their civic duties, and seek the good of their country. Indeed, Christian people should encourage the state to perform its God-given duty to reward those who do right and punish those who do wrong (Rom. 13:1–7; I Pet. 2: 1:13–15; cf. Jer. 29:7).

What happens if the state abuses its authority, however, and either forbids what God commands or commands what God forbids? The principle is clear. We are to obey the state (whose authority comes from God) right up to the point where obedience to it would involve us in disobedience to him. In that extreme circumstance alone, it is our Christian duty to disobey the state in order to obey God.

This has an evangelistic implication. It was when the Sanhedrin forbade the apostles to preach in the name of Jesus that Peter said, 'We must obey God rather than men', and, 'We cannot but speak of what we have seen and heard' (Acts 4:17–20; 5:27–29). Those of us who live in free countries are in no position to tell our brothers and sisters in totalitarian situations how they should respond to government attempts to silence them. We do not think they necessarily should defy the authorities with the outspoken boldness of the apostles. They may consider it wiser at least in many cases to bear testimony more by deed than by word. On the other hand, they will be unable to give the state complete allegiance in this matter, since witness to Jesus is an inalienable part of our obedience to him.

Turning to social action, the Bible records a noble succession of men and women who risked their lives by courageously defying a human authority in the name of the God of justice. We have been reminded of Nathan, who confronted King David over his adultery with Bathsheba and his murder of her husband; of Elijah, who denounced King Ahab for annexing Naboth's vineyard by having him assassinated; of Daniel and his friends, who between them refused either to worship an image or to stop worshipping the true God; of Queen Esther, who dared to present herself, though unbidden, to King Ahasuerus in order to plead for her people unjustly condemned to be massacred; and of John the Baptist, who told King Herod that his marriage to Herodias his sister-in-law was unlawful, and who lost his life as a result.

With these biblical precedents we should not be surprised that they have their modern counterparts. Three African examples have particularly impressed us. When the President of Chad, in the name of cultural revolution, tried to force Christians to submit to pagan initiation rites, some compromised, others were killed, and the church leaders were unable to act in unison. A single layman, however, wrote an Open Letter to the President to explain why he could not submit, even if it meant that he must die. His letter was received and respected.

Although Kenya does not fall into the category of a repressive dictatorship, and Christians (who are in the majority) enjoy freedom, yet the church has on occasions suffered and has taken a firm stand against injustices. In 1969, some Kikuyu leaders tried to unite their tribe by requiring an oath of loyalty to it. Many Christians refused to take the oath because, they said, their supreme loyalty was to Christ, and their next loyalty was to their nation, not their tribe. Some were killed. So a group of church leaders went together to President Kenyatta, and as a result the oathing was stopped.

That confrontation with a President was successful. Another, in the neighbouring country of Uganda, led to tragedy, although God turned it to the church's good. During Amin's reign of terror, the house of bishops of the Anglican Church of Uganda wrote him a joint letter to complain of the cruelty and malpractices of his soldiers, and of the total disregard for human life in the country. Archbishop Janani Luwum was summoned to appear before an assembly of leaders and soldiers, and then was falsely accused, mocked, and shortly afterwards assassinated. The other bishops stood in solidarity with him at this time of suffering.

These examples of courage have greatly challenged us. We believe that such confrontations should be reserved for extreme situations only and that in such circumstances church leaders, if possible, should act together and only after the most thorough consultation.

Nevertheless, there are occasions of moral principle in which the church must take its stand, whatever the cost. For the church is the community of the Suffering Servant who is also the Lord, and it is called to serve and suffer with him. It is not popularity which is the authentic mark of the church, but prophetic suffering, and even martyrdom. 'Indeed all who desire to live a godly life in Christ Jesus will be persecuted' (II Tim. 3:14). May we be given grace to stand firm!

CONCLUSION: A CALL TO OBEDIENCE

We have come to the end of our report. It has been a great joy for us to be together for this week. Despite our different backgrounds and traditions, we have deeply appreciated one another and the rich multi–cultural fellowship which God has given us.

We have talked, listened, pondered, debated and prayed. We also have warned one another of the dangers of such prolonged analysis, categorization and reflection, while outside — beyond the delightful campus of the Reformed Bible College where we have been accommodated so comfortably — are living those lost, oppressed and needy people about whom we have been speaking.

Now the time has come for us to stop discussing them and start serving them, to leave 'the mountain of glory' and descend to 'the valley of problems and opportunities' (about which Bishop David Gitari preached during our opening service of worship).

Jesus our Lord is calling us to put into practice what we have written, and to determine afresh by his grace to reach all peoples with the Gospel. Challenged by the humility of his incarnation, inspired by the love of his cross, relying on the power of his resurrection, and eagerly awaiting the glory of his return, we are resolved to obey his call. We hope that others who read our report will be moved by the same Lord to the same resolve and the same obedience.

We request the Lausanne Committee for World Evangelization and the World Evangelical Fellowship, who jointly sponsored our consultation, and other bodies of like mind, to call Christians and churches around the world to a more costly commitment to the lost, the needy and the oppressed, for the greater glory of God, Father, Son and Holy Spirit.

Grand Rapids, Michigan
26 June 1982

APPENDIX A

Members of the Consultation

'*Members*' *is an inclusive term referring to several groups of persons involved in CRESR 82: ex officio individuals, participants invited on a regional basis, and consultants from various fields of expertise. In this list they are placed in alphabetical order, irrespective of the category to which each belonged.*

Tokunboh Adeyemo,
  Nigeria/Kenya
Sarah F. Anders, USA
Pedro Arana-Quiroz, Peru
Gonzalo Baez-Camargo, Mexico
Peter Beyerhaus, West Germany
Klaus Bockmuehl, Canada
David J. Bosch, South Africa
Hector Camacho, USA
Robinson Cavalcanti, Brazil
John C. Cho, South Korea
Wilson W. Chow, Hong Kong
Wade Coggins, USA
Harvie M. Conn, USA
Edward R. Dayton, USA
Eva Den Hartog, Holland/USA
Mariano di Gangi, Canada
Carmen Canelo Donoso, Chile
Leighton Ford, USA
David M. Gitari, Kenya
Samuel Habib, Egypt
Michael Haynes, USA
Arthur P. Johnston, USA
Peter Kuzmic, Yugoslavia
Harold Lindsell, USA
Robert Matzken, Netherlands
Lois McKinney, USA

Gordon Moyes, Australia
Ludwig Munthe, Norway
Abel Ndjerareou, Chad
Bruce Nicholls, N.Z./India
Agne Nordlander, Sweden
Emilio A. D. Nunez, Guatemala
Samuel A. Olson, Venezuela
Gottfried Osei-Mensah,
  Ghana/Kenya
C. René Padilla, Argentina
John Perkins, USA
Soeti Rahayoe, Indonesia
John R. Reid, Australia
D. John Richard, India
Bong Rin Ro, Taiwan
Vinay K. Samuel, India
Kefa Sempangi, Uganda
Ronald J. Sider, USA
Tom Sine, USA
John Stott, Britain
Christopher Sugden, Britain/India
Tite Tiénou, Upper Volta
Dick L. Van Halsema, USA
Agustin B. Vencer, Philippines
C. Peter Wagner, USA
David F. Wells, USA

211

APPENDIX B

The Papers and their Writers

Day One: Church History and Modern Theologies

1. The Perspective of Church History — Bong Rin Ro
   Response: David Wells
2. Perspectives on Evangelism and Social Responsibility in
   Contemporary Theology (1954 to present) — Tokunboh Adeyemo
   Response: David Bosch

Day Two: Salvation and Kingdom

3. How Broad is Salvation in Scripture? — Ronald Sider
   Response: Ludwig Munthe
4. The Kingdom in Relation to the Church and the World — Arthur
   P. Johnston
   Response: René Padilla

Day Three: History and Eschatology

5. Evangelical Views — Peter Kuzmic
   Response: Emilio Antonio Nunez
6. A Biblical Encounter with Some Contemporary Non-Christian or
   Un-Evangelical Views — Peter Beyerhaus
   Response: Gordon Moyes

Day Four: The Mission of the Church

7. The Mission of the Church in Relation to Evangelism and Social
   Responsibility. A Biblical Study — Vinay Samuel and Chris Sugden
   Response: Harold Lindsell
8. A second presentation — John Chongnahm Cho
   Response: Tite Tiénou

212

POSTSCRIPT

A book containing the revised papers and some of the responses to them was edited by Bruce J. Nicholls and published by the Paternoster Press in 1985. It was entitled *In Word and Deed*, and sub-titled 'Evangelism and Social Responsibility'.

After a Preface by Bong Rin Ro and Gottfried Osei-Mensah, the co-chairmen of the consultation, the book concentrates on four main areas — first, historical and contemporary perspectives on the relation between evangelism and social responsibility (chapters 1–3), secondly, the meaning and extent of God's 'salvation' and 'kingdom' (chapter 4 and 5), thirdly, the relations between history and eschatology (chapters 6 and 7), and fourthly, the nature and priorities of the Christian mission (chapter 8 and 9).

8

— 1984–1988 —

Four Consultations and their supporting Documents

♦♦♦♦♦

Seoul — Oslo — Singapore — Hong Kong

—Four Consultations—

CONTENTS

1. THE INTERNATIONAL PRAYER ASSEMBLY FOR WORLD EVANGELIZATION

(June 1984 — Seoul, Korea)

This was the first of four further Lausanne-inspired events which took place during the five–year period 1984–1988.

The June 1984 Assembly was designed to explore the relations between prayer and world evangelization. It was sponsored and organized by LCWE's Intercession Working Group and by the Korean Evangelical Fellowship.

Twenty-three representative messages given at the Assembly were edited and compiled by Vonette Bright and Ben A. Jennings, and published by Moody Press in 1989 under the title *Unleashing the Power of Prayer*. After some introductory material, which includes 'The International Call to Prayer', the book is divided into five parts.

Part I is entitled 'Prayer for Personal Renewal' (the source and cost of revival); Part II 'Learning How to Pray' (principles and hindrances); Part III 'Prayer for the Revival of the Church' (the conditions and fruits of spiritual awakenings); Part IV 'Prayer and Regional Evangelization' (strategies for regional and national prayer movements); and Part V 'Prayer Strategy for World Evangelization' (what God is doing and could do in response to his people's prayers).

THE INTERNATIONAL CALL TO PRAYER

Adopted by the full International Prayer Assembly for World Evangelization, meeting in June 1984 in Seoul, Korea.

Introduction

God in his calling and providence has brought us together in Seoul, Korea, from sixty-nine nations. We have sought his face and his guidance. He has impressed on us an urgency to call for an international prayer movement to accomplish spiritual awakening and world evangelization.

World Evangelization and Prayer

World evangelization is a sovereign work of the triune God, through the ministry of Christ's church. The forces of darkness, which block the spread of truth and the growth of the church, cannot be displaced by human plans and efforts. Only the omnipotent and omniscient Holy Spirit, applying the fruits of the finished work of Christ, through a church constantly awakened through prayer, can deliver the lost from the power of Satan (Acts 26:18), as the Lord adds daily those who are being saved (Acts 2:47).

The awakening of the church is thus essential to the completion of world evangelization. The renewed church in Acts 2:42–47 was strengthened by apostolic teaching, the Lord's Supper and sharing fellowship. But these means of grace can be empowered for us today only through fervent and persistent prayer to the Father in the name of the crucified and risen Christ. Even after Pentecost, the apostles repeatedly turned to prayer for the church to be filled afresh with the Spirit and empowered to proclaim the Gospel with boldness, despite Satanic resistance (Acts 4:23–31).

Prayer is God's appointed means whereby the Spirit's power is released in evangelism. By prayer the Spirit both empowers our witness and opens Satan-blinded unbelievers to seek and desire the Lord Jesus Christ as Savior. The Lord's promise that his Father will answer us, if we ask according to his will and in his name, is our strong encouragement in believing prayer.

Before the Lord's return, to judge all Satanic rebellion and to consummate his kingdom in power and glory, the Gospel must and will be preached, and disciples made, among every people on earth (Matt. 24:14; 28:19, 20; Mk. 13:10). The explicit agreement and visible union of God's people in extraordinary prayer, for the renewal of the church and world evangelization, is essential to the extension of the kingdom of Christ through the preaching of the Gospel.

We rejoice that in the last few years in many parts of the world, through the work of the Holy Spirit, there has been a growing dependence on God, which has led to increased unity in prayer in the body of Christ, transcending denominational, national, ethnic and cultural divisions.

Our failures in prayer

We confess that too often prayer is offered only for personal, physical and financial needs, rather than also for spiritual needs in the church, the neighborhood and the world.

We confess that frequently there is a lack of meaningful prayer by the congregation in the services of the local church, as well as a general lack of personal and family prayer.

We confess that there is not enough emphasis on, training for, and dependence upon, prayer from our pulpits and in Christian training institutions.

We confess that too often dependence on the Holy Spirit's role in prayer has been minimized, and that prayer has been mobilized without reliance on him.

A call to prayer

We are constrained to call the body of Christ worldwide to mobilize intercession for spiritual awakening in the church and for world evangelization. We call specifically for the following:

1. The formation of interdenominational *prayer committees*, whenever possible through existing structures, on local, national, regional, continental and international levels.
2. The convening of national, regional, continental and international *prayer assemblies*, as soon as this can be adequately implemented, and thereafter at regular intervals.
3. The establishing of *information networks* through personal visitation, literature, audio-visual means etc. for prayer needs, emergencies, reports of prayer movements worldwide, and prayer ministry resources.
4. The promotion and nurture of *the prayer life* through seminars, workshops, literature and audiovisuals.
5. The giving of *priority to prayer* (in life and ministry) by churches and parachurch organizations, by seminaries and other Christian institutions, and by Christian leaders and pastors.
6. The cooperation and participation of churches worldwide in the observance of designated *days of prayer*.

Conclusion

We therefore call all believers to a specific and personal commitment to become prayer warriors for spiritual awakening and world evangelization.

2. THE CONSULTATION ON THE WORK OF THE HOLY SPIRIT AND EVANGELIZATION

(May 1985 — Oslo, Norway)

This international consultation was jointly sponsored by LCWE's Theology Working Group and WEF's Theological Commission. It brought 46 participants together, evangelists, theologians, pastors and church leaders, both charismatic and non-charismatic. About 25 papers were contributed, covering biblical, historical, theological, missiological and personal themes. A number of case studies were contributed, and the participants prayed as well as studied together.

It was decided at the end of the consultation that the best way to share its deliberations with the wider church would be through a book rather than a statement, and Professor David Wells was invited to write it. He took the papers and the tape-recordings of the debate as his basis, worked them into a report, and submitted it to the small, authorized editorial committee, chaired by Bishop John Reid. This committee considered the manuscript, made a few minor modifications, and approved the text. In this sense it may justly be regarded as carrying the authority of the consultation.

The book is entitled *God the Evangelist* and sub-titled 'How the Holy Spirit works to bring men and women to faith'. It was published in 1987 by Eerdmans and Paternoster.

After an introduction by Dr. J. I. Packer entitled 'On Being Serious about the Holy Spirit', Dr. Wells writes six chapters in which the biblical doctrine of the Holy Spirit is thoroughly unfolded. Chapter 1 ('Spirit of the Living God') considers the place of the Spirit in the Old Testament, the New Testament and the church fathers. Chapter 2 ('The World and its Religions') draws a careful distinction between God's presence in creation and history, and his work of redemption. Chapter 3 ('The Gospel made Effective') insists on the indispensability of the work of the Spirit according to both Scripture and church history. Chapter 4 ('God's Message and God's People') argues that the church is both a product and a model of the Gospel. Chapter 5 ('Spiritual Power Encounters') emphasizes liberation through the Gospel from the flesh, the world and the devil, and opens up the question of 'signs and wonders'. Chapter 6 ('Spirit of the living God, Fall Afresh on Us') urges us to hold together the Spirit's three major functions in relation to truth, holiness and power.

This valuable book concludes with five appendices. Two of them are case studies from China and East Africa, and the other three consider the work of the Spirit in relation to people groups, local church worship and evangelistic Bible studies.

3. A CONFERENCE OF YOUNG LEADERS
(June 1987 — Singapore)

About 100 younger evangelical leaders from the six continents were invited
to come together, in order to share the vision for world evangelization and to
pass the Lausanne torch to the rising generation. The challenge and inspiration were considerable, but no report was issued.

A North American *Young Leaders' Conference*, with similar objectives,
was held in Washington DC in June 1988.

4. THE CONSULTATION ON CONVERSION AND WORLD EVANGELIZATION

(January 1988 — Hong Kong)

Like the Oslo consultation on the work of the Holy Spirit (1985), the Hong Kong consultation on Conversion (1988) was jointly sponsored by LCWE's Theology Working Group and WEF's Theological Commission. Its convener was Robert Godfrey, and the joint chairmen were Bishop John Reid (LCWE) and Dr. Wilson Chow (WEF). Participants came from a wide diversity of countries and cultures, and from both academic and pastoral ministries. The twenty-three papers presented reflected biblical-theological, psychological and cultural-anthropological perspectives, and ensured an informed, vigorous, inter-disciplinary debate.

As in Oslo, so in Hong Kong, Dr. David Wells was invited to use the papers as the basis for a book and to supplement their contents both with his own understanding of the subsequent discussion and with 'fresh material where needed to fill in between the cracks'. This commission David Wells fulfilled with his customary depth and breadth of treatment. The result is entitled *Turning to God* and sub-titled 'biblical conversion in the modern world'. It was published by Paternoster Press and Baker Book House in 1989.

In his Introduction David Wells rejects the two popular ecumenical trends which he calls 'social gospel theologies' and 'visions of a world religion'. In their place he puts the biblical alternative that conversion is both 'supernatural' (God's grace being its cause) and 'unique' ('Conversion is not uniquely Christian, but Christian conversion is unique and uniquely true'). Eight chapters follow this introduction.

Chapter 1 ('Christian Conversion') examines the relevant biblical vocabulary and then introduces the helpful distinction between 'insider conversions' (involving people who already have a substantial set of Christian beliefs) and 'outsider conversions' involving people who have little or no prior Christian knowledge). Yet in both cases authentic conversion will be evidenced in a life of God-centred convertedness and baptized community membership.

Chapter 2 ('Insiders') begins with a study of Saul's conversion, asking which aspects of it are normative and which are not. Then children are taken as exemplifying 'insider conversion'.

Chapter 3 ('How and Why we Turn') argues that conversion is a complex process involving thought and struggle. Three questions are then asked and answered. Are some people more susceptible to conversion than others? How much knowledge is necessary for salvation? What is the appropriate motivation and preparation for conversion?

Chapter 4 ('The Church's View of Conversion') asks whether conversion is 'by grace through faith' or 'dispensed through the church', and finds a combination of these two models in Augustine. The catholic and the evangelical understandings are then considered separately, and a historical conclusion on 'Revivals and Missions' shows how during the last 250 years evangelism has tended to be detached from the church, truth to be replaced by experience, and the sovereignty of grace to be forgotten.

Chapters 5 to 7 are careful and informed studies of 'outsiders' — first 'religious' outsiders (Jews and Muslims in Chapter 5, Hindus and Buddhists in Chapter 6) and then 'materialistic' outsiders in Chapter 7, in particular secularists and Marxists. These chapters offer rich resources for messengers of the Gospel who are called to work and witness among the people described. The need, nature, implications, hindrances and consequences of conversion are faithfully considered. It is emphasized that people come to faith in stages.

Chapter 8 ('Into the Future') declares television and popular psychology to be two streams of fantasy hostile to the truth, reminds us that the Gospel focuses on Christ crucified, resurrected, reigning and coming to judge, and insists that even in our age of technological omnicompetence self-conversion and self-salvation are impossible.

9

— 1989 —

The Manila Manifesto: an elaboration of The Lausanne Covenant 15 years later

◆◆◆◆◆

The Second International Congress on
World Evangelization (Lausanne II),
Manila, Philippines, 11–20 July 1989

CONTENTS

CONTENTS

FOREWORD

The participants in Lausanne II, the Second International Congress on World Evangelization, held in Manila in the Philippines in July 1989, deliberated on the prospects for the fulfillment of the Great Commission of our Lord Jesus Christ.

The subject was looked at from every conceivable angle, with an attempt to be true to the Holy Scriptures in the analysis. The results were summarized in *The Manila Manifesto*. Its second draft was submitted to all the participants. They made many comments and suggestions, which were carefully considered in the preparation of the final document. The following motion was then put to the whole Congress in plenary session: 'We accept the Manila Manifesto as an expression, in general terms, of our concerns and commitments, and we commend it to ourselves, to churches and to Christian organizations for further study and response'. This motion passed by an overwhelming majority.

The Executive of the Lausanne Committee for World Evangelization has directed that The Manila Manifesto never be published apart from The Lausanne Covenant, of which it is an extension fifteen years later [and which is printed in chapter 1 of this book. The Covenant has been translated into more than twenty languages.]

The Lausanne Committee recognizes that reflection on the Great Commission needs to be a continuous process, and would therefore welcome responses to both the Covenant and the Manifesto, so that we may discern better the nature of our task in mission in the last decade of the second millennium AD.

TOM HOUSTON
International Director, LCWE

INTRODUCTION

In July 1974 the International Congress on World Evangelization was held in Lausanne, Switzerland, and issued the Lausanne Covenant. Now in July 1989 over 3,000 of us from about 170 countries have met in Manila for the same purpose, and have issued the Manila Manifesto. We are grateful for the welcome we have received from our Filipino brothers and sisters.

During the 15 years which have elapsed between the two congresses some smaller consultations have been held on topics like Gospel and Culture, Evangelism and Social Responsibility, Simple Lifestyle, the Holy Spirit, and Conversion. These meetings and their reports have helped to develop the thinking of the Lausanne movement.*

A 'manifesto' is defined as a public declaration of convictions, intentions and motives. The Manila Manifesto takes up the two congress themes, 'Proclaim Christ until he comes' and 'Calling the Whole Church to take the Whole Gospel to the Whole World'. Its first part is a series of 21 succinct affirmations. Its second part elaborates these in 12 sections, which are commended to churches, alongside the Lausanne Covenant, for study and action.

*These reports appear in chapters 2–8 of this book.

TWENTY-ONE AFFIRMATIONS

1. We affirm our continuing commitment to the Lausanne Covenant as the basis of our cooperation in the Lausanne movement.

2. We affirm that in the Scriptures of the Old and New Testaments God has given us an authoritative disclosure of his character and will, his redemptive acts and their meaning, and his mandate for mission.

3. We affirm that the biblical gospel is God's enduring message to our world, and we determine to defend, proclaim and embody it.

4. We affirm that human beings, though created in the image of God, are sinful and guilty, and lost without Christ, and that this truth is a necessary preliminary to the Gospel.

5. We affirm that the Jesus of history and the Christ of glory are the same person, and that this Jesus Christ is absolutely unique, for he alone is God incarnate, our sin-bearer, the conqueror of death and the coming judge.

6. We affirm that on the cross Jesus Christ took our place, bore our sins and died our death; and that for this reason alone God freely forgives those who are brought to repentance and faith.

7. We affirm that other religions and ideologies are not alternative paths to God, and that human spirituality, if unredeemed by Christ, leads not to God but to judgment, for Christ is the only way.

8. We affirm that we must demonstrate God's love visibly by caring for those who are deprived of justice, dignity, food and shelter.

9. We affirm that the proclamation of God's kingdom of justice and peace demands the denunciation of all injustice and oppression, both personal and structural; we will not shrink from this prophetic witness.

10. We affirm that the Holy Spirit's witness to Christ is indispensable to evangelism, and that without his supernatural work neither new birth nor new life is possible.

11. We affirm that spiritual warfare demands spiritual weapons, and that we must both preach the word in the power of the Spirit, and pray constantly that we may enter into Christ's victory over the principalities and powers of evil.

12. We affirm that God has committed to the whole church and every member of it the task of making Christ known throughout the world; we long to see all lay and ordained persons mobilized and trained for this task.

13. We affirm that we who claim to be members of the body of Christ must transcend within our fellowship the barriers of race, gender and class.

14. We affirm that the gifts of the Spirit are distributed to all God's people, women and men, and that their partnership in evangelization must be welcomed for the common good.

15. We affirm that we who proclaim the Gospel must exemplify it in a life of holiness and love; otherwise our testimony loses its credibility.

16. We affirm that every Christian congregation must turn itself outward to its local community in evangelistic witness and compassionate service.

17. We affirm the urgent need for churches, mission agencies and other Christian organizations to cooperate in evangelism and social action, repudiating competition and avoiding duplication.

18. We affirm our duty to study the society in which we live, in order to understand its structures, values and needs, and so develop an appropriate strategy of mission.

19. We affirm that world evangelization is urgent, and that the reaching of unreached peoples is possible. So we resolve during the last decade of the twentieth century to give ourselves to these tasks with fresh determination.

20. We affirm our solidarity with those who suffer for the Gospel, and will seek to prepare ourselves for the same possibility. We will also work for religious and political freedom everywhere.

21. We affirm that God is calling the whole church to take the whole Gospel to the whole world. So we determine to proclaim it faithfully, urgently and sacrificially, until he comes.

A. THE WHOLE GOSPEL

The Gospel is the good news of God's salvation from the powers of evil, the establishment of his eternal kingdom and his final victory over everything which defies his purpose. In his love God purposed to do this before the world began and effected his liberating plan over sin, death and judgment through the death of our Lord Jesus Christ. It is Christ who makes us free, and unites us in his redeemed fellowship.

Col.2:15
1 CO. 15:24-28
Eph. 1:4;
Col. 1:19
Tit. 2:14

1. Our Human Predicament

We are committed to preaching the whole Gospel, that is, the biblical Gospel in its fullness. In order to do so, we have to understand why human beings need it.

Ac. 20:27

Men and women have an intrinsic dignity and worth, because they were created in God's likeness to know, love and serve him. But now through sin every part of their humanness has been distorted. Human beings have become self-centered, self-serving rebels, who do not love God or their neighbour as they should. In consequence, they are alienated both from their Creator and from the rest of his creation, which is the basic cause of the pain, disorientation and loneliness which so many people suffer today. Sin also frequently erupts in anti-social behavior, in violent exploitation of others, and in a depletion of the earth's resources of which God has made men and women his stewards. Humanity is guilty, without excuse, and on the broad road which leads to destruction.

Ge. 1:26, 27
Ro. 3:9-18
2 Ti. 3:2-4
Ge. 3: 17-24
Ro. 1:29-31
Ge. 1:26, 28; 2:15
Ro. 1:20; 2:1; 3:19
Mt. 7:13

Although God's image in human beings has been corrupted, they are still capable of loving relationships, noble deeds and beautiful art. Yet even the finest human achievement is fatally flawed and cannot possibly fit anybody to enter God's presence. Men and women are also spiritual beings, but spiritual practices and self-help techniques can at the most alleviate felt needs; they cannot address the solemn realities of sin, guilt and judgment. Neither human religion, nor human righteousness, nor socio-political programs can save people. Self-salvation of every kind is impossible. Left to themselves, human beings are lost forever.

Mt. 5:46; 7:11
1 Ti. 6:16
Ac. 17:22-31
Ro. 3:20
Eph. 2:1-3

So we repudiate false gospels which deny human sin, divine

Gal. 1:6-9
2 Co. 11:2-4

233

judgment, the deity and incarnation of Jesus Christ, and the necessity of the cross and the resurrection. We also reject half-gospels, which minimize sin and confuse God's grace with human self-effort. We confess that we ourselves have sometimes trivialized the Gospel. But we determine in our evangelism to remember God's radical diagnosis and his equally radical remedy.

1 Jn. 2:22, 23; 4:1–3

1 Co. 15:3,4

Jer. 6:14; 8:11

2. Good News for Today

We rejoice that the living God did not abandon us to our lostness and despair. In his love he came after us in Jesus Christ to rescue and re-make us. So the good news focuses on the historic person of Jesus, who came proclaiming the kingdom of God and living a life of humble service, who died for us, becoming sin and a curse in our place, and whom God vindicated by raising him from the dead. To those who repent and believe in Christ, God grants a share in the new creation. He gives us new life, which includes the forgiveness of our sins and the indwelling, transforming power of his Spirit. He welcomes us into his new community, which consists of people of all races, nations and cultures. And he promises that one day we will enter his new world, in which evil will be abolished, nature will be redeemed, and God will reign for ever.

Eph. 2:4

Lk. 15; 19:10

Ac. 8:35

Mk. 1:14, 15

2 Co. 5:21; Gal. 3:13

Ac. 2:23, 24

2 Co. 5:17

Ac. 2:38, 39

Eph. 2:11–19

Rev. 21:1–5; 22:1–5

This good news must be boldly proclaimed, wherever possible, in church and public hall, on radio and television, and in the open air, because it is God's power for salvation and we are under obligation to make it known. In our preaching we must faithfully declare the truth which God has revealed in the Bible, and struggle to relate it to our own context.

Eph. 6:19–20; 2 Ti. 4:2

Ro. 1:14–16

Jer. 23:28

We also affirm that apologetics, namely 'the defense and confirmation of the Gospel', is integral to the biblical understanding of mission and essential for effective witness in the modern world. Paul 'reasoned' with people out of the Scriptures, with a view to 'persuading' them of the truth of the Gospel. So must we. In fact, all Christians should be ready to give a reason for the hope that is in them.

Php. 1:7

Ac. 18:4, 19:8, 9

2 Co. 5:11

1 Pe. 3:15

We have again been confronted with Luke's emphasis that the gospel is good news for the poor and have asked ourselves what this means to the majority of the world's population who are destitute, suffering or oppressed. We have been reminded that the law, the prophets and the wisdom books, and the teaching and ministry of Jesus, all stress God's concern for the materially poor and our consequent duty to defend and care for them. Scripture also refers to the spiritually poor who look to God alone for mercy. The Gospel comes as good news to both. The spiritually

Lk. 4:18, 6:20; 7:22

Dt. 15:7–11

Am. 2:6, 7:

Zec. 7:8–10

Pr. 21:13

Zep. 3:12

poor, who, whatever their economic circumstances, humble themselves before God, receive by faith the free gift of salvation. There
is no other way for anybody to enter the kingdom of God. The
materially poor and powerless find in addition a new dignity as
God's children, and the love of brothers and sisters who will
struggle with them for their liberation from everything which
demeans or oppresses them.

We repent of any neglect of God's truth in Scripture and
determine both to proclaim and to defend it. We also repent where
we have been indifferent to the plight of the poor, and where we
have shown preference for the rich, and we determine to follow
Jesus in preaching good news to all people by both word and deed.

3. The Uniqueness of Jesus Christ

We are called to proclaim Christ in an increasingly pluralistic
world. There is a resurgence of old faiths and a rise of new ones.
In the first century too there were 'many gods and many lords'.
Yet the apostles boldly affirmed the uniqueness, indispensability
and centrality of Christ. We must do the same.

Because men and women are made in God's image and see in
the creation traces of its Creator, the religions which have arisen
do sometimes contain elements of truth and beauty. They are not,
however, alternative gospels. Because human beings are sinful,
and because 'the whole world is under the control of the evil one',
even religious people are in need of Christ's redemption. We,
therefore, have no warrant for saying that salvation can be found
outside Christ or apart from an explicit acceptance of his work
through faith.

It is sometimes held that in virtue of God's covenant with
Abraham, Jewish people do not need to acknowledge Jesus as
their Messiah. We affirm that they need him as much as anyone
else, that it would be a form of anti-Semitism, as well as being
disloyal to Christ, to depart from the New Testament pattern of
taking the Gospel to 'the Jew first . . .'. We therefore reject the
thesis that Jews have their own covenant which renders faith in
Jesus unnecessary.

What unites us is our common convictions about Jesus Christ.
We confess him as the eternal Son of God, who became fully
human while remaining fully divine, who was our substitute on
the cross, bearing our sins and dying our death, exchanging his
righteousness for our unrighteousness, who rose victorious in a
transformed body, and who will return in glory to judge the world.
He alone is the incarnate Son, the Savior, the Lord and the Judge,

Mt. 5:3

Mk. 10:15

1 Jn. 3:1

Ac. 2:44, 45;
4:32–35

1 Co. 8:5

Ps. 19:1–6;
Ro. 1:19, 20

Ac. 17:28

1Jn. 5:19;
Ac. 10:1, 2;
11:14, 18;
15:8, 9

Jn. 14:6

Ge. 12:1–3;
17:1,2

Ro. 3:9; 10:12

Ac. 13:46;
Ro. 1:16, 2:9,
10

Ac. 13:38, 39

Jn. 1:1, 14, 18:

Ro. 1:3, 4

1 Pe. 2:24;
1 Co. 15:3

2 Co. 5:21

1 Co. 15:1–11

and he alone, with the Father and the Spirit, is worthy of the Mt. 25:31, 32; Ac. 17:30, 31
worship, faith and obedience of all people. There is only one Rev. 5:11–14
Gospel because there is only one Christ, who because of his death
and resurrection is himself the only way of salvation. We therefore Ac. 4:12
reject both the relativism which regards all religions and spiritu-
alities as equally valid approaches to God, and the syncretism
which tries to mix faith in Christ with other faiths.

Moreover, since God has exalted Jesus to the highest place, in Php. 2:9–11
order that everybody should acknowledge him, this also is our
desire. Compelled by Christ's love, we must obey Christ's Great 2 Co. 5:14
Commission and love his lost sheep. But we are especially moti- Mt. 28:19,20
vated by 'jealousy' for his holy name, and we long to see him Jn. 10:11, 16
receive the honour and glory which are due to him. 2 Co. 11:2, 3

In the past we have sometimes been guilty of adopting towards
adherents of other faiths attitudes of ignorance, arrogance, disrespect and even hostility. We repent of this. We nevertheless are
determined to bear a positive and uncompromising witness to the 1 Ti. 2:5–7
uniqueness of our Lord, in his life, death and resurrection, in all
aspects of our evangelistic work including inter-faith dialogue.

4.   The Gospel and Social Responsibility

The authentic Gospel must become visible in the transformed lives 1 Th. 1:6–10
of men and women. As we proclaim the love of God we must be 1 Jn. 3:17
involved in loving service, and as we preach the kingdom of God Ro. 14:17
we must be committed to its demands of justice and peace.

Evangelism is primary because our chief concern is with the Gos- Ro. 10:14
pel, that all people may have the opportunity to accept Jesus Christ
as Lord and Savior. Yet Jesus not only proclaimed the kingdom of Mt. 12:28
God, he also demonstrated its arrival by works of mercy and power.
We are called today to a similar integration of words and deeds. In a 1 Jn. 3:18
spirit of humility we are to preach and teach, minister to the sick, feed Mt. 25:34–46
the hungry, care for prisoners, help the disadvantaged and handicapped, and deliver the oppressed. While we acknowledge the diver-
sity of spiritual gifts, callings and contexts, we also affirm that good Ac. 6:1–4
Ro. 12:4–8
news and good works are inseparable. Mt. 5:16

The proclamation of God's kingdom necessarily demands the Jer. 22:1–5;
11–17; 23:5–6
prophetic denunciation of all that is incompatible with it. Among
the evils we deplore are destructive violence, including institutionalized violence, political corruption, all forms of exploitation of Am. 1:1–2; 8
people and of the earth, the undermining of the family, abortion
on demand, the drug traffic, and the abuse of human rights. In Is. 59
our concern for the poor, we are distressed by the burden of debt Lev. 25
in the two-thirds world. We are also outraged by the inhuman

conditions in which millions live, who bear God's image as we do.   Job 24:1–12

Our continuing commitment to social action is not a confusion of the kingdom of God with a Christianized society. It is, rather, a recognition that the biblical Gospel has inescapable social implications. True mission should always be incarnational. It necessitates entering humbly into other peoples' worlds, identifying with their social reality, their sorrow and suffering, and their struggles for justice against oppressive powers. This cannot be done without personal sacrifices.

Eph. 2:8–10

Jn. 17:18;
20:21

Php. 2:5–8

We repent that the narrowness of our concerns and vision has often kept us from proclaiming the lordship of Jesus Christ over all of life, private and public, local and global. We determine to obey his command to 'seek first the kingdom of God and his righteousness'.

Ac. 10:36

B.   THE WHOLE CHURCH

The whole Gospel has to be proclaimed by the whole church. All
the people of God are called to share in the evangelistic task. Yet
without the Holy Spirit of God all their endeavors will be fruitless.

5.   God the Evangelist

The Scriptures declare that God himself is the chief evangelist. For
the Spirit of God is the Spirit of truth, love, holiness and power,
and evangelism is impossible without him. It is he who anoints the
messenger, confirms the word, prepares the hearer, convicts the
sinful, enlightens the blind, gives life to the dead, enables us to
repent and believe, unites us to the body of Christ, assures us that
we are God's children, leads us into Christ–like character and
service, and sends us out in our turn to be Christ's witnesses. In
all this the Holy Spirit's main preoccupation is to glorify Jesus
Christ by showing him to us and forming him in us.

All evangelism involves spiritual warfare with the principalities
and powers of evil, in which only spiritual weapons can prevail,
especially the Word and the Spirit, with prayer. We therefore call
on all Christian people to be diligent in their prayers both for the
renewal of the church and for the evangelization of the world.

Every true conversion involves a power encounter, in which the
superior authority of Jesus Christ is demonstrated. There is no
greater miracle than this, in which the believer is set free from the
bondage of Satan and sin, fear and futility, darkness and death.

Although the miracles of Jesus were special, being signs of his
messiahship and anticipations of his perfect kingdom when all
nature will be subject to him, we have no liberty to place limits on
the power of the living Creator today. We reject both the skepti-
cism which denies miracles and the presumption which demands
them, both the timidity which shrinks from the fullness of the
Spirit and the triumphalism which shrinks from the weakness in
which Christ's power is made perfect.

We repent of all self-confident attempts either to evangelize in
our own strength or to dictate to the Holy Spirit. We determine
in future not to 'grieve' or 'quench' the Spirit, but rather to seek
to spread the good news 'with power, with the Holy Spirit and
with deep conviction'.

Marginal references:
2 Co. 5:20
Jn. 15:26, 27
Lk. 4:18
1 Co. 2:4;
Jn. 16:8–11
1 Co 12:3;
Eph. 2:5
1 Co. 12:13;
Ro. 8:16
Gal. 5:22, 23
Ac. 1:8
Jn. 16:14;
Gal. 4:19
Eph. 6:10–12
2 Co. 10:3–5
Eph. 6:17
Eph. 6:18–20;
2 Th. 3:1
Ac. 26: 17, 18
1 Th. 1:9, 10
Col. 1:13, 14
Jn. 2:11;
20:30, 31
Jn. 11:25;
1 Co. 15:20–28
Jer. 32:17
2 Ti. 1:7
2 Co. 12:9, 10
Jer. 17:5
Eph. 4:30;
1 Th. 5:19
1 Th. 1:5

238

6. The Human Witnesses

God the evangelist gives his people the privilege of being his 'fellow-workers'. For, although we cannot witness without him, he normally chooses to witness through us. He calls only some to be evangelists, missionaries or pastors, but he calls his whole church and every member of it to be his witnesses. [2 Co. 6:1 / Ac. 8:26–39; 14:27 / Eph. 4:11 / Ac. 13:1–3 / Ac. 1:8, 8:1, 4]

The privileged task of pastors and teachers is to lead God's people (*laos*) into maturity and to equip them for ministry. Pastors are not to monopolize ministries, but rather to multiply them, by encouraging others to use their gifts and by training disciples to make disciples. The domination of the laity by the clergy has been a great evil in the history of the church. It robs both laity and clergy of their God-intended roles, causes clergy breakdowns, weakens the church and hinders the spread of the Gospel. More than that, it is fundamentally unbiblical. We therefore, who have for centuries insisted on 'the priesthood of all believers', now also insist on the ministry of all believers. [Co. 1: 28 / Eph. 4:11–12 / Mt. 28:19; 2 Ti. 2:2 / 1 Th. 5:12–15 / 1 Co. 12:4–7; Eph. 4:7]

We gratefully recognize that children and young people enrich the church's worship and outreach by their enthusiasm and faith. We need to train them in discipleship and evangelism, so that they may reach their own generation for Christ. [Mt. 21:15, 16 / 1 Ti. 4:12]

God created men and women as equal bearers of his image, accepts them equally in Christ, and poured out his Spirit on all flesh, sons and daughters alike. In addition, because the Holy Spirit distributes his gifts to women as well as to men, they must be given opportunities to exercise their gifts. We celebrate their distinguished record in the history of missions and are convinced that God calls women to similar roles today. Even though we are not fully agreed what forms their leadership should take, we do agree about the partnership in world evangelization which God intends men and women to enjoy. Suitable training must therefore be made available to both. [Ge. 1:26–27 / Gal. 3:28 Ac. 2:17–18 / 1 Pe. 4:10 / Ro. 16:1–6, 12 / Php. 4:2, 3]

Lay witness takes place, by women and men, not only through the local church (see section 8), but through friendships, in the home and at work. Even those who are homeless or unemployed share in the calling to be witnesses.

Our first responsibility is to witness to those who are already our friends, relatives, neighbors and colleagues. Home evangelism is also natural, both for married and for single people. Not only should a Christian home commend God's standards of marriage, sex and family, and provide a haven of love and peace to people who are hurting, but neighbors who would not enter a church usually feel comfortable in a home, even when the Gospel is discussed. [Mk. 5:18–20; Lk. 5:27–32 / Ac. 28:30, 31 / Ac. 10:24,33; 18:7, 8; 24–26]

Another context for lay witness is the work-place, for it is here that most Christians spend half their waking hours, and work is a divine calling. Christians can commend Christ by word of mouth, by their consistent industry, honesty and thoughtfulness, by their concern for justice in the work-place, and especially if others can see from the quality of their daily work that it is done to the glory of God.

1 Co. 7:17–24
Tit. 2:9, 10
Col. 4:1
Col. 3:17, 23, 24

We repent of our share in discouraging the ministry of the laity, especially of women and young people. We determine in the future to encourage all Christ's followers to take their place, rightfully and naturally, as his witnesses. For true evangelism comes from the overflow of a heart in love with Christ. That is why it belongs to all his people without exception.

Ac. 4:20

7.   The Integrity of the Witnesses

Nothing commends the Gospel more eloquently than a transformed life, and nothing brings it into disrepute so much as personal inconsistency. We are charged to behave in a manner that is worthy of the Gospel of Christ, and even to 'adorn' it, enhancing its beauty by holy lives. For the watching world rightly seeks evidence to substantiate the claims which Christ's disciples make for him. A strong evidence is our integrity.

2 Co. 6:3, 4
Php. 1:27
Tit. 2:10
Col. 4:5, 6
Pr. 11:3

Our proclamation that Christ died to bring us to God appeals to people who are spiritually thirsty, but they will not believe us if we give no evidence of knowing the living God ourselves, or if our public worship lacks reality and relevance.

1 Pe. 3:18
1 Jn 1:15, 6
1 Co. 14:25, 26

Our message that Christ reconciles alienated people to each other rings true only if we are seen to love and forgive one another, to serve others in humility, and to reach out beyond our own community in compassionate, costly ministry to the needy.

Eph. 2:14–18
Eph. 4:31–5:2
Gal. 5:13
Lk. 10:29–37

Our challenge to others to deny themselves, take up their cross and follow Christ will be plausible only if we ourselves have evidently died to selfish ambition, dishonesty and covetousness, and are living a life of simplicity, contentment and generosity.

Mk. 8:34
Mt. 6:19–21; 31–33
1 Ti. 6:6–10, 17, 18

We deplore the failures in Christian consistency which we see in both Christians and churches: material greed, professional pride and rivalry, competition in Christian service, jealousy of younger leaders, missionary paternalism, the lack of mutual accountability, the loss of Christian standards of sexuality, and racial, social and sexual discrimination. All this is worldliness, allowing the prevailing culture to subvert the church instead of the church challenging and changing the culture. We are deeply ashamed of the times when, both as individuals and in our

Ac. 5:1–11
Php. 1:15–17
1 Co. 5:1–13
Jas. 2:1{4
1 Jn. 2:15–17
Mt 5:13

Christian communities, we have affirmed Christ in word and Mt. 7:21–23
denied him in deed. Our inconsistency deprives our witness of 1 Jn. 2:4
credibility. We acknowledge our continuing struggles and failures. But we also determine by God's grace to develop integrity Eph. 4:1
in ourselves and in the church.

8. The Local Church

Every Christian congregation is a local expression of the body of 1 Co. 12:27
Christ and has the same responsibilities. It is both 'a holy priesthood' to offer God the spiritual sacrifices of worship and 'a holy
nation' to spread abroad his excellences in witness. The church is 1 Pe. 2:5, 9
thus both a worshiping and a witnessing community, gathered and Jn. 17:6, 9, 11, 18
scattered, called and sent. Worship and witness are inseparable. Php. 2:14–16

We believe that the local church bears a primary responsibility
for the spread of the Gospel. Scripture suggests this in the pro-
gression that 'our Gospel came to you' and then 'rang out from 1 Th. 1:5, 8
you'. In this way, the Gospel creates the church which spreads the
Gospel which creates more churches in a continuous chain reaction. Moreover, what Scripture teaches, strategy confirms. Each Ac. 19:9, 10
local church must evangelize the district in which it is situated, and
has the resources to do so.

We recommend every congregation to carry out regular studies
not only of its own membership and program but of its local
community in all its particularity, in order to develop appropriate
strategies for mission. Its members might decide to organize a Col. 1:3–8
visitation of their whole area, to penetrate for Christ a particular
place where people assemble, to arrange a series of evangelistic Ac. 13:1–3; 14:26–28
meetings, lectures or concerts, to work with the poor to transform
a local slum, or to plant a new church in a neighboring district or
village. At the same time, they must not forget the church's global
task. A church which sends out missionaries must not neglect its
own locality, and a church which evangelizes its neighborhood
must not ignore the rest of the world.

In all this each congregation and denomination should, where Php. 1:27
possible, work with others, seeking to turn any spirit of competition into one of cooperation. Churches should also work with
para-church organizations, especially in evangelism, discipling
and community service, for such agencies are part of the body of
Christ, and have valuable, specialist expertise from which the
church can greatly benefit.

The church is intended by God to be a sign of his kingdom, Lk. 12:32
that is, an indication of what human community looks like
when it comes under his rule of righteousness and peace. As Ro. 14:17
with individuals, so with churches, the Gospel has to be 1 Th. 1:8–10

embodied if it is to be communicated effectively. It is through our love for one another that the invisible God reveals himself today, especially when our fellowship is expressed in small groups, and when it transcends the barriers of race, rank, sex and age which divide other communities.

1 Jn. 4:12; Jn. 13:34, 35: 17:21, 23

Gal. 3:28; Col. 3:11

We deeply regret that many of our congregations are inward-looking, organized for maintenance rather than mission, or pre-occupied with church-based activities at the expense of witness. We determine to turn our churches inside out, so that they may engage in continuous outreach, until the Lord adds to them daily those who are being saved.

Ac. 2:47

9. Cooperation in Evangelism

Evangelism and unity are closely related in the New Testament. Jesus prayed that his people's oneness might reflect his own oneness with the Father, in order that the world might believe in him, and Paul exhorted the Philippians to 'contend as one person for the faith of the gospel'. In contrast to this biblical vision, we are ashamed of the suspicions and rivalries, the dogmatism over non-essentials, the power-struggles and empire-building which spoil our evangelistic witness. We affirm that cooperation in evangelism is indispensable, first because it is the will of God, but also because the Gospel of reconciliation is discredited by our disunity, and because, if the task of world evangelization is ever to be accomplished, we must engage in it together.

Jn. 7:20, 21

Php. 1:27

Php. 1:15, 17; 2:3, 4

Ro. 14:1–15:2

Php. 1:3–5

Eph. 2:14–16; 4:1–6

Eph. 4:6, 7

'Cooperation' means finding unity in diversity. It involves people of different temperaments, gifts, callings and cultures, national churches and mission agencies, all ages and both sexes working together.

We are determined to put behind us once and for all, as a hangover from the colonial past, the simplistic distinction between First World sending and Two-Thirds World receiving countries. For the great new fact of our era is the internationalization of missions. Not only are a large majority of all evangelical Christians now non-western, but the number of Two-Thirds World missionaries will soon exceed those from the west. We believe that mission teams, which are diverse in composition but united in heart and mind, constitute a dramatic witness to the grace of God.

Ac. 20:4

Our reference to 'the whole church' is not a presumptuous claim that the universal church and the evangelical community are synonymous. For we recognize that there are many churches which are not part of the evangelical movement. Evangelical attitudes to the Roman Catholic and Orthodox Churches differ widely. Some evangelicals are praying, talking, studying Scripture and working with these churches. Others are strongly opposed to any form of dialogue or cooperation with them. All evangelicals are aware that serious theological differences between us remain. Where appropriate, and so long as biblical truth is not compromised, cooperation may be possible in such areas as Bible translation, the study of contemporary theological and ethical issues, social work and political action. We wish to make it clear, however, that common evangelism demands a common commitment to the biblical Gospel.

Some of us are members of churches which belong to the World Council of Churches and believe that a positive yet critical participation in its work is our Christian duty. Others among us have no link with the World Council. All of us urge the World Council of Churches to adopt a consistent biblical understanding of evangelism.

We confess our own share of responsibility for the brokenness of the body of Christ, which is a major stumbling-block to world evangelization. We determine to go on seeking that unity in truth Jn. 17:11, 20–23, for which Christ prayed. We are persuaded that the right way forward towards closer cooperation is frank and patient dialogue on the basis of the Bible, with all who share our concerns. To this we gladly commit ourselves.

C. THE WHOLE WORLD

The whole Gospel has been entrusted to the whole church, in order that it may be made known to the whole world. It is necessary, therefore, for us to understand the world into which we are sent.

Mk. 16:15

10. The Modern World

Evangelism takes place in a context, not in a vacuum. The balance between Gospel and context must be carefully maintained. We must understand the context in order to address it, but the context must not be allowed to distort the Gospel.

Ac. 13:14–41;
14:14–17;
17:22–31

In this connection we have become concerned about the impact of 'modernity', which is an emerging world culture produced by industrialization with its technology and by urbanization with its economic order. These factors combine to create an environment, which significantly shapes the way in which we see our world. In addition, secularism has devastated faith by making God and the supernatural meaningless; urbanization has dehumanized life for many; and the mass media have contributed to the devaluation of truth and authority, by replacing word with image. In combination, these consequences of modernity pervert the message which many preach and undermine their motivation for mission.

In AD 1900 only 9% of the world's population lived in cities; in AD 2000 it is thought that more than 50% will do so. This worldwide move into the cities has been called 'the greatest migration in human history'; it constitutes a major challenge to Christian mission. On the one hand, city populations are extremely cosmopolitan, so that the nations come to our doorstep in the city. Can we develop global churches in which the Gospel abolishes the barriers of ethnicity? On the other hand, many city dwellers are migrant poor who are also receptive to the Gospel. Can the people of God be persuaded to re-locate into such urban poor communities, in order to serve the people and share in the transformation of the city?

Modernization brings blessings as well as dangers. By creating links of communication and commerce around the globe, it makes unprecedented openings for the Gospel, crossing old frontiers and penetrating closed societies, whether traditional or totalitarian. The Christian media have a powerful influence both in sowing the seed of the Gospel and in preparing the soil. The major missionary broadcasters are committed to a Gospel witness by radio in every major language by the year AD 2000.

We confess that we have not struggled as we should to understand modernization. We have used its methods and techniques uncritically and so exposed ourselves to worldliness. But we determine in the future to take these challenges and opportunities seriously, to resist the secular pressures of modernity, to relate the lordship of Christ to the whole of modern culture, and thus to engage in mission in the modern world without worldliness in modern mission.

Ro. 12:1, 2

11. The Challenge of AD 2000 and Beyond

The world population today is approaching 6 billion people. One third of them nominally confess Christ. Of the remaining four billion half have heard of him and the other half have not. In the light of these figures, we evaluate our evangelistic task by considering four categories of people.

First, there is the potential missionary work force, the committed. In this century this category of Christian believers has grown from about 40 million in 1900 to about 500 million today, and at this moment is growing over twice as fast as any other major religious group.

Secondly, there are the uncommitted. They make a Christian profession (they have been baptized, attend church occasionally and even call themselves Christians), but the notion of a personal commitment to Christ is foreign to them. They are found in all churches throughout the world. They urgently need to be re-evangelized.

Thirdly, there are the unevangelized. These are people who have a minimal knowledge of the Gospel, but have had no valid opportunity to respond to it. They are probably within reach of Christian people if only these will go to the next street, road, village or town to find them.

Fourthly, there are the unreached. These are the two billion who may never have heard of Jesus as Savior, and are not within reach of Christians of their own people. There are, in fact, some 2,000 peoples or nationalities in which there is not yet a vital, indigenous church movement. We find it helpful to think of them as belonging to smaller 'people groups' which perceive themselves as having an affinity with each other (e.g. a common culture, language, home or occupation). The most effective messengers to reach them will be those believers who already belong to their culture and know their language. Otherwise, cross-cultural messengers of the Gospel will need to go, leaving behind their own culture and sacrificially identifying with the people they long to reach for Christ.

There are now about 12,000 such unreached people groups within the 2,000 larger peoples, so that the task is not impossible. Yet at present only 7% of all missionaries are engaged in this kind of outreach, while the remaining 93% are working in the already evangelized half of the world. If this imbalance is to be redressed, a strategic redeployment of personnel will be necessary.

A distressing factor that affects each of the above categories is that of inaccessibility. Many countries do not grant visas to self-styled missionaries, who have no other qualification or contribution to offer. Such areas are not absolutely inaccessible, however. For our prayers can pass through every curtain, door and barrier. And Christian radio and television, audio and video cassettes, films and literature can also reach the otherwise unreachable. So can so-called 'tent-makers' who like Paul earn their own living. They travel in the course of their profession (e.g. business people, university lecturers, technical specialists and language teachers), and use every opportunity to speak of Jesus Christ. They do not enter a country under false pretenses, for their work genuinely takes them there; it is simply that witness is an essential component of their Christian lifestyle, wherever they may happen to be. Ac. 18:1–4; 20:34

We are deeply ashamed that nearly two millennia have passed since the death and resurrection of Jesus, and still two-thirds of the world's population have not yet acknowledged him. On the other hand, we are amazed at the mounting evidence of God's power even in the most unlikely places of the globe.

Now the year 2000 has become for many a challenging milestone. Can we commit ourselves to evangelize the world during the last decade of this millennium? There is nothing magical about the date, yet should we not do our best to reach this goal? Christ commands us to take the Gospel to all peoples. The task is urgent. We are determined to obey him with joy and hope. Lk. 24:45–47

12. Difficult Situations

Jesus plainly told his followers to expect opposition. 'If they persecuted me', he said, 'they will persecute you also'. He even told them to rejoice over persecution, and reminded them that the condition of fruitfulness was death. Jn. 15:20 Mt. 5:12 Jn. 12:24

These predictions, that Christian suffering is inevitable and productive, have come true in every age, including our own. There have been many thousands of martyrs. Today the situation is much the same. We earnestly hope that *glasnost* and *perestroika* will lead to complete religious freedom in the Soviet Union and other Eastern bloc nations, and that Islamic and Hindu countries will become more open to the Gospel. We deplore the recent brutal suppression of China's democratic movement, and we pray that it will not bring further suffering to the Christians. On the whole, however, it seems that ancient religions are becoming less tolerant, expatriates less welcome, and the world less friendly to the Gospel.

In this situation we wish to make three statements to governments which are reconsidering their attitude to Christian believers.

First, Christians are loyal citizens, who seek the welfare of their nation. They pray for its leaders and pay their taxes. Of course, those who have confessed Jesus as Lord cannot also call other authorities Lord, and if commanded to do so, or to do anything which God forbids, must disobey. But they are conscientious citizens. They also contribute to their country's well-being by the stability of their marriages and homes, their honesty in business, their hard work and their voluntary activity in the service of the handicapped and needy. Just governments have nothing to fear from Christians. _{Jer. 29:7; 1 Ti. 2:1, 2; Ro. 13:6, 7; Ac. 4:19, 5:29}

Secondly, Christians renounce unworthy methods of evangelism. Though the nature of our faith requires us to share the Gospel with others, our practice is to make an open and honest statement of it, which leaves the hearers entirely free to make up their own minds about it. We wish to be sensitive to those of other faiths, and we reject any approach that seeks to force conversion on them. _{2 Co. 4:1, 2}

Thirdly, Christians earnestly desire freedom of religion for all people, not just freedom for Christianity. In predominantly Christian countries, Christians are at the forefront of those who demand freedom for religious minorities. In predominantly non-Christian countries, therefore, Christians are asking for themselves no more than they demand for others in similar circumstances. The freedom to 'profess, practise and propagate' religion, as defined in the Universal Declaration of Human Rights, could and should surely be a reciprocally granted right.

We greatly regret any unworthy witness of which followers of Jesus may have been guilty. We determine to give no unnecessary offense in anything, lest the name of Christ be dishonored. However, the offense of the cross we cannot avoid. For the sake of Christ crucified we pray that we may be ready, _{2 Co. 6:3; 1 Co. 1:18, 23: 2:2; Php. 1:29}

by his grace, to suffer and even to die. Martyrdom is a form of witness which Christ has promised especially to honor. _{Rev. 2:13;}

Rev. 2:13; 6:9–11; 20:4

CONCLUSION:
PROCLAIM CHRIST UNTIL HE COMES

'Proclaim Christ until he comes'. That has been the theme of Lausanne II. Of course we believe that Christ has come; he came when Augustus was Emperor of Rome. But one day, as we know from his promises, he will come again in unimaginable splendor to perfect his kingdom. We are commanded to watch and be ready. Meanwhile, the gap between his two comings is to be filled with the Christian missionary enterprise. We have been told to go to the ends of the earth with the Gospel, and we have been promised that the end of the age will come only when we have done so. The two ends (of earth space and time) will coincide. Until then he has pledged to be with us.

Lk. 2:1–7

Mk. 13:26, 27

Mk. 13:32–37

Ac. 1:8

Mt. 24:14

Mt. 28:20

So the Christian mission is an urgent task. We do not know how long we have. We certainly have no time to waste. And in order to get on urgently with our responsibility, other qualities will be necessary, especially unity (we must evangelize together) and sacrifice (we must count and accept the cost). Our covenant at Lausanne was 'to pray, to plan and to work together for the evangelization of the whole world'. Our manifesto at Manila is that the whole church is called to take the whole gospel to the whole world, proclaiming Christ until he comes, with all necessary urgency, unity and sacrifice.

POSTSCRIPT

A compendium of all the documents relating to Lausanne II, entitled *Proclaim Christ Until He Comes*, and subtitled 'Calling the whole church to take the whole gospel to the whole world', was edited by J. D. Douglas and published by World Wide Publications, Minneapolis, in 1990.

After some introductory material (including the Lausanne Covenant and the Manila Manifesto) and the Opening Addresses (including Billy Graham's video message and Leighton Ford's fine speech which set the scene for the Congress), the body of the book consists of the plenary papers and supporting video texts. The material is divided into three sections.

The first section, 'The Whole Church', contains the plenary papers on the primacy of the local church, the mandate of the laity, the work of the Holy Spirit, living the Christ-life, and evangelism in challenging settings.

The second section, 'The Whole Gospel', contains the plenary addresses on good news for the poor, sin and lostness, cross-cultural evangelism, the challenge of other religions, the Gospel and salvation, and cooperation in evangelism, and also the eight biblical expositions of Romans 1–15.

The third section, 'The Whole World', contains the plenary papers on urban evangelism, the impact of modernization, social concern, the uniqueness of Christ, communication, and sacrifice.

Then follow the closing addresses, which look both back and forward, and contain reflections and exhortations by several leaders.

The postscript consists of the reports of forty-two 'Tracks', each of which was divided into a number of workshops covering a very wide variety of topics.

APPENDIX

The Uppsala Consultation on Faith and Modernity (1993)

Because the parameters of this book are the fifteen-year period from Lausanne 1974 to Manila 1989, the Uppsala Consultation of 1993 does not strictly belong. Nevertheless, it owed its inspiration to Manila, so that at least a brief reference to it is appropriate.

One of the most stimulating addresses given at Manila 1989 was Dr. Os Guinness's paper 'Faith and Modernity'. The participants' positive response to it led the Lausanne Committee's Theology Working Group to convene an international consultation in order to delve more deeply into this topic. It took place in Uppsala, Sweden, in June 1993.

No official report was issued, but the papers read at it were assembled in a symposium entitled *Faith and Modernity*, edited by Philip Sampson, Vinay Samuel and Chris Sugden, and published by Regnum Books International (1994).

In the Introduction the editors acknowledge the ambiguity of the epithets 'modern' and 'post-modern', since they are used in at least two senses. On the one hand, 'modernity' denotes 'the intellectual and cultural heritage of the Enlightenment project' (especially the autonomy of the human reason), and 'post-modernity' is a self-conscious rejection of this. On the other hand, 'modernity' and 'post-modernity' refer to 'different cultural and social developments' which the church tends to absorb even while rejecting Enlightenment self-confidence.

The papers themselves are grouped into three 'levels'. Level One is 'The Analysis of Modernity'. Level Two is 'Modernity and Christianity in Tension'. It is much longer than the other two sections, and discusses the relations of modernity to authority, theology, anthropology, morality, eschatology, spirituality, New Age, economics, information technology, the church, and mission. Level Three, entitled 'Strategies in Confronting Modernity', is Os Guinness's Manila paper (1989) revised for the Uppsala Consultation (1993). The distinguished international team of authors includes James Houston, James Hunter, Lesslie Newbigin, Elaine Storkey and David Wells.

The contributors would probably agree that the book is stronger on 'modernity' than on 'faith', stronger on social analysis than on mission strategy. But then accurate diagnosis is the indispensable preliminary to prescription and cure.

INDEX OF SUBJECTS

INDEX OF BIBLICAL REFERENCES